MY RELIGION:
REEL OR REAL?

A Post-modern Catholic's Assessment on his Faithjourney

REV. BENJAMIN A. VIMA

Order this book online at www.trafford.com
or email orders@trafford.com

Most Trafford titles are also available at major online book retailers.

Printed in the United States of America.

ISBN: 978-1-4907-1364-9 (sc)
ISBN: 978-1-4907-1366-3 (hc)
ISBN: 978-1-4907-1365-6 (e)

Library of Congress Control Number: 2013916178

Trafford rev. 09/24/2013

 www.trafford.com

North America & international
toll-free: 1 888 232 4444 (USA & Canada)
fax: 812 355 4082

Contents

Dedication

I sincerely and with overwhelming appreciation I dedicate this book to three persons who have been rolemodels to me in practicing authentically the Realreligion in this post-modern world:

* Saint Pope John Paul II who has been a model for People-oriented Leadership;
* Pope Benedict XVI, a pattern for Status-ripped Leadership;
* Pope Francis, an example for Humble and Simple Leadership.

Introduction:
The Realreligion

At the onset I must avow that in no way I try to compare and contrast religions or faiths abounding around the globe. I don't have such caliber and experience in the study of all religions and sects. While I am good at a few, I know very nominally little of all the others. My primary focus here is on the attitudes and behaviors of two groups of people affiliated to my religion, specifically Catholic Christianity. In this too, I am only assessing my personal holdings and performances as a Catholic Christian religious person, all in the light of Scriptures, Traditions and Signs of the Time.

These days people are fed up seeing only the *fiction-TV*. Rather they prefer and choose what is called 'the *reality-TV*.' This is true with our approach to religion. Even though our lips profess the faith of resurrection, our hearts beat for reality religion. Some years back I happened to read an article in the magazine 'America: The National Catholic Review', written by Cardinal Avery Dulles S.J. Its title was *Vatican II: The Myth and the Reality.* It inspired me to coin the title for this book *"My Religion: Reel or Real."*

At every age, the cradle-religion I belong to has been probing into her managing and conserving of the Mysterious Treasures entrusted to her. In particular the enlightenment, offered by Vatican Council II, helped me judging my own handling of Catholic Christian Faith. Describing the intention of the gathering of the Sacred Synod as Vatican council II as 'being to teaching of previous councils, to unfold now more fully to the faithful of the Church and to the whole world its own inner nature and universal mission, the Church fathers underlined the necessity of it: *"The present-day conditions of the world add greater urgency to this work of the Church so that all men, joined more closely today by various social, technical and cultural ties, might also attain fuller unity in Christ."* (LG para-1) The words 'Present-day conditions' certainly refer to the 'Signs of the Times', which Blessed Pope John XXII spoke about in his inaugural address. Simultaneously Council fathers insisted that their intention for this august gathering was to scrutinize and interpret the same 'Signs of the Times' in the 'light of the Gospel of Jesus.' (GS Para 4) I observe Vatican Council has been one such effort in my time. I was enlightened by Vat II's deliberations which now assist me in the effort of probing into my personal religious adherence, and practice. Personally I don't want to fall short of my faith and trust in Realreligion, as my friends of reelreligion, who consider renewal or renovation of one's religious life as deviating or totally drifting away from what our Mother-Religion entrusted to us. It would be a grave mistake and I don't buy it.

What is the meaning of 'Religion'?

Before entering into a discussion on a debatable topic like *'My Religion: Reel or Real?'* I would like to clarify certain terms I use in this book. First the term 'religion': From its Latin root meaning 'rebinding' (*Re-ligare*) usually in conservative circle it denotes the re-relationship of humans to God. In spiritual sense it is a pedestal for God and humans holding a re-sitting discussion and communication in order to renew their agreement or covenant made and violated in the past. Also in a socio-political sense it is a forum where like-minded people come together again and again to re-bind together, to re-new their fellowship and re-strengthen their bond. Generally in modern communication languages 'religion' is used to mean people's beliefs and opinions concerning the existence, nature, and worship of a deity or deities, and divine involvement in the universe and human life. It refers to an institutionalized or personal system of beliefs and practices relating to the divine. It also means a set of strongly-held beliefs, values, and attitudes that somebody lives by. It indicates to an object, practice, cause, or activity that somebody is completely devoted to or obsessed by.

From all these divergent definitions I can derive at the core meaning of religion: It is a human endeavor that starts from the spiritual realm or dimension of a person being nourished, fed, and strengthened by one's sensual, emotional and physical and intellectual abilities of listening, seeing, interacting and learning. It comes out vehemently and immediately through the same way it entered, namely one's physical, emotional, sensual, intellectual rituals and practices. In all this process one core and center that stays eternal is the human spiritual realm. This is indeed more personal and private than social or public. In any action or reaction or proaction of humans there is this core realm that acts as source, origin, basis, center and destination. Though all other human acts that are performed during religion's in-and-out process are unequivocally needed for religion's survival in individual's life, they are in no way to be esteemed as essential to the fact of religion. What is going on inside the spiritual realm of the individual is the most essential to form a person's religion.

Spiritual realm in me is nothing but my true self. The basic self within me over the years has been formed, groomed, shaped, molded and caricatured into what I call 'my personality' contrived with its character, characteristics, qualities, abilities and dreams. Once I take hold of that inner self, I work on it and work with it, first and foremost for my best survival, then for my relationship, my life's basic necessities, my growth and my fulfillment. There is no sense of construing any altruistic motivation to human deeds. All the actions, reactions or proactions that are generated from an individual are only out of selfism in the right meaning. All arise from the spiritual source hidden in depth of every human being.

Religion essentially personal but formally social

With my personal study on the existence of different religions, I can boldly say, even though religions seem like community-oriented in their essence, there exist in this world as many religions as there are individual humans existing here on earth. Religion is basically personal and individualistic but formally social. I can offer innumerable proofs for such observation. For example: If I ask my parishioners about their religious affiliation surely each one would with no hesitation say 'I am Catholic.' However if I question them about their individual or personal likings and dislikes each one would differ from each other in their answers: "I like all that I was taught about my beliefs except papacy." "I follow everything my religion says except on birth control." "I sincerely believe that God exists but I hesitate to put my belief in Jesus as God." "I like Sunday Services but I attend them only if they are held at my convenient time." "Undoubtedly I need God to forgive my sins but not through some men." "I regularly offer my tithe to Church only if this priest of my skin, race, color and caste is my pastor." Such above-quoted statements of my parishioners are only a few out of millions of proofs to show that religions exist as many as the existing individuals. There is nothing wrong in making choices of beliefs and dogmas as long as freedom hails on high. My emphasis is about the fact of religion: Religion is basically personal but formally communal.

The existence of multifarious religions

From the above-mentioned central concept of 'religion' I can understand the multifarious attitudes, approaches and affiliations human beings hold on religion. Let me illustrate it in this way: Recent age clearly shows the grand exodus of Christians moving from their original churches or mainline denominations to the so-called non-denominational or inter-denominational churches manufactured and promoted by skilled salespersons of religion. They call themselves 'Evangelists' or 'self-designated' prophets of God. People endorse such efforts and flock in for services and conventions. What is the reason behind all this behavior of baptized Christians? Some criticize them and label them as 'quitters' not able to withstand the human problems existing in each one's church environment.

But if I relate this sort of modern behavior of the original Christians to the core meaning of religion I can figure out the true cause of this exodus. Every individual human being holds a religion of his/her own according to the spiritual impulses coming out of one's inner spiritual realm. He /she has got already certain clue or concept of religion for his/her survival and success. When that clue is not found in what he/she had been thrusted into in his/her early childhood he/she jumps out to make peace with one's own spiritual self. If any situation in that matter comes to him/her where he/she would lose his/

her spiritual balance or peace surely he/she would not tolerate it. This is historical truthful fact.

That insight offers us a valid answer to why we have so many religions in the world. Either they are the inspirations plumbed out of human spiritual realm or consolidation of different spiritual experiences of different people at various times. Because such individualistic and personal origin, in every world religion there are so many sects and branches: Among the Christians are Catholics, Eastern Orthodox Church, and Protestants etc. Sunnis and Shias belong to two different major branches of Islam apart from Sufis and other distinct groups. Two major divisions of Buddhism are Hinayana and Mahayana. Hinduism is split into hundreds of sects and beliefs. The differences in hundred thousands of religions and sects are based on distinctive cultures, nationalities, social environments, natural climates and so on.

Even though people state that they belong to a religion that is already framed and organized, in actual situation every one of us framed of our own religion setup and follow it. In my childhood and even in my adolescent life I never thought this way. Later when I took priestly life, not just as a profession, but as a life of service and moving from one community to another as pastor I witnessed this truth hundred percent sure in my adult parishioners. They need not be only of the well-sophisticated group or educated elite but also of the uneducated, poor and tribal groups. Even within my priests' circle, bishops and cardinals, theologians and other experts and authors in the Church every one of them possesses a certain way of dealing with their religious affiliations and that proves to me each one holds on to one's own religion. This is why I boldly assert I hold on to my own religion in the midst of many religions.

The use of terms: Reel and Real

There are many ways of differentiating religions according to each one's upholding, history, culture, and results. In this book I prefer to underline two most prevalent major divisions in practicing religions: Either they are reel or real. The term *real*, as all of us know, is an adjective pointing out a thing, a person or any matter dealt, used and applied is actual, factual, genuine, authentic, original, sincere, truthful, unfeigned and so on. Commonly we consider the opposite of 'real' is false, dishonest, artificial, fictional, and moot and so on. In this book I substitute to all those opposites of 'real' by the word *'reel'* for the right reason: The term 'reel' is used in dictionaries both as noun and verb. As a noun *'reel'* means a revolving wheel-shaped device, around which something such as thread, film, or wire, can be wound for storage. For example, storing device used as a spool, where movie films were wound up in earlier days before digital age; in fishing it means a winding device attached to a fishing rod that holds the fishing line and enables it to be cast and wound back. As a verb, *'to reel'* is to move in a sudden and uncontrolled fashion, especially backward as if struck by a blow; to move or whirl around in circles; to move unsteadily, staggering or swaying from side to side; to feel giddy or shocked and confused; in other words, to give way or fall back; sway, waver, or stagger as from being struck; to lurch or stagger about, as from drunkenness or dizziness; and to go around and around.

Related to dealing with religion, the word 'reel', in the light of its root meaning, refers to a religion which is simply a bundle of rituals and activities that are performed routinely, with no commitment to the centrality and basis of religion; it also points out a religion which is practiced unsteadily, in confusion, staggering and swaying from side to side being tossed around in flux; sometimes it also denotes to a religion which is practiced as if in drunkenness and dizziness. Added to all these, I use this term as handled by younger generation of my native place in India. When their elders-parents, principals, professors and even their peers offer some healthy but long and tedious advice, they show their aversion or dislike by using the term 'reel' with the gesture of wheeling. This means, according to the youngsters, what they are told is either a lie or folly. There is one more very important factor regarding the term 'reel' as used in non-digital movie circles. If there was a 30-minute movie picture rolled in a movie wheeler (reel) there are almost 43200 still images on a strip of plastic which when run through a projector and shown on a screen created the illusion of moving plus speaking images. This brings out the fictional and unreal and imaginative characteristics of a movie experience. Applying this factor to a religion, we discover so many religion-practioners live and move and wheel around in their lives only enjoying certain kind of fictional, unreal and very subjective experience of their religions.

The Realreligion Vs Reelreligion

A preacher writes in one of his sermons that 'religion is a human tool made of faith, worship and charity in order to relate or rebind oneself to a Supreme Being. It becomes real, true and genuine if it is observed with truthful spirit. And this is highlighted by Christ in his teachings.' I find he is correct when I browse the Gospels in the Bible. As much as I know with the help of Scriptures, any Realreligion is always concerned with: rereading; rewriting; revisiting; reliving; renewing; reviving and reforming itself in every moment and movement of its lifespan. But the Reelreligion is commonly seen as a religion of superstition; religion of fear; religion of ignorance; religion of pride; religion of convenience; and a religion of easy-go and easy-come.

I ascertain that a religion becomes reel or real according to its origin and in its day-today practices with clear understanding of its genuine endresults. Its origin may be originated from tribal fear, imaginative myths and dreams of humanity. It may be based on 'they said', 'it is said', 'faith of my fathers and mothers' or on the absence of proper rationality and the active presence of vibrating emotionality, or on the fear of being shattered by natural calamities, fear of sickness, or on the inability to rise up and walk in times of troubles and crises, and above all fear of death, of being annihilated, of becoming dust unto dust and of turning out to be nothing after a glorious period of living and achieving so many things in life. If the above-said were solely the reasons and sources for a religion then we can label it unquestionably a reel religion. On the contrary if it is generated out of true and genuine experiences of a Supreme Being, beyond all that exist in the universe and if that Being holds certain and confirmed and provable connection with the human person or persons then we can name it a real religion.

The second qualification to make a religion reel or real is derived from how that religion is practiced at present. Again it can contain practices that are superstitious, impractical, pharisaical, made of human imaginative, creative, convenient; it can be filled with unjust, undemocratic, doubtful, scrupulous, meticulous and authoritative applications of the ideals of religion and above all, endorsing pluralistic interpretations on the truths it holds and binding every member under burdens of fear and anxiety. Such religion is truly a reel religion. In contrast, real religion's qualifications are: its ultimate goal is possessing fuller life or qualitylife already, but not yet; performing its rituals in spirit and in truth; it is grasped and held both by rationality and faith; expounded in myths and facts; practicing a morality based on humanistic freedom and revelatory experience; and total concern for present world in love and justice.

Realreligion is one practiced in Spirit and Truth

Once, Master Jesus was sharing with a Samaritan woman one of his dreams about his followers and their religious performances. He said: *"The hour is coming, and is now here, when true worshipers will worship the Father in Spirit and truth; and indeed the Father seeks such people to worship him. God is Spirit, and those who worship him must worship in Spirit and truth."* (Jn. 4: 23-24) Anything I perform in the name of my Realreligion, according to my Master, must be done only in Spirit and truth. It can be a spiritual exercise, a sacramental act, a ritual practice or a good work for others. All these must be acted out in Spirit and truth. This means, first of all we should be very clear about the Triune God who is Supreme Spiritual Being. We deal with things pertaining to spiritual realm. Therefore the Spirit of the Lord must individually inspire us to do certain things in the name of God and for the name of God. We must be ready to listen to His promptings and also try to discern its credibility and genuiness; because we should remember we have our own human spirit which has been already tarnished by sin and which possesses its own trickery and deceptiveness.

This is why I love to qualify my Realreligion as 'human spiritual life-management in-situations. What I mean by this is that religion is not just a 'social institution' as any secular systems but also mainly a personal spiritual lifemanagement strategy 'in-situations.' To me religion is simply an environment to put into practice the twofold command or will of God for humans: "Love your Lord God with your whole heart, whole mind, whole soul, whole body and whole strength. And love your neighbor as yourself." Religion is a situation conducive to fulfill such will of God. By nature human person is inclined to one's own self. It is very difficult to go out of oneself, to withdraw from Ego and to love a Being who is beyond all beings, a Life beyond all lives and to love others as oneself. Religion offers an environment to perform certain exercises, practices, rituals and duties to enhance the observance of those commands of God. Religion, therefore, is not an institution but it is a situation. All institutions in the name of religions are simply human systems, man-made strategies to make the religion as situation-in. That is why they are called 'in-situations' or 'institutions'. The true religion is the heart pulse of every human being. The seat of religion is the human heart. That is why the Lord offered the twofold command of love, which is closely related to the heart. When human beings begin to analyze, reflect, think, reason out those heartbeats of religion, they turn to be institutions. Until the human mind does not intervene into the hearts' endeavors regarding God, the religion of humans is plain, simple and genuine. Once the mind starts its 'ancilla-business'—its handmaid job of analyzing and reasoning out—then all the complexities of religions come to exist.

This sort of my approach to religion may be labeled as humanistic, secular, new age, revolutionary or natural and so on. I personally do not accept any such label to my approach. I simply call it for my own convenience 'the heart-religion.' Every human being is born with an environment of religion, because everyone has got a heart, which is the seat of religion. It craves for love in its infinity. It craves for life in its eternity. It longs for fulfillment in its totality. Also everyone is born in an in-situation of religion that is in a system of exercises of religion. If that in-situation does not help the human person to go deeper to the inner religion of the heart, then such an institution must be deserted and the human person should go in search of another 'in-situations'.

Jesus too declared and foretold that his followers would worship God in Truth. He meant that we too must be consecrated to the truth which is absolute as it is found both in Scriptures and Tradition. Since it is crucial but hard to be always attuned to truth, Jesus made a special prayer for this consecration of ours in the truth at his Last Supper: *"Consecrate them in the truth. Your word is truth. As you sent me into the world, so I sent them into the world. And I consecrate myself for them, so that they also may be consecrated in truth."* (Jn. 17: 17-19) Jesus Christ who identified himself as 'the Truth', and told Pilate that he was *born and came to this world in order to testify to the truth.* Now, it is good to know what he meant by 'truth'. 'What is the 'truth'? This was the question asked by Pilate then might be in a sarcastic way or with some suspicion and doubt; but today the same question surely arises in the hearts of every person who desires to follow Jesus. What does the Lord Jesus mean by 'truth'? By analyzing the entire Scriptures, especially the NT Books, I can sum up the meaning of truth under three important factors:

The first dimension of the truth is that every human being is a sinner, offending God and his goodness, disobeying his commandments and because of their sins they undergo so many maladies, pains, sufferings and lead unwanted and unpleasant and unfair lives. Another part of the truth is that love and mercy of God presented itself in the form of the Cross and death of Jesus. The Death of Jesus Christ is the performance in history of the very Mind of God. There is no room for looking on Jesus Christ as a martyr; His death was not something that happened to Him which might have been prevented: His death was the very reason why He came. Never esteem of forgiveness and never base it on the fact that God is our Father and He will forgive us because He loves us. It is untrue to Jesus Christ's revelation of God; it makes the Cross unnecessary. If God does forgive sin, it is because of the Death of Christ. God could forgive men in no other way than by the death of His Son, and Jesus is exalted to be Savior because of His death. And thirdly all who hold Jesus as their Savior in that way turns out to be his citizens and he becomes the Lord and King to them. This means even though I walk through the dusty and muddy road of earthly life, because of Jesus' death I am cleansed from my sins; if I die the same death as his, namely denying, detaching and even losing my worldly and earthly pleasures and possessions, I am chosen to be his soldier, bodyguard, courtier and even his ambassador in my own territory. One thing is certain. The more I am consecrated in Truth the clearer I can listen to Jesus. That is what he prophesied: *"Everyone who belongs to the truth listens to my voice."*

There is one more meaning to the saying of Jesus: 'in Spirit and truth.' Members who belong to Jesus' Kingdom in this world are very human who constitute both soul and body; spiritual and physical; earthly and heavenly. This dichotomy of human existence is the reality. Make-up of two elements is the truthful fact of humanness. So in our dealing with humans if we choose the one element and ignore the other, we are untruthful. Jesus emphasizes this fact in performing our religious observances. In particular in the worship we offer to God this soul-and-body factor must be attended to. Hence the necessity of Rituals, which include involvement of all human senses, all human kinetic communications, and all aesthetic and artistic creativities! Humans, unquestionably, can worship God through meditation and recollection; they can also go so far as encountering mystic intimacy in Spirit; however as God commanded us, we have to love our God with all our heart, with all our mind, with all our strength and with all our being. He demanded from us a total and wholistic worship. Besides, Jesus Christ encouraged us to be together in prayer and worship as a family. It is there, he told us, he would be present and he would grand whatever we request him. The Church takes this wish of Jesus very seriously and makes us gather together as one Body, one Community of disciples in a liturgical environment during which we sing, dance, kneel and stand, raise and hold our hands together. We, the members who follow Realreligion, make sure that we don't participate in any liturgical services like immovable stone or dead cadaver but take strenuous efforts to involve both our soul and body in living, rejoicing and communing with God and our neighbors. It is in this bodily and emotional worship the role of rituals is so essential. And it is thus we fulfill our Master's demand of worshipping wholeheartedly in Spirit and in truth.

Realreligion is a sort of 'Mountaineering University'

In the light of Scriptures and Tradition I am told to esteem my life's ultimate goal is to reach God the Most Holy and enjoy eternal joy and peace in His Presence. I am also instructed to consider this Holy Residence of God is like the Mountain. Invariably in all religions, especially in Judeo-Christianity, mountains are the symbols of mighty God's dwelling place. Prophet Isaiah records the prerequisites for those who dream of dwelling on the high peak of God's Mountain as: Walking righteously; speaking honestly; spurning what is gained by oppression; brushing their hands free of contact with a bribe; stopping their ears lest they hear of bloodshed; and closing their eyes lest they look on evil. (Ref. Is. 33: 15-16) This is why the Psalmist repeats in his songs inviting us to climb up the Mountain of the Lord. He indicates who are capable of reaching the

Lord's Mountain and dwell there for eternity: *Whoever walks without blame, doing what is right, speaking truth from the heart; who does not slander with his tongue, does no harm to a friend, never defames a neighbor; who disdains the wicked, but honors those who fear the LORD; who keeps an oath despite the cost; who lends no money at interest and who accepts no bribe against the innocent.* (Ps. 15: 2-5) The Psalmist again sings in Psalm 24 first questioning: *"Who may go up the mountain of the LORD? Who can stand in his holy place?"* and then answering: *"The man with clean hands and pure heart, who desires not worthless things, who has not sworn so as to deceive his neighbor."*

In the light of Jesus Christ I understand that a religion is a Way for reaching the Heights of God's Mountain and all that I am asked to do and perform as religious deeds are learning, practicing, and taking strenuous efforts to be qualified for attaining my ultimate goal. Though the Psalmist as Isaiah don't use the word religion James in his Letter splendidly exposes the true identity of a religion which is nothing but attempting to covet those prerequisites to reach and dwell in God's Heights. He sums up what the Psalmist and the Prophet wrote on this matter: *"Religion that is pure and undefiled before God and the Father is this: to care for orphans and widows in their affliction and to keep oneself unstained by the world."* (Jas. 1: 27)

Religion, therefore, is a God & man-made 'Mountaineering University' to equip and train myself for continued act of climbing the Mountain of the Lord in this world. It is where I learn and understand what it takes to succeed in the Holy Mountain, pulling together many strands of knowledge and skills; to plan and execute mountaineering expedition, for which my Realreligion prepares me offering lots of helps on many different levels according to my age, gender, culture, and so on. As a matter of mountaineering, anyone who intends to climb any mountain needs to possess the most obvious set of mountaineering skills of technical ability and knowledge of how to climb and how to manage the inherent risks involved. For example, if I plan to climb an earthly mountain like Himalayas, I need to know at least the rudimentary matters like how to set a belay, how to rope up to cross a snow covered glaciers, how to move in steep terrain. The same thing is absolutely true in climbing the Holy Mountain of God. My Realreligion does offer intense, stable, truthful, total, wholistic, and effective assistance in my personal endeavor of climbing the Mountain of my Supreme God.

Like the deer that yearns for running streams, so my soul is yearning for you, my God. My soul is thirsting for God, the God of my life; when can I enter and see the face of God? (Ps. 42) The last sentence in the verse is paraphrased in one of the daily Psalter prayers' antiphon as: *When will I come to the end of my pilgrimage and enter the presence of God?*

Reelreligion of Graveyard

While my Realreligion is full of life and growing, reelreligion looks to me as a religion dead. Whenever I come into a small or big town I am surprised to see a graveyard well-furnished and maintained at the entrance of the town. That scene reminds me of one more graveyard inside the town which many are not aware of. It is called cemetery of the living in contrast and in parallel to the cemetery of the dead. I am not referring only to ghost towns but also many homes is housed by humans who are leading life of isolation, never care of what is going on in neighbor's home or in the community. These self-centered people are in one way dead humans walking. These people religion is literally a reel religion in which there is no life and steam to move on giving life to others. A man passed a funeral parlor. There in the window stood a bold sign that said: 'Why walk around half dead when we can bury you for fifty dollars'. This is how many move around in their lives. In this kind of reel-religion its members feel and live half dead.

In my short tenure of earthly life I sense clearly that a real religion esteems itself not as an end but only as means to an End. A real religion if it is genuinely true must not be esteemed and practiced as an end in itself. It is a big mistake of many humans who are fully satisfied with certain religious practices and rituals and end with it; their religion turns out to be merely an environment for temporary solace. In contrast to this thought a real religion is to be handled only as a way, a channel, or a strategy to covet an eternal goal of human aspiration to become fully part of the Divine. This is why in the days of Apostles after the risen Lord ascended to heaven the whole bundle and package of all the rituals and practices-ethical and spiritual, was called 'the Way.'

Reelreligion is practiced in blindness

Many humans, among both irreligious and religious as well, are not ready to accept that they are blind. It's called the blindness of the blindness. If you are truly sleeping, I can wake you up. But if you act as if you are sleeping, I can't do anything. If you accept that you are blind, then there is the possibility of curing. But if you are blind to your own blindness, then there can be no healing. This is why Jesus pronounced the judgment on the Pharisees. We hear him say, 'If you were blind, there would be no sin in that. But you say that you see, and that is why your sin remains.' The man born blind accepted his weakness, his sickness and his need of healing. Jesus then could heal him. Only those who feel they are sick need Doctor. These persons can never reach out to Jesus for healing by his anointing.

There was a married man in his middle age experienced a crisis in his prayer life. He was very intensively praying to God for nearly 6 months for a gift from Him. No response came from the Upstairs. So very much frustrated he sought some counseling from many priests, pastors and evangelists. They advised him, as much as they could, referring to all kinds of Scriptural quotations. The man tried again with full trust and confidence as he was directed. It did not help. He found God very silent and distant. Finally he approached a priest who was famous in his straightforward and down to earth counseling. The priest, as soon as he listened to the man's complaint about God's indifference toward his prayer, asked him: 'My dear man, would you please tell me what sort of gift you asked from the Lord?" the man replied: "I asked him to give me one more wife." This is how we are blind or blindfolded in many things related to God and to others. It's called our 'inner blindness.'

Many humans are spiritually blind to know, to love and to serve their God as Creator and Redeemer. They are blind in their sinfulness to be conscious of God's active presence in and around their lives. Secondly they are blind to see outside of them what their inner hearts tell them. That is about the human relationships that surround as from their birth as parents, brother, sisters, relatives and friends. Thirdly they too are blind to see those human beings outside of their territory or campus who are handicapped, physically, mentally and socially challenged and neglected by the society. They are prone to be complacent within their four walls and say 'Am I my brother's keeper?' Thus they are grown spiritually empty, judgmental, envious, suspicious, afraid, autonomous, depressed, lonely, disconnected, and out of energy. As Scriptures say, they are blind to see the world, life and the whole universe as God sees. They are fully satisfied with their fake judgment based on outward appearances while God sees through the hearts.

In this modern world there are two groups of spiritually blind people: While on one side of the world where poverty and ignorance dominate people grope in darkness, being blind in superstitious practices and even turn out to be religious terrorists, on the other side we notice so many being blind of the presence of God and the need of connections with him in faith, hope and love. Blindness of not seeing the meaning of human life, its goal, its destiny and its power makes many of us dislike religion, especially the organized religions, religious and spiritual practices like Lenten disciplines. There are millions in this world who never see through the importance of God, his commandments and religions. Following such trend of thought there are millions of people, Catholics and Christians as well stopped going to church and being fully busy making money and getting fame and power.

For example, many who belong to a reel religion either misuse it, or abuse it or carelessly take it for granted. They consider it as any social dinner where they greet, converse, hug, sometimes dance, other times gossip, fill their body and a little bit their emotions. That remains for a short duration. They forget that once all the food is digested. That is how they consider the Eucharistic Meal. By such approach I do not think this breaking of the Bread is going to be an entrypoint for God into their lives nor it would pave the way for turningpoints.

In 'reelreligion' I include also irreligion, which is a lack of religion, indifference to religion, or hostility to religion. Depending on the context, irreligion may be understood as referring to atheism, agnosticism, deism, skepticism, free thought, secular humanism or general secularism. Irreligious people may have convictions equal in depth to those of religious adherents. For instance, followers of the life stance of Humanism regard themselves as just as deeply believing in their life stance as corresponding to any religious belief. In reelreligion there are irreligious Theists; although people classified as irreligious might not follow any religion, not all are necessarily without belief in the supernatural or in deities; such a person may be a non-religious or non-practicing theist. In particular, those who associate organized religion with negative qualities, but still hold spiritual beliefs, might describe themselves as irreligious. People claim that their religion preaches love, and do not hesitate to explain the philosophy of their religion. But the very same people are behind the riots perpetrated against the people of other religion and caste. Why these communal riots happen? What are the reasons behind them? The clashes between groups of different religions and castes have become a great social disease of many countries. Nobody can deny that bigotry is the root cause behind all these conflicts. Until or unless this bigotry is removed from the minds of the people, there is no other way for the people to get enlightened and awakened.

My Unique Religious Journey

Questions are inevitable in our lives. Without questions we do not grow in knowledge, wisdom and understanding. As we all know in our education system these questions play a vital role, not just to get good grade in tests and exams, but more for discovering already existing truths and facts and searching and finding new things too. As any boy of seven I too asked many questions from my brother. Once as he compelled me to go to church I reluctantly got out of my bed and went with him. On our way as we passed a Hindu temple I asked 'why do we go to church? He answered 'To worship God.' I again asked why don't we go to this Temple or Mosque? He said, 'it is because Our God does not want us to go.' Why does he not want us to go here and only to our church? Because Jesus is present only in our churches. Who is Jesus? Jesus is God's Son. How do we know Jesus is God's Son? We know from our Sacred Scriptures. My Hindu friends also told me their Scriptures say that God is present and his saints are present in their temples too? Our Jesus and his Book are the true sources from the true God. Who said it? Jesus himself said it. We believe him because he is the Messiah. Why do we say he is our Messiah? By this time we reached the entrance of our church. My brother stopped and said to me, 'You go inside. I will come later.' I went and joined with other boys and girls in prayer. When I came out of the church I noticed my brother still sitting at the entrance of the church. I asked him 'Why did you not come inside the church?' He got wild. He was furious. 'Stop there,' he said. 'I will come or I won't. It is none of your business.' I could not understand why he got angry that way. Only later when I was interrogated this way by my students in the catechism class I could clearly understand my brother's desperate situation in answering my hundreds of questions.

Some of my atheistic friends confronted me many times in my life with a question that put me on spot and never left me until I decided to find a legitimate answer. That dangerous question is: "Is your religion reel or real?" At first hearing the question I was truly irritated like my brother. I had been thinking that I belong to a religion that is real and not fake, truthful and not superstitious, based on truths and not myths, and above all, that is the one and only religion that is wholistic, total and full. That is how I ended up with a religion, which I call the 'Realreligion.' I hopefully dream that a day will come in everyone's life at which he/she, after searching untiringly, will be satisfied with the religion of the heart, a real religion where all will find God, all will love him and all will love their neighbors as themselves.

My friends and myself who are staunchly practicing Realreligion have gone through a faithjourney which is so breathtaking when we browse our journals and diaries of olden days. We either jumped, or hopped, or swimming against or floating on the current at every step or phase of our religious and spiritual life: From drinking milk to eating meat as Paul would say. From Blind Faith to Reasonable Faith; From Impersonal God to Personal God; Not much formal but more spontaneous prayer; From my God to our God; From Historical Jesus to Mystical Jesus; From Institutional Church to Pilgrim Church (moving, growing); From Ritualistic Faith to Monumental Faith (Approaching sacraments, rituals not by itself but with reciprocal relation to its efficacy); From Receiving Personality to Giving Personality; From single-track View of life to Open-ending View of it; From Sin-avoiding Spirituality to Holy Mountaineering Spirituality; From Spot-light Winning to Dark-night Diving (Suffering, Retirement and Old Age)

My Realreligion is primarily a personal endowment

Unquestionably the religion I hold is certainly a lion's share taken from the Religion labeled us Christianity. However when I started appropriating it as my own, developing it through my intelligence, prayer and with the cooperation of others belonging to the same and applying it fully in my day today life, it turns out to be 'my religion.' There may be certain discrepancies between mine and others in how I understand how I grip it and how I handle and manage it according to my personality, my culture, my social milieu and my human abilities. This disparity in no way changes its very root and basis. It is as if a son's share of his father's inheritance. Though he makes it grow more and enlarge its territory-at some times may seem dissimilar in its shape and size, it is after all the inheritance of the father which is shared the same as this son. Once a religion becomes my own endowment as part and parcel of my life it turns out to be very exclusive and very personal. Still my religion remains as the sole inheritance of the heavenly Father received through my elder Brother Jesus Christ. What I possess now as my own inheritance is very little compared to what the heavenly Father's Possessions. I reflect in this book only about the creed-package I personally uphold within me and how I act upon it in my personal life.

The Twofold Religious Gift-package

Generally a religion, if it is true to its name, contains two gift-packages offered to its members: A package of values and a package of practices. While the wallet of values fills the emotional, intellectual and spiritual dimensions of humans with magnificent logics, goals, visions, and rewards regarding religious membership, the second gift-pack contains commandments, ritual observances, religious and spiritual practices. The Church, in which I practice my Realreligion, truly offered to me this twofold package on the first day of my entrance to it. Since I was too little a baby at that time my elders got it on my behalf. They too made the first vow in my place as my proxies. As I grow older I used my reason and education and appropriated those two religious gift-packs and began unwrapping them and slowly learned why and how of all that were contained in those packs. I listened attentively to the voice of my Realreligion regarding those gifts offered to me by my Mother Religion.

Intrinsic connection between Religion and Life

In the spirit of my Guru Jesus my Realreligion always holds that any true religion cannot be separated from life. Religion, according to Jesus, is nothing but the way of life. Like my earthly life my religion is divided as private and public, inner and outward. The fundamental choice I have made regarding my God in Jesus is not only the starting point of my religion but also its core and base. While such an intimate relationship with an invisible God and the spiritual resurrected there is one more important component in my religion. The former is only the inner side of my religion whereas the latter is an outward dimension of it. It is the practice and exercise of the choice I have made in religion. A true religion is a combination of both the choice of God and its practice. This is why my Realreligion upholds very faithfully the twofold commandment of God, namely loving God as my only Lover and expressing it with my neighborly love. The first one is my inner religion and the second, my outward religion.

In Scriptures I come across many words of God emphasizing this truth. In James' Letter I read: 'Be doers of the choice you made and not just hearers.' In other words, not simply be spiritual but also religious. Practice it in day-to-day life. And he adds: *"Religion that is pure and undefiled before God and the Father is this: to care for orphans and widows in their affliction and to keep oneself unstained by the world."* God handed down his Commandments to his people who pledged to love him wholeheartedly telling them to observe them faithfully. My God wants me therefore to observe outside what I believe inside of my heart; not making my religion as mere lipservice, rather a life brimming with lovedeeds.

True religion does not end there. With the two as observed by James there is one more that my realreligion teaches me to observe is the performing of certain rituals and rites personal and communal to show our connections with God the Lover, to worship Him as my Creator, to exercise and experience certain kind of heavenly connections in this world. Through these rites and rituals I am to receive power from on High to live the life as God wants us to live.

All these four dimensions of my Realreligion, namely total love for God, selfless and sacrificial love of neighbors, good moral behavior and religious rituals, are contained in the Ten Commandments God gave to me as a summary. Unfortunately most of my friends in reelreligions either undo the entire commandments or overdo them. My Guru Jesus never endorses, rather chides, those who overdo it. Those are the people who are very meticulous and scrupulous in adding to what the Lord intended them to observe. Many times some of them burden other people with overdoses. Others concentrate only on outward observances and not on the inner attitude.

In those days of my formation my superiors were very strict with me in obeying what they proposed to me as rules and regulations of the institution. For example, Rule of sacred silence; Rule of Touch; and Rule of speaking English. My superiors were very meticulous and very much concerned with rules they made for their convenience but always telling us 'keep these rules and the rules will keep you; observe these things for the greater glory of God.' As a young man I did violate many times such rules daily. Such violation hurt me so much that whenever I went for weekly confession my only confession was about violating these rules sometimes hundred times a week and asking God's pardon for my sins. Now I understand my superiors' goodwill and over-anxiety to make out of me a perfect priest. But very sadly they have instilled in me a feeling of more concerned with outward observances than inner connections with the eternal Lover.

My Realreligion today is my way of life basing and centering everything in my life on total love for God and expressing such inner drive through observing certain outward deeds. It demands to be moral in private and in public; it urges me to do kind deeds to the needy; it compels me to perform certain regular rituals and rites both inside and outside the church campus as private, personal and communal prayer and worship. All these outward deeds are to be observed or performed as vital, real and truthful. I can use all my talents and creative power to enhance all these things. But I should make sure that my mind, heart and body are blended together and everything I do outside come out of the total love for my God in Jesus. Anything I perform as religious rituals must be with purity of intention and always in connection with what I say and do in my private, family and community life. Consequently I firmly believe all that I labor with sweat and blood become a source of joy, peace, and heavenly rewards here and after death.

Realreligion shuns hypocrisy in religious performances

It is most disgusting to observe how so many members, who practice reelreligion inside the Church, perform their religious obligations in a very hypocritical manner. Realreligion makes sincere attempt to shun such despicable religiosity. It reminds itself frequently what its divine Teacher Jesus Christ instructed on this matter: *"Take care not to perform righteous deeds in order that people may see them; otherwise, you will have no recompense from your heavenly Father."* In following chapters I discuss how I, with other friends of Realreligion, preserve a clear mindsetup regarding all earthly things and matters, especially our religious observances and rituals which are proposed to us by our Mother religion-the Church and how we conduct ourselves in handling and performing them in Spirit and in truth in the light of the risen Lord Jesus.

Rituals abused by Reelreligion's members

A Sage decided to spend several years in solitude, meditating on the presence of God in all things. When he returned to his family and friends, his eyes shone with the beauty of what he had experienced in solitude. Many seekers came to ask him for his truth, yet he hesitated to answer them, refusing to try to put his experience into words. Under pressure, he finally relented and wrote down what he knew was only a feeble hint of what he had discovered. His admirers memorized his words. They wrote them down; held conferences so others could hear them; created volumes of books analyzing them and finally formed a religious organization so they would be reverenced forever. Soon, repeating his words became so important that no one remembered that they were originally about a profound experience. As his words spread, the Sage became disheartened. He wept and said: "I had hoped to help but perhaps I should not have spoken at all."

This story reminds us of what Jesus might have been thinking as the reelreligion's members participate every time in the Mass. Words to them have become more important than messages! That is how these rituals turn out to be total distractions to the experiences they are supposed to offer! Our Lord Jesus established his Church as and His Spirit moves the Church to impart all promised heavenly experiences and blessings through many rituals.

In this Book

My book discusses about the values of my Realreligion I uphold to. While I describe about the true and genuine values I too talk in contrast about their corrupted version as found in the Reelreligion. There are indeed numerous faith elements in my Realreligion in the form of Dogmas, Doctrines and Traditions and so on. I have taken a few of them not at random or by lot. Rather, I picked up those faith-elements that I personally esteem as most crucial and beneficial to my personal and communal life—the life of one of BabyBoomers; of a person born out of Age of Enlightenment; an adult crawling in the midst of aftermath shocks of post-modern world.

Though I began 10 years back gathering all that I could to write on this subject, I started putting everything into a book form only after the Catholic Church announced the Year of Faith. Pope Benedict XVI announced the 'Year of Faith' beginning on 11 October 2012, the fiftieth anniversary of the opening of the Second Vatican Council, and ending on the Solemnity of Our Lord Jesus Christ, Universal King, on 24 November 2013. The starting date of 11 October 2012 also marks the twentieth anniversary of the publication of the Catechism of the Catholic Church. Pope's motivation for such announcement was, as he quoted in his Apostolic Letter *'Porta Fidei'* from Pope VI, to offer a solemn moment for the whole Church to make an authentic and sincere profession of the same faith; and that faith is to be confirmed in a way that was individual and collective, free and conscious, inward and outward, humble and frank. In this way the whole Church could reappropriate exact knowledge of the faith, so as to reinvigorate it, purify it, confirm it, and confess it.

Taking the Church's Year of Faith invitation seriously and for several months I pondered over my personal religion and examined those values of faith sincerely. I asked myself 'whether religion I uphold is truly: Real or reel? True or false? Genuine or false? Authentic or artificial? Heartfelt or routine? Fruitful or poisonous? Original or counterfeit? Single-hearted or double-hearted?' This is how this book was conceived and shaped. This book can be considered as a self-imposed act of examining my conscience about the identity, nature and application and practice of religion in my life. I attempt to confess whether I have done my best to blossom my personal religion into a real one as oppose to reel or false one. I hope and pray this effort of mine will surely assist my readers do the same not only during this Year of Faith but also later on in life when tumult of waves and trials daunting against our faith and religion.

Every one of us has to go through in religious life different stages of uphill or downhill, emptiness or fullness, and sometimes of hostility or indifference toward one's religious practices. I am not exempted at all in this kind of zigzag religious journey. However thanks to God, my Mother Church and religious authors I read, I was able to rise up and walk again in religious faith and fidelity. Above all, as the days went by, I realized within me an overwhelming taste for reading and reflecting over the words of God in the Bible which became the most powerful and resourceful means for expounding my Realreligion. The Prophets testify: "When I found your words, I devoured them; they became my joy and the happiness of my heart, because I bore your name, O Lord, God of hosts." (Jer. 15:16) That happened in my ministry of communication and journalism. Consequently my readers may notice in all my works, especially in this book, Scriptural words are abounding.

Every 'in-out-in' religious conversion of this sort was not a sudden one but a gradual one in accordance with my analytical and rational nature. On this basis of my life-conversions I am fully confident of the fact that my readers too will experience slowly but steadily the same genuine conversions in practicing their Realreligion in faith and reason as they read through this book unhurriedly but analytically.

Fr. Benjamin A. Vima

Chapter-1:
Faith according to my Realreligion

"I believe"

Generally the word 'Faith' is considered as a synonym of 'Religion.' The main reason is that every religion is based and made of certain faith-formulas called 'Creed.' That is the source and sign of a religion. My realreligion is not exempted in this. However there are many misgivings and misuses of the virtue 'faith' found among my fellow-humans, who are named by me the members of reelreligion. Hence, before discussing the principles and practices of my Realreligion, first I want to talk about my Realreligion's faith in 'Faith.'

True meaning of 'faith'

Before I discuss about my assessment on my own faith, I have to clarify how I use in this book the term 'faith'. The English word 'faith' is a translation of a Latin *fidem*, or *fidēs,* meaning trust, akin to *fidere* to trust. It is very much close to a *Yiddish term 'Chutzpah' which derives from the Hebrew word ḥuṣpâ.* It indicates the quality of audacity in humans, for good or for bad, but it is generally used negatively. However we notice this term applied to faith by the Gospel writers many times. *Chutzpah has lot more in its meaning: It indicates the supreme self-confidence or nerve that allows someone to do or say things that may seem shocking to others; it's* a nearly

1

arrogant courage; utter audacity or impudence; it makes a person shameless in doing or speaking certain things which to others seem like crazy or freaky behavior.

In conjunction with its root meaning therefore faith is simply the confident belief or trust in the truth of or trustworthiness of a person, idea, or thing. This term faith is applied generally to any simple trust a human person holds on another human person's outward behavior, even inward convictions that are communicated outside through words, promises and actions. In common usage inner faith can refer to confidence in a person or thing; adherence to an obligation of loyalty to a person, organization, or idea; holding to things your reason has once accepted, in spite of your changing moods; belief in a proposition or belief system without proof. When I relate here all these definitions to my own faith I deliberate candidly how my 'Faith'—outer, communal and my 'faith'-inner, personal, are either interrelated to each other or at odds with each other.

Abiding by the same 'root-formula', in religious circle and theological studies faith is used in two ways. I too follow the same in this book: First, it is used to point at a 'Package of Creed' containing all convictions, values, directives and guidelines about God, the relationship between Him and His creations and their covenantal dealings going on in the spiritual and social realm. This faith is also renamed as religion. Secondly, faith also describes a person's inner attitude toward the 'creed-package' of values and convictions taught and preached outside and followed by millions of people as religion This inner side of faith is in general influenced by the persuasion of the mind which subdues the will to accept and live the outside life according to it. As Oswald Chambers writes, I firmly hold that to believe means to commit: mentally we commit ourselves to certain things, values or persons and abandon all that is not related to that commitment; morally we commit ourselves to this way of confidence and refuse to compromise with any other. As a specific example, I can say that through my Christian faith I commit myself spiritually to Jesus Christ, and determine in everything I do, to be dominated by the Lord alone.

In order to assess the identity and impact of one's own faith, it is necessary to understand several highly complex and deeply entrenched challenges that accompany with it. Although each one's faith remains radically the same, an individual's temperament, personal growth, age, formation, peergroup, and societal environment, and so on, change the style, understanding, communication, performance and application of his/her faith. Every Christian is demanded by our Master Jesus to uphold his radical faith-Chutzpah. This radical faith can differ from each other in the individual style through which we demonstrate it. Look at our two Popes of the modern world: Benedict and Francis. While we notice in both of them the one and only radical faith there is a difference in style of it. Both are two historical figures of the highest faith, whose relationship with life is completely anchored in God. However this radical faith is shown in Pope Benedict's shy and kind bearing but in Pope Francis it is revealed by his immediate sweetness and spontaneity. I have been in my pastoral ministries encountering the same radicalness of faith in most of my parishioners but differing from each other in their style of performing it.

Notable role of 'faith' in humans' lives

As a matter of fact, a person's faith in the 'Faith' he/she upholds plays a great role in one's religious, social and spiritual life. As many philosophers and theologians in religious campuses have advocated, faith is truly the basis of all knowledge. St. Augustine is quoted saying: *"Crede, ut intelligas"* ("Believe in order that you may understand"). This adage holds good not just in religious matters but encompasses the totality of knowledge. In the process of human knowledge faith must be present in order to know anything. Human act of knowing something or somebody is based primarily on the knower's quality and quantity of assumption, belief or faith in the credibility of a person, place, thing, or idea from outside; even the kind of inner intuition of an individual needs largely the faith upheld within as its startup.

When I browse my own past life I discover this fact very truthful. As a child I held my parental teaching as credible, in spite of my lack of sufficient research to establish such credibility empirically; my parental teaching, however fallible, became a foundation upon which my future knowledge has been built. My faith in my parents' teaching was based on a belief in their credibility. Until my belief in my parents' credibility was superseded by a stronger belief, their teaching did serve as a filter through which other teachings had been processed and evaluated. Later days I came to a realization that my parents, on whose instructions and directions I relied fully for my lifemanagement, were not infallible. Some of what I learned from them seemed to me later wrong, and therefore I consciously rejected them. Parental instruction had been the historical foundation of my future knowledge but that does not necessarily make it a structural foundation. Such human development process found in my life proves to me that faith is the fundamental basis of all knowledge every human being has.

Even when I became adult I realized that the basis for some of my knowledge can be attributed to so-called "authorities" in a given field of study. This is true because I simply do not have the time or resources to evaluate all of my knowledge empirically and exhaustively. I often depend on my faith. It is very interesting to know that sometimes even scientific knowledge is dependent on 'faith.' Namely the more I hold strong faith in the credibility of the scientist's competence and honesty, the greater is my adherence to his/her empirical conclusion. As Michael Polanyi, a distinguished chemist and philosopher, argues, any scientific discovery begins with a scientist's faith that an unknown discovery is possible. Scientific discovery thus requires a passionate commitment to a result that is unknowable at the outset.

Complexity of 'faith'

I fully agree with St. Cyril of Jerusalem who says that there are two kinds of faith and both are equally important in human life that craves for intimate relationship with the things related to God and His realm. *One kind of faith concerns doctrines. It involves the soul's ascent to and acceptance of some particular matter.* According to my personal perception, this sort of faith is more akin to human intellect and emotionality. So it can end up as mere natural faith which is a necessity to survive in this world as social, cultural human being. Our human survival, and even for success, practically depends on natural faith. As I have discussed earlier, from womb to tomb every human being hang on to believing certain people or some established traditions and systems for one's life's welfare. The same is true in interactions between God and humans. Human faith in God is 99%

4

very human and natural; it is based on humans' physical, emotional and intellectual cooperation throughout life, especially in its initial stage. All, that are taught to humans, as Scriptural passages, their interpretations, as catechetical lessons, as dogmas, doctrines and surely the creed, the summary-bundle of one's faith, are the outcome of humans' ability of understanding, perceiving and communicating. So we can assert a large portion of my faith is natural that is the basis of my faith.

However St. Cyril of Jerusalem adds one more kind of faith to this natural faith. Let me quote him: *"The other kind of faith is given by Christ by means of special grace. Now this kind of faith, given by the Spirit as a special favor, is not confined to doctrinal matters, for it produces effects beyond any human capability."*

St. Cyril is absolutely right in his statement on twofold faith. Once I fully uphold and adhere to what the Church teaches and how I personally grasp them and apply them to my daily life, I need to make this natural faith grow into a spiritual one. This I can never accomplish. I need the gratuitous cooperation of the Spirit of the risen Lord to whom I can cry out as his disciples did, 'Lord, increase my faith.' Then the Lord comes to my assistance to make my fragile human faith into stronger, truer, more genuine and more fruitful. In John's Gospel narratives about the apparitions of the resurrected Lord, I hear about the increase of human faith of all his disciples, especially Thomas. Thomas did have some sort of initial natural faith; but as any other humans he wanted to be smarter than others to look for tangible testimony for his faith, he wanted to touch the risen Lord's body and strengthen his faith. The risen Jesus, being happy about Thomas' natural faith and how he was longing for the increase of that faith, came near him and showed his readiness to comply with the disciple's quest. At that very moment something 'deeper touching' was happening. Jesus touched the heart of Thomas and made his faith stronger. This is why even before he touched Jesus' wounds, he cried out with faith 'My Lord and My God.' When such a historical transformation was occurring in Thomas, Jesus, praising our human attempt of showing and improving our natural faith, teaches us through Thomas that we should always live by faith and not by sight alone.

God in Jesus is always looking for chance to increase our human faith as he wants, especially at the time of human trials. Most of us drop out of our natural faith in God and his realm only in those moments of human sufferings and trials. As the Lord proclaimed, 'blessed are those who live by faith and not by sight.' And this was repeated by Paul too. As I reflected on this blessedness of faith, I began rewriting it for my personal use. I wrote in my journal: "I live not by sight but by 'vision'. A passage from the book of Revelation gave me such audacity to claim. John, the writer of this Book, wrote it, as Scriptural scholars point out, in his venerable old age and in his exile. His opponents exiled him to an isolated island for murdering him. Even at this horrible moment of his life John testifies his faith as well as expresses his heartbeats for the increase of his faith. In the beginning chapter of his Book he writes: *I, John, your brother, who share with you the distress, the kingdom, and the endurance we have in Jesus, found myself on the island called Patmos because I proclaimed God's word and gave testimony to Jesus.* We know from his own writing how the Lord increased his faith encouraging him: *"Do not be afraid. I am the first and the last, the one who lives. Once I was dead, but now I am alive forever and ever. I hold the keys to death and the netherworld.*

This is the regular experience of every disciple committed to Jesus. Despite of my agonizing period of pain and suffering, I do my best to profess and praise the Lord with the limited faith I possess. During this kind of period of renewing and increasing my faith, as other disciples of Jesus, my natural faith-by-sight turns out to be faith-of—vision; the risen Lord makes me perform marvelous deeds; I am aware that they may not be all the time miracles that are enumerated in the Bible. However every ordinary and routine thing I perform and go through drudgeries of daily life with the spiritual faith in the risen Lord they become extraordinarily fruitful and effective.

The faith I cherish within me is first and foremost purely a gracious gift from God; and simultaneously a product of my intellect in its making. Let me clarify my statement. The faith I possess as my own, though it appears as the product of my inner self, made of intellect and will, is after all an infused virtue, by which the intellect is perfected by a supernatural light, in virtue of which, under a supernatural movement of the will, it assents firmly to the supernatural truths of Revelation, not on the motive of intrinsic evidence, but on the sole ground of the infallible authority of God revealing. *My faith, which is truly the nerve in my human dealings with God, still* is totally the gift of my Supreme Master. In my upholding of faith I am fully aware of the fact that the faith I hold about my life with God is totally a gift from Him only.

There is an intrinsic connection between faith and grace. Without the grace of God we cannot do any spiritual efforts including believing God and His interactions with us. Faith is purely a gift of God. It is only through His grace our faith can be nourished, developed, matured and would reap the expected results. Paul emphasizes in his Letters that our justification, namely liberation from sinfulness and sanctification like unto Him, can be realized only by our faith and adherence to His grace.

Here I want to add one author's explanation of the intrinsic connection existing between grace and faith: The word, "justify", besides its forensic implications, it also relates to carpentry and to type-setting. A carpenter uses a plumb line (a cord weighted at one end to determine vertical and right angles) to establish right angles or determines depth. A vertical line can be described as 'justified' when the line is straight. The line is "right." It is "upright." It does not lean one way or list another. The line is "just." Applied to us it suggests that grace 'justifies' us by helping us stand up straight and walk in balance. Our faith in grace makes us "just," or "upright" when it heals our limp, straightens our back, or heals our back humped over from carrying burdens. We walk in righteousness with God when we help free others from their burdens as well.

Though my faith is very human it is also esteemed as divine, not much because of its content is all about the Supreme Spiritual Being and about all that surrounded Him, but mostly because it is purely a gratuitous gift from God. This is why the disciples prayed to their Master: *"Lord, increase our faith."* (Lk.17:5) God's grace from above must descend upon us to believe and continue to believe in Jesus: *"No one can come to me unless the Father who sent me draws him."* (Jn.6:44, 65) *"For flesh and blood has not revealed this to you, but my heavenly Father."* (Mt.16:17) Faith is a sheer bequest from God. *"For by grace you have been saved through faith, and this is not from you; it is the gift of God."* (Eph.2:8)

My faith and my Reason

Very amazingly the truthful fact about 'my faith' which I unquestionably claim as the gratuitous gift from God, by the same firm state of mind I declare it is also a my personal product-in-making. In other words there is no more blind-leaping in my faith. There is an intrinsic connection between my faith and my reason. There are many efforts taken in the past as well as today to save the Faith as the Society of Christian Philosophers (SCP), a sub-group of the American Philosophical Association; the Evangelical Philosophical Society; the save the Faith Movement and so on.

My faith depends on the service of my intellect which is supposed to be its handmaid. Though there is an amazing unity between my faith and my reason, there is an undisputable chasm between them: The truths and facts that are proposed and elaborated by my reason regarding God and religion are interiorly ordered to my faith, finding in the latter their entire truth. It is also true that my faith, recognizing the necessity of my reason, reciprocally embraces and makes its own whatever my reason points out to it. In fact both tend to unveil the same mystery, the mystery of me, a human person, who is destined to realize the human dignity and human endowments of freedom, justice, and love. However the difference between the two lies in the fact that while my reason stands by itself with no help or hope whatsoever outside of its weak and fragile background, such as sense-perceptions, my faith claims that all the human endowments are the gratuitous gifts from God who created humans in his image and likeness, plus these endowments are to be realized fully only in Christ. As Paul instructs, I walk by my faith and not by my brittle sight.

Essentially, my faith, which I as a cradle Catholic inherited, learned, exercised-with amusement but sometimes with irritation, and renovated, consists of many incredibles which my reason is unable to digest. For example, my faith that God is triune: Father, Son and the Spirit; that Jesus is the Word, Logos, already existing with the Father God before creation; that he is God's Son but in the fullness of time he was conceived as human being; that he was born of a woman who became a mother to Him before her wedding. This means His mother brought him forth even though she had no any relations with a man; that he was born of a family tree in which many of his ancestors were holy people of God but few others were sinful and even prostitutes; that he was born in hidden way and in a very poor rejected condition; that at his birth while angels were singing and the heavens were bright with beautiful lights as a theatrical background certain poor and rustic shepherds visited and greeted him with his mother; that there was also a shining star that appeared in the sky that brought three magi to see him and pay their homage.

Besides all the above-mentioned, my faith too holds on some more incredibles on the basis and in the light of Scriptures and Tradition: That Jesus, sent by God, through his blood has brought redemption to me. This means from his death and resurrection I've received ever-victorious grace to win all spiritual battle against evils, including my death; that I live, move and have my being in the resurrected Jesus; that his Spirit moves me, overpowers me and executes all that God intends for me; that a day will come when the same resurrected Lord will come back in glory. When the judgment day shall come, and when all humans must rise to meet their both reward and punishment as they deserve and I will be one among them; that in the meantime Jesus has left to me and my friends his Church, His own mystical Body, which is my guiding star, teaching Guru, and nourishing mother through the sacraments and rituals.

There are many other incredibles, such as I above enumerated, in the form of dogmas which the Faith, I am affiliated to, expects me to believe them all strongly with no hesitation, to cherish them in my heart and float around in that air of incredibles. As I said earlier, my reason is not very much pleased with such incredibles, though they have numerous eyewitnesses for them to be claimed worth holding. Pope Francis, in his visit to Brazil, 25 July 2013, was quoted saying to people: *"Please, do not 'liquidize' your faith in Jesus Christ. We liquidize oranges, apples, bananas, but please—do not drink liquidized faith. Faith is whole, it cannot be liquidized or reduced."* Human reason always tries to liquidize or oversimplify the whole truth of all incredibles Church offers me for my human convenience. But that is not the right way to handle my faith.

In the Letter to the Hebrews after enlisting so many faith-holders in the past, the author writes: *"Therefore, since we are surrounded by so great a cloud of witnesses, let us rid ourselves of every burden and sin that clings to us and persevere in running the race that lies before us while keeping our eyes fixed on Jesus, the leader and perfecter of faith."* (Heb. 12: 1-2) John, in his Book of Revelation describing about his vision of heaven writes: *"After this I had a vision of a great multitude, which no one could count, from every nation, race, people, and tongue. They stood before the throne and before the Lamb, wearing white robes and holding palm branches in their hands."* (Rev. 7: 9) He also adds his conversation with an elder who points out who those people are: *"These are the ones who have survived the time of great distress; they have washed their robes and made them white in the blood of the Lamb."* (Rev. 7: 14) All, who the Faith I belonged to glorifies as Martyrs and Saints are those people vested in white garment. Through their life-stories I come to know how strong they were in upholding all the incredibles I have inherited.

There is one more factor which forces me to accept the credibility of those incredibles. In human development process holding on to incredibles is the only way to realize my human dreams. Let me explain myself this way: Every human being is brought up with stories, fables and fairy tales. Most of us did not get sleep as babies until our mom or dad sat near us and told us a bedtime story that shrouded with incredibles. We are built up by fables and incredibles. As children we crave and thirst for such incredibles. Look at our boys and girls. The whole world of children looks for novels like Harry Potter's Adventures and movies like Superman and Spiderwoman and stories like 'The Lion, the Witch and the Wardrobe.' Even as adults we long to read and hear such incredibles happened or happening in our midst. If the journalism or arts world are thriving and booming today thanks to their frequent and regular offers of such incredible stories in the form of news, documentaries, and biographies and so on. We cannot survive without hearing or at least dreaming about incredible things. We always dream bigger than ourselves, greater than what we possess and hold.

If the humanity has produced so much technological and scientific things and has reached to this modern age it is all thanks to human dreaming about greater things. The same is true about our dreams about the incredibles of God's identity, existence and his deeds. Human development in all its dimensions entirely depends on how much a human being possesses an ability to believe in incredibles, which means believing in something higher than oneself, bigger than one's material possessions and greater than even one's own life.

Thanks to God and His Messengers, I am gifted with a huge package of numerous incredibles about my God and my religious Faith. God invites me to believe and hold them in my heart very fervently and to long, to pray and to wish such incredibles happening in my life and in my friends' lives. One of the most fruitful and necessary incredibles is that the same God wishes I should imitate Him in His holiness and compassion; and the same God loved me so much that He sent His only Son for my rescue from evils and in order to become divine follow His Jesus as my Way. Therefore the Faith I hold as my faith induces me to proceed with all my personal and communal endeavors focused on the ultimate goal of becoming like God's Son, and in turn I become incarnated being as an 'Emmanuel' in my family, in my community and in the whole universe. Consequently my life turns out to be one of those incredibles as the lives of countless men and women. To be an Emmanuel in this hurry berry, confused, distracted, and selfish world is an incredible occurring in this funny world. And the irony of this incredible is I will reach my ultimate goal of life though my innate nature is not that much favorable and cooperative to me.

Faith is source of chivalrous life of endurance

Besides its distinguished part played in human life, there are innumerable benefits gained from one's true faith. Without faith no true relationship is built among humans. Without faith in God the individuals, though they have accomplished so many philanthropic achievements, have ruined themselves at the end or lived unhappily with no peace of mind.

My faith, besides being the source and basis of all that I perform and speak in all dimensions of my life, especially my religious and spiritual undertakings, is also an attitude of patience or endurance in life, especially at the times of crisis. My faith, as a spiritual author puts it, is simply living always in the hands of God as a bow and arrow in the hands of an archer. My Creator and Provider is aiming at something I cannot see; most of the times He seems stretching and straining it; and even at times I feel "I cannot stand anymore." I am so vexed to discover so many unanswered prayers at my praying pews;

He does not heed. In His Faith Package He admonishes me to stay put to it there. This enduring faith is not a pathetic sentiment, but hearty and vigorous confidence (Chutzpah) built on the fact that God is holy love. I cannot understand what He is doing, but I know Him. Faith is the heroic effort of my life, a reckless confidence on God.

Ever-challenging conundrum of faith

Prayer of complaint has become an integral part of my daily routines toward God. Especially after seeing and listening to many horrible incidents like the Twin tower Tragedy at New York it has turned to be consistent one. I tell the God of my faith: "I see everywhere violence and terror. Unfortunately I don't know why you are not intervening? Why do you let me see ruin? Why must I look at misery? Destruction and violence are before me. There is strife and clamorous discord. I cry to you for help but you do not listen! Why? Why?" This prayer of complaint is not anything spontaneous or informal. It's a formal prayer I picked up from the Bible. It's the prayer of prophet Habakkuk (Hab.1/2-3). And the Lord consistently answers me, "Wait for my promise to be fulfilled; wait for your dreams and visions come true." He adds, "Don't rush. The rash one has no integrity; but the just one because of his faith shall live."

Such a cold but persistent response of the God whom I worship induces me to doubt about His Presence. My faith in Him as a way and destiny is shattered. I even doubt about the very concept of faith. I don't enjoy having faith in my own faith. I hear many modern philosophers calling it a mere human psychological 'complex' to find a balance in this unfair game of life. Communists label it as the refuge of the oppressed and the weaklings of the society. Majority of the humanity not just survive but thrive without adhering to a faith. Worst still, people who register themselves to a faith use their faith either as a magical lamp of Aladdin, or as a mask to hide their wrong doings, or justify their social evil doings, or to uphold their political power over the common people. Through this faith many deceive themselves and cheat others too.

Against this background, the God of Jesus insists that the just man lives only by faith. In Scriptures He explains the need of faith, the results of faith, and the kind of true faith. He offers me ample proof for the positive and negative approaches to faith among humans.

People who misused their faith or upheld a wrong approach to faith have only hurt themselves and the entire humanity as we experienced in many cruel acts of terrorists.

Jesus my Leader has declared: 'If you have faith the size of a mustard seed, you would say to this mulberry tree, 'be uprooted and planted in the sea,' and it would obey you'. (Lk. 17/6) This is version of Luke. Matthew goes further and describes the power of faith: 'Amen I say to you, if you have faith the size of a mustard seed, you will say to this mountain, 'Move from here to there,' and it will move. Nothing will be impossible for you.' (Mt.17/20) The question arises here: What kind of mustard-size-faith should I have to release such enormous power?

In the same Scriptures with the guidelines of a preacher I come across some details about the true and powerful faith: Faith is character and not just knowledge and acceptance of some values. It's simply a spirit of power, love, and self-control. Faith is patiently waiting and enduring the process of running until we reach the destiny. Faith is an untiring quest to seek God the beyond. Faith is a continuous begging from the Supreme to give His wisdom first to know His will, secondly to share His power with us to execute His will, and thirdly to offer us His love to bear the consequences of His will. Faith is a sense of servitude to an Invisible but personal Being who is the Sovereign of the Universe.

Very sadly I don't come across any of the above-cited characteristics of faith in the dictionary of modern world. They are hard to digest. This kind of faith surely degrades the scientific, technological and enlightened human prestige. This is why human faith is underestimated and devalued. And with sour-grape attitude it is labeled as 'complex', 'refuge of weaklings', 'Mechanism of Power-Politics', and even as a 'source of terrorism'.

The faith, an incredible and rare gift endowed to us from above, must be properly handled and managed as long as we live in this world where our faith is challenged sometimes crudely by the sight-oriented earthly life. *"We live by faith and not by sight."* Faith, as Paul says, is a deposit handed down to us. Therefore we have to safeguard it. Faith is a high-maintenance gift. Faith, a rare gift from heaven, is to be personalized, appropriated. Yes, it's true that, whether we are cradle or converted Catholics, we inherit this wonderful faith from our families or from the community or from some of our friends. However this faith should not always stay as 'our faith' or their faith. It must become personal, part and parcel of each person. It should grow as 'my faith.' It is then only faith would show its true color, its power and identity. *"Your faith has saved you; go in peace."* *(Lk.7/50)*

Undoubtedly our faith is to be safeguarded and protected as if tending a burning lamp. Until our faith remains in its childhood it is to be treated that way. As our parents and grandparents did to us while we were children we have to take good care of our faith not to be easily contaminated, polluted or twisted by external malicious influences. We were told not to read this book or that, threatened with parental warnings if we browse any filthy and anti-faith webs or TV channels. Faith in the childhood was very vulnerable. Hence it had to be protected that way.

But once we become grown up, matured in our reasoning, judging, and discerning we have to take that lamp of faith burning within our hearts outside of us and try to burn down some evils in the society, to brighten the lives of people who struggle in darkness and to ignite the same fire of faith in other people who feel empty within their souls. We should go on keeping the lamp of faith as the light on the mountain. Even though we have the faith of the Mountain, we have to carry it down to the valley of tears and take the risks of love and service. It is to be developed by strengthening our interpersonal relationships by committing oneself to others in friendship, marriage, family and community, as the command of Jesus and following Him even to lay down one's life for the commitment. Our faith is to be nurtured by being near to people of faith. It is also to be nourished by prayer and Scripture.

If our faith is not approached and handled the way the Word of God teaches us, it would turn to be a source of curse, source of hurt, and source of hate and source of terrorism. This why I personally time to time examine my faith and purify it and/or renew it as it demands. The 'Year of Faith' is an apt opportunity to perform this act of purifying my faith. I present this book to my readers as a sort of manual for their own examination of conscience about their personal faith.

What is true faith?

With my Realreligion-friends I ask myself in this book 'whether the faith I uphold is: True or not? Genuine or false? Real or simply a reel (routine)? Fruitful or pernicious? Original or counterfeit?' Sincere answers to these questions will add more credibility to my Realreligion.

We know from the Gospel that the Apostles were begging Jesus to increase their faith. Being aware of the limitation of their understanding of the true meaning of faith Jesus is quoted replying to them that if they hold on to genuine faith even be it the size of mustard seed that will bear great fruits. (Ref. Lk. 17: 5-6) This is why we beg the Lord to increase not mere faith but a true faith. *"Nourished by these redeeming gifts, we pray, O Lord, that through this help to eternal salvation true faith may ever increase. Through Christ our Lord. Amen."* The Church prays in her Liturgy on 4th Sunday in Ordinary Time as prayer after communion. It is an earnest prayer for increasing of not just an ordinary faith but a true faith.

A faith-filled traveler came through customs in the airport. The inspector asked if he had anything to declare. He said, 'Nothing at all.' The suspicious inspector asked, 'What is in the bottle?' The faith-filled man declared, 'it's only holy water'. The inspector opened the bottle out of curiosity. He smelt and even tasted it. His eyebrows went up and down. He shouted, 'Aha . . . It's whisky!' Immediately the faith-filled man jumped and raised his hands and shouted, 'Glory to God! It's a miracle'.

This is the way many of us make our religious faith to work on. It is held to cheat others, to put on mask on our weakness and to close tight the skeletons in our closets. We want our faith bring lot of magic to our life, to add spice and color into the drudgery of daily routine schedule. Fortunately faith is more than magic. It's a human virtue, received as a gift from God, earned by human efforts and used as the most powerful instrument in human hands to win the battle of life.

Faith is one of those cardinal or theological virtues: faith hope and charity. Faith is the basis and starting point of other virtues. Even though all virtues are gifts of God, they are maintained and grown by human efforts. The book of Wisdom today tells us that faith is simply a human ascend of intellect and will. *That night was known beforehand to our Fathers; with sure knowledge of the oaths in which they put their faith."* (Wis.18/6) In Letter to the Hebrews we read: *"Faith is confident assurance concerning what we hope for, and conviction about things we do not see."* (Heb.11/1) Faith therefore is a reality of human capacity to dream dreams. It's an ascent of human intellect and will toward a reality which is not there at present, which is unseen, unheard, a virtual reality. It's simply a human thing.

Faith is a virtue of perseverance in pursuing certain things that are not available at present. It is 'chutzpah', the human spirit of impudence, certain nerve or guts to put out into deep water, to launch some daredevil activities without any tangible hold. As the Lord Jesus indicates, faith is the spirit of a faithful and farsighted steward, waiting and waiting for great things to happen. *"Let your belts be fastened around your waists and your lamps be burning ready. Be like humans awaiting their master's return from a wedding."* (Lk.12/35) Faith also is a virtue maintained and grown by human efforts. It is true *'A just man lives by faith'*. But the *faith of the just man lives by his performance.* Simply storing certain truths and values in our intellect, even showering certain emotional kudos or appreciation toward them will not nurture faith. Rather with the seed of faith the humans have to work on. The book of wisdom says, *'with the faith and hope they had, the holy children, namely the Israelites in secret were offering sacrifice and putting into effect with one accord the divine institution'* (Wis.18/9). The Author of the Hebrews reports, *'Our forefathers did not obtain what had been promised but saw and saluted it from afar, still they were searching for a better homeland, a heavenly home.'* (Heb. 11/1ff) Now we can understand why the church and church leaders are hard on their faithful to observe certain religious practices and regular rituals. Look at those faith healing conventions and mega-churches' activities. They induce, elicit the virtue of faith in us by asking us to offer them or church their tithes, their contributions, their voluntary services. All are for the growth and maintenance of our faith.

Once this virtue of faith gets matured and stronger, then it does marvelous job in our lives. Faith is a powerful instrument to handle the unfairness of life successfully. Jesus said, *If you have faith the size of a mustard seed, you will say to this mountain, 'move from here to there', and it will move. Nothing will be impossible for you'.* (Mt.17/20) Faith changed the entire course of the lives of Biblical heroes; it took them to places they would have never dreamed of; gave them innumerable material blessings and enabled them to survive the ultimate test of life. According to the recent study done by the Gallup Institute's religious Research Center in New Jersey, approximately 13% of believers were found to be most religiously committed. This means those 13% of Christians are fully engaged in doing something with their faith seed, very faithful in their religious practices. The empirical evidences show that the benefits of faith in those people's lives are numerous: Their vibrant faith has transformed them into more ethical and honest; more tolerant, respectful and accepting of persons of different ethnicity, race, social, political or economic background; more apt to perform acts of kindness, offer charitable services, volunteer and so on; more concerned about the betterment of society; and far happier than those with little, weak or no faith to sustain them.

Faith grows by faith: How?

Faith is an indwelling spirit within a human being. Its seat is largely concentrated in the right side of the brain that deals with all human activities of imagination, memory, art. Faith is a package of dreams, visions, imaginations, longings, hopes. If such an unearthly or immaterial storage in the brain is to be grown, developed, matured and strengthened it should be done only by the human acts generated by the same faith. This is how religion becomes very handy in this faith-development. Every religion proposes a list of practices and exercises of faith such as: prayer, yoga, meditation, rituals, recitation and repetition of the essentials of the faith which is called 'the creed', reading, listening singing and memorizing the Scriptures, and their interpretations named as 'dogmas'. Unless a human of faith does at least a few in the list his/her faith will never grow. Faith and its increase is not something magic or miraculous downpour from the sky as 'manna'. From Scriptures: Jesus therefore asked us to repeat prayer telling: Ask, knock and seek. Increase of faith also depends on other people's faith witnessing. Others by their faith practice familiarize and identify my faith. There is a mutual transaction going on between my faith and others' faith. Others' faith is not just a support but a resource to my faith.

Prayer of complaint has become an integral part of my daily routines toward God. Especially after seeing and listening to many horrible incidents like the Twin tower Tragedy at New York it has turned to be consistent one. I tell the God of my faith: "I see everywhere violence and terror. Unfortunately I don't know why you are not intervening? Why do you let me see ruin? Why must I look at misery? Destruction and violence are before me. There is strife and clamorous discord. I cry to you for help but you do not listen! Why? Why?" This prayer of complaint is not anything spontaneous or informal. It's a formal prayer I picked up from the Bible. It's the prayer of prophet Habakkuk (Hab.1/2-3). And the Lord consistently answers me, "Wait for my promise to be fulfilled; wait for your dreams and visions come true." He adds, "Don't rush. The rash one has no integrity; but the just one because of his faith shall live."

Such a cold but persistent response of the God whom I worship induces me to doubt about His Presence. My faith in Him as a way and destiny is shattered. I even doubt about the very concept of faith. I don't enjoy having faith in my own faith. I hear many modern philosophers calling it a mere human psychological 'complex' to find a balance in this unfair game of life. Communists label it as the refuge of the oppressed and the weaklings of the society. Majority of the humanity not just survive but thrive without adhering to a faith. Worst still, people who register themselves to a faith use their faith either as a magical lamp of Aladdin, or as a mask to hide their wrong doings, or justify their social evil doings, or to uphold their political power over the common people. Through this faith many deceive themselves and cheat others too.

Against this background, the God of Jesus insists that the just man lives only by faith. In Scriptures He explains the need of faith, the results of faith, and the kind of true faith. He offers me ample proof for the positive and negative approaches to faith among humans. People who misused their faith or upheld a wrong approach to faith have only hurt themselves and the entire humanity as we experienced in many cruel acts of terrorists.

Jesus my Leader has declared: 'If you have faith the size of a mustard seed, you would say to this mulberry tree, 'be uprooted and planted in the sea,' and it would obey you'. (Lk. 17/6) This is version of Luke. Matthew goes further and describes the power of faith: 'Amen I say to you, if you have faith the size of a mustard seed, you will say to this mountain, 'Move from here to there,' and it will move. Nothing will be impossible for you.' (Mt.17/20) The question arises here: What kind of mustard-size-faith should I have to release such enormous power?

Demands of faith

Such an incredible and rare gift endowed to us from above must be properly handled and managed as long as we live in this world where our faith is challenged sometimes crudely by the sight-oriented earthly life. *"We live by faith and not by sight."* Faith, as Paul says, is a deposit handed down to us. Therefore we have to safeguard it. Faith is a high-maintenance gift. Faith, a rare gift from heaven, is to be personalized, appropriated. Yes, it's true that, whether we are cradle or converted Catholics, we inherit this wonderful faith from our families or from the community or from some of our friends. However this faith should not always stay as 'our faith' or their faith. It must become personal, part and parcel of each person. It should grow as 'my faith.' It is then only faith would show its true color, its power and identity. *"Your faith has saved you; go in peace."* *(Lk.7/50)*

Undoubtedly our faith is to be safeguarded and protected as if tending a burning lamp. Until our faith remains in its childhood it is to be treated that way. As our parents and grandparents did to us while we were children we have to take good care of our faith not to be easily contaminated, polluted or twisted by external malicious influences. We were told not to read this book or that, threatened with parental warnings if we browse any filthy and anti-faith webs or TV channels. Faith in the childhood was very vulnerable. Hence it had to be protected that way.

But once we become grown up, matured in our reasoning, judging, and discerning we have to take that lamp of faith burning within our hearts outside of us and try to burn down some evils in the society, to brighten the lives of people who struggle in darkness and to ignite the same fire of faith in other people who feel empty within their souls. We should go on keeping the lamp of faith as the light on the mountain. Even though we have the faith of the

Mountain, we have to carry it down to the valley of tears and take the risks of love and service. It is to be developed by strengthening our interpersonal relationships by committing oneself to others in friendship, marriage, family and community, as the command of Jesus and following Him even to lay down one's life for the commitment. Our faith is to be nurtured by being near to people of faith. It is also to be nourished by prayer and Scripture. If our faith is not approached and handled the way the Word of God teaches us, it would turn to be a source of curse, source of hurt, and source of hate and source of terrorism.

In my Realreligion Jesus advises me how to deal with my faith in God as I am moving energetically with my businesses, duties and other worldly commitments. He wants me to behave as a faithful servant and steward of God in handling, managing, possessing, saving and using all my resources and goods of this world with the fear of God, with the obedience and surrender to him and with the love and hope he expects me to hold toward him. He demands from me an unshaken faith which is nothing but a strong feeling, a bright sense of God's values I hold. It is not impossible for human beings to cleave to this unshaken faith. I think all of us have strong opinions on certain things we handle in our lives. We never change and move a bit out of those ideas or judgments till we die. As we are able to hold unshaken attitude about material and worldly things and persons, so it is also possible for us to hold such unshaken faith in spiritual things too.

Faith becomes unshaken only when we put that faith in unshaken things. What are those unshaken things? Once I listened to a preaching of an Evangelist on Radio. He said there are three things on which we can put our unshaken faith. Precisely because they are truly unshaken values: 1. Faith in an unshaken God who is eternal and never-changing in His nature and behavior. 2. Faith in unshaken Revelation in Scripture which were written by God's Spirit through the hands of humans. 3. Faith in our unshaken relationship with Christ Jesus. *"What will separate us from the love of Christ? Will anguish, or distress, or persecution, or famine, or nakedness, or peril, or the sword? As it is written: "For your sake we are being slain all the day; we are looked upon as sheep to be slaughtered." No, in all these things we conquer overwhelmingly through him who loved us. For I am convinced that neither death, nor life, nor angels, nor principalities, nor present things, nor future things, nor powers, nor height, nor depth, nor any other creature will be able to separate us from the love of God in Christ Jesus our Lord."* (Rom. 8: 35-39)

Chapter-2:
God of the Realreligion

I believe in God, the Father almighty, Creator of heaven and earth. (Apostles Creed)

Once Peter Berger, a rationalist, wrote and admitted in his *'Desecularization of the world'* that 'the world today is as furiously religious as it ever was . . . Experiments with secularized religions have generally failed; religious movements with beliefs and practices dripping with reactionary supernaturalism have widely succeeded. Berger's statement is a genuine assessment on today's postmodern world.

For example, as Meera Nanda, an Indian columnist writes in her article on *'The Rush of the Gods'* regarding an uprising enthusiasm for religious piety among Indians even in this modern world of technology and growing economy. She claims that 'India today, even more than its past, is teeming with millions of educated, relatively well-to-do men and women who enthusiastically participate in global networks of science and technology. The Indian economy is betting its fortunes on advanced research in biotechnology and the drug industry, whose very existence is a testament to the naturalistic and disenchanted understanding of the natural world. And yet a vast majority of these middle-class beneficiaries of modern science and technology continue to believe in supernatural powers supposedly embodied in idols, "god-men" or "god-women," stars and planets, rivers, trees and sacred animals. By all indications, they treat supernatural beings and powers with utmost earnestness and reverence and go to great lengths to please them in the hopes of achieving their desires.' Nanda's statement about India is absolutely true also in many parts of the world. It may not be in the form of idol worship but surely the large portion of humanity of modern world still upholds millions of varieties of god-figures according to individualistic whims and fancies and needs. In this chapter I want to analyze and spell out to myself how I think of God as I sincerely plan to observe a Realreligion.

God in human spirituality

My Realreligion holds firmly that there is a Supreme Supernatural Being, labeled by Scriptural writers and theologians as 'GOD.' This upholding removes my religion from the traditional and modern attempts of containing all human religious endeavors as mere natural religions. The philosophy of nature-religion denies God and any systematized religion but offers a belief professing: That every human can follow a spirituality that is innate in human nature as ethical, moral and innocent; that all human spiritual efforts need not be connected to any outside phenomenon as its goal or to a system for its support; and that there is an inner spirit within every human being that knows what is right or wrong and how one should be good and doing good.

My Realreligion never denies that it is natural for humans to be spiritual because of the Biblical fact that God created humans in His likeness and image. Unfortunately when some of the humans take a leave of absence from their Creator and Redeemer and withdraw from His Presence and interaction, as world history testifies, they fall victims of the other dimension of dyadic humanity, namely the unguarded, unenlightened mere human spirit, the flesh as Paul calls it. Consequently natural spirituality without being God-related loses its mighty power and its resourcefulness. This is why individuals get help and support from their community and Scriptures and writings of their rolemodels to preserve the likeness and image of God within them intact. Almost all true religions were established and managed only for this august purpose. And that is where my Realreligion stands.

Realreligion Vs Deism

Before entering into the deliberation of my personal view about my God I have to contend clearly there is a vast difference between mine and the view of Deism. My Realreligion holds a belief in a personal God, one who designed all creations, responds favorably to prayers and interferes in daily events; this indicates its identity as Theism opposite of atheism. My religion doesn't agree with the belief of Deism according to which God the Creator who after his creative act set the universe in motion with all the physical laws and both sacred and learned commentaries, but has been absent after that.

God in my Realreligion is Triune

From my childhood the Religion I was born in introduced to me only one God and with Paul it installed in my mind and heart what Paul writes: *"Indeed, even though there are so-called gods in heaven and on earth (there are, to be sure, many "gods" and many "lords"), yet for us there is one God, the Father, from whom all things are and for whom we exist . . ."* (1 Cor. 8: 5-6) Simultaneously it also educated me from my primary school that the same one God is Trinity. My catechism teachers made me memorize the entire Penny Catechism of the Catholic Church; I think it contained 7 chapters of questions and answers. In the first chapter on the faith in God this is what I learned about the Trinity: Q. *Is there only one God? A. There is only one God. Q. Are there three Persons in God? A. There are three Persons in God: God the Father, God the Son, and God the Holy Spirit. Q. Are these three Persons three Gods? A. These three Persons are not three Gods: the Father, the Son, and the Holy Spirit are all one and the same God. Q. What is the mystery of the Three Persons in one God called? A. The mystery of the three Persons in one God is called the mystery of the Blessed Trinity. Q. What do you mean by a mystery? A. By a mystery I mean a truth which is above reason, but revealed by God.* For many years, even till this day (I am now 67) only those answers stayed with me. Certainly I accepted my God is in Three Persons; yet in my youth days I began questioning those answers in order to get the right and understandable explanation of God's identity. The following are some of the gleanings of my findings about my God:

From the beginning of human race people felt an inner and intrinsic connection between themselves and that God. While they experienced Him and his presence they could not explain about him totally and fully. When their children asked them to explain about their God they tried to offer some explanations but always incomplete: Some said he was wisdom, others a power, a force. Some others he is the Nature itself. Many thought he is pleasure in itself. They always described him with their own human symbols as man, woman or both together, a father or a mother, a spouse, a friend, a king, a judge, a shepherd and so on. Some define him as just a power, some others a father, or mother or both. There are others who consider God as a judge, as a destroyer, as a policeman, or as a sleeping beauty. Many fell short of words that either most of them failed or were incomplete or they even spoiled the integrity of God. Due to so many above-mentioned and more versions and holdings and convictions about this name "GOD" millions of human beings are drifting away from that name which we hold as the only life-giving force.

Humans, the most intelligent creatures of God as we are, want to dig into God's identity. The cynical French deist Voltaire once wrote in his diary: *"God made man in his image and likeness, and man has paid him back."* Over the centuries all religions tried to understand and define God to picture Him in the form of their theological studies. Most of them failed or were incomplete in their descriptions of God; rather, many gods and goddesses are mostly patterned after their own worshippers; some define him as just a power, some others a father, or mother or both; there are others who consider God as a judge, as a destroyer, as a policeman, or as a sleeping beauty. For example: The God of certain religious sects demands immolation or sacrifice of human or animal blood. Some others' God loves to drink round the clock. Some others worship a God who sleeps twenty-four hours a day. There is a God of some who always sits at the riverbank stalking ladies in their bathing suits. I have read about the God of certain religions marries many wives as his sexual urge demands from him, plus owning thousands of concubines. You can imagine then how these kinds of concepts of God inspire the devotees to commit immoral and perverted actions.

Such a difference found in humans' findings about God is the result of two factors: First the God we try to probe into is a unique

Being beyond physicality, in other words, metaphysical, purely spiritual. Second reason for our faulty as well as flawed descriptions about God is our own human limitation. On a Father's Day as the children were giving their gifts to their dad, the dad asked his children to say to him honestly what they feel or think about their dad. There were 12 children 11 answered very promptly. There were 11 descriptions about the dad. When the 12th's turn came, he was hesitant and was ready to give any answer. Finally father approached the baby of the family and coaxed him to tell something about him. The boy finally got up and retorted, 'I do not believe whatever my elder brothers and sisters described of my dad. I myself cannot say anything about my dad because too young to describe about him. I want to hear from our mom who has been with our dad nearly 50 years. I am sure we will get the real description of our dad." So everybody requested their mother to say something about their dad. The mother got up and said, "I have nothing to say about him, because though I have lived with him for 50 years, still I cannot understand him."

As a matter of fact, we are indeed mystery to each other; we therefore find it hard to understand each other correctly; some years back it was too difficult for humans to understand how and why the body functions both through its outer and internal organs. We know now through scientific and technological inventions why everyone of us gets sick. But still it is hard for each one of us to understand the behavior and personality of another in depth. Even through psychological studies we come to know of a person very incomplete. It is because we are spiritual beings embedded in physical cover-up. If it is so with us, what about God who is the sole spiritual being. If we accept God as we think He should be, then He is supposed to be a mystery impenetrable, indescribable and unfathomable. This is why St. Thomas warned us: *"The greatest thing we can know about God is that we cannot know God."* And centuries before that, St. Augustine said: *"If you understand it, it is not God."*

My Realreligion proudly expounds that the God I worship is one in three Persons: Father, Son and Spirit. Every day I pray before my God saying, *"O Father who sought me; O Son who bought me; O Spirit who taught me."* *(A* Celtic Prayer) As St. Augustine would acknowledge, this description is still limited because the terms and language used here is very culturally restricted and humanly projected. It is the revelation of Jesus, which brought me to this level of understanding God. He used the vocabulary of his time and of his culture. And so were his disciples. Though Jesus has delivered his revelation as complete and total, still I humbly acknowledge, I the limited human have to struggle to understand it. In every age solid attempts have been made to know this explanation of Jesus about the 'Triune God-Mystery' a little more clearly. In this post-modern age, possessing all kinds of research studies of different religions and their description of God and combining what my Church proclaims my friends and relatives uphold this dogma on Trinity firmly.

The Christian Religion's belief of God, which I have inherited, is fully based on Scriptures and Traditions. In Scriptures we find God revealing himself as a person not just as a power or force or as a fairytale mega super being; rather He showed himself as the creating person, a parental figure. He proclaimed to Moses His lifestyle of abounding in love. *"So the LORD passed before him and proclaimed: The LORD, the LORD, a God gracious and merciful, slow to anger and abounding in love and fidelity."* And Jesus, the God's Word, emphasizing this truth called God as *Abba, Father*. The same God manifested himself as the redeeming person in the form of a human being called Jesus who called himself as the Son of God. In the Gospel Jesus attested: *"God so loved the world that he sent his only begotten Son."* When Jesus the Emmanuel was lifted up to heaven he consoled his disciples saying that he would not leave them orphans. He made lot of references of God as their guide and companion staying with them till the end of ages. The sovereign God, as we notice in the Book of Acts, exhibited himself as a sanctifying and unifying and inspiring and guiding person in the form of wind and fire and dove. Jesus asked his disciples to call him the Holy Spirit. As for my personal faith about this Triune God, besides by my ability of reasoning and analyzing the Scriptural references and the teachings of the Church, I got the help of my mentors, theologians and preachers for explaining out this Mystery of Trinity in my own version:

My God is a *Life-giving Person* which means He is a source of Life: Our God is the Parent of the entire creation who creates everything in it, especially the humans; he provides for them all they need to survive and succeed in life and leads them to their final destiny. This is what the Psalmist sings: *When I see your heavens, the work of your fingers, the moon and stars that you set in place. What is man that you are mindful of him, and a son of man that you care for him? Yet you have made him little less than a god; crowned him with glory and honor. You have given him rule over the works of your hands; put all things at his feet: All sheep and oxen, even the beasts of the field; the birds of the air, the fish of the sea, and whatever swims the paths of the seas."* (Ps. 8: 4-9) The Hebrew term Father; Abba denotes the creativeness of God. He is the Source of all things in the universe; He maintains it; He protects it and destroys it. Everything is functioning according to His Will. This is what Moses tells his people about their God who was interacting with them as they made their journey to the Promised Land.

My God is a *Loving Person* denoting that He is a Source of Love: God is love is a theme of my Realreligion and Scriptures. Jesus showed in his Incarnation by being the Son of God, suffered and died for love of God and love of people. God becomes a victim of love, a sacrifice of love. He loved me first. He is the source of love, act of love and end of love. He expects an intimacy of love in him and around him. Paul speaks in his Letters about the intimacy of love that exists between God and Jesus and us. He too invites us to follow Jesus in addressing God as 'Abba, Father.'

My God is also a *Communing Person* in the sense that He is a source of Communion: God is a communion floating in love. The Spirit, Jesus introduced to us as third Person in Trinity, is the symbol of God's communion. In the Gospel Jesus has described the functions of the Spirit: "The Spirit of truth will guide you to all truth. He will not speak on his own, but he will speak what he hears, and will declare to you the things that are coming. He will glorify me, because he will take from what is mine and declare it to you." (Jn. 16: 13-14) The Spirit connected the Father with the Son Jesus and now He is connecting them with every one of us. This is what the Gospel of Jesus all about. *'Go to all nations and bring everyone to this communion. I shall be there among you until the end of ages.'* It is the Father's and Jesus' Spirit of communion that remains forever with us.

What makes our faith so exceptional, so unique is the belief that our God is a family! We are told that God created the humans, male and female, "in the image and likeness of God." The particular Hebrew word employed for "image" is the same word our sacred authors use when talking about idols of pagan gods and goddesses. When someone in sixth-century B.C.E. Palestine asked why Israelites had no idols of Yahweh, the response was, *"We do. Each of us is an image of our God. Our God is as diverse as we are."* However the same diversified God is after all One. He is a Community, a Family, yet he is One. Our God is a community of persons, a fellowship of Love that has burst forth in ecstasy to the point that St. Paul can say: *"The love of God has been poured into our hearts by the Holy Spirit which has been given to us"* (Romans 5:5). The Apostle declares that God, whom we worship, is constantly communicating infinite Love within the Trinity between the Father, the Son and the Holy Spirit. Our God is a sharing God, a God who wants us to build and maintain similar community of love among ourselves-as microfamily, as Church, as parish, as nation and surely as a global human family. Here I am reminded of Jesus' prayer for 'union' at his Last Supper: *"That they may all be one, as you, Father, are in me and I in you, that they also may be in us, that the world may believe that you sent me. And I have given them the glory you gave me, so that they may be one, as we are one, I in them and you in me, that they may be brought to perfection as one, that the world may know that you sent me, and that you loved them even as you loved me."* (Jn. 17: 21-23) Our God, then, is not only a model for how we are to be in relationship with one another but also through every family we form His Trinitarian Family is being revealed.

From the moment I am baptized in the Name of the Father, Son and Holy Spirit every day I testify and proclaim that my God is a Community. Especially as my Realreligion's members enter into their church for Mass until they leave the church, not less than 10 times they say and hear together about the glorious Community of the Triune God. Quoting Paul, the celebrant reminds them their valuable identity of being God's own Community: *"May the grace of Our Lord Jesus Christ, and the love of God, and the communion of the Holy Spirit be with you all."* On this greeting of Paul St. Athanasius writes: *'For grace and the gift of the Trinity are given by the Father through the Son in the Holy Spirit. Just as grace is given from the Father through the Son, so there could be no communication of the gift to us except in the Holy Spirit. But when we share in the Spirit, we possess the love of the Father, the grace of the Son and the fellowship of the*

Spirit himself.' Paul, as he went town to town and establish so many small churches, felt the revealing power of each church community and therefore relentlessly preached about its togetherness generated by the Triune God: *"There are different gifts but the same Spirit; there are different ministries but the same Lord; there are different works but the same God who accomplishes all of them in everyone."* (1 Cor. 12: 4-6)

Why do I accept my God as Triune?

Theologian Theron Price was once asked by a young person why the Trinity is important. He offered four suggestions. First, "It is important that we take seriously what our forbearers have formulated with great wisdom and devotion." Second, "However, one does not become a Christian by believing ideas they have formulated." Third, "The doctrine of the Trinity is the Church's way of trying to say in one piece what the Bible seems to be saying in many pieces." Fourth, "The Trinity is an attempt to express as an *idea* what Christians have learned through *experience."* This is what makes me continue to hold the truth of Trinity. My realreligion with full conviction is conformed to the dogma of Holy Trinity of God for the following reasons:

The concept of Trinity portrays my identity

If you go to a psychologist and ask him to help you to find out who you are he will answer you: "First you tell me who your friend is then I will tell you who you are." But if you come to a religious, spiritual counselor with the same question of 'who am I?' he will surely reply: "First you tell me what kind of God you profess and worship. I will surely tell you who you are." It is a truthful fact of human behavior that its large portion is being influenced by each person's approach to the God figure. It is a sociological fact that most of our attitudes and actions are deeply prejudiced by our approach to the existence of God-either negatively or positively. Even among the believers of God there is a vast difference in our attitudes and behaviors because of the difference found in our concepts about God. My faith in God as Trinity reminds me so vividly my true identity. I am a child of God who loves me so much that He created me out of nothing, that He redeemed me out of my inner darkness, that He decided to stay with me as Emmanuel through Jesus, and that He continues to act in me as Spirit, and through me to offer fuller life to the entire human family and the universe.

Faith in Trinity enhances my personality

I hear my mentors say, 'show your friend, I will point out what personality you are'. This saying echoes the understanding of my personality through Trinity: 'Show me the God of your faith, I can read your personality'. I need not explain this because world witnesses how different people of different religions behave different ways. The God of some make them suicide bombers; the God of many allows them to eat and drink and make life's pleasures as the only goal of life. A member of Realreligion worshipping the Triune God lives and moves by His love, His commands and His inspiration; he/she cannot just be individualistic but he/she is to be community-oriented; his/her life fulfillment and joy by being united, being connected with family, group, team, and community he/she never excludes anyone on earth because of his/her differences; he/she belongs to one and only one family of God's children; he/she cannot think himself/herself a lonely island; being child of God is his/her pride; belonging to a family or community is his/her strength.

Trinity-concept satisfies my human dream

Being endowed with an inner craving for becoming godly I with other human beings yearn for a God-concept that satiates my spiritual hunger. I am so blessed that I come across such a God in my Christian Scriptures: The God of the Bible seems to be the Almighty, Powerful One who created the whole universe; He is seen as the most skillful CEO runs the whole show of nature. As prophet Daniel proclaims, my God carries a name that is holy and glorious; He is enthroned as the King of the universe and being worthy of receiving all our praises. While my dream—God is like a powerful King I too want Him to be a kind-hearted and loving Parent to me and to my fellowhumans. This is what I read in the Bible God saying to Moses: "The Lord, the Lord, a God merciful and gracious, slow to anger, and abounding in steadfast love and faithfulness." I personally love to encounter God more as a loving Parent and not just a Parent of rules and discipline. God proved Himself in human history as a loving Father and Mother to all his creatures.

At the same time I don't want Him to be always seated there above in heaven; I long to see Him in my earthly environment. That is what Moses requested from God: "If now I have found favor in thy sight, O Lord, let the Lord, I pray thee, go in the midst of us." I join with Moses encountering my God to be with me as Emmanuel, God with us. Undoubtedly I am delighted to read from New Testament Books that that dream has been fulfilled. John points out that God the Father sent his beloved Son Jesus to us out of love for us. Jesus is quoted saying: "God so loved the world that he gave his only Son." Matthew in his Gospel writes: *All this took place to fulfill what the Lord had said through the prophet: Behold, the virgin shall be with child and bear a son, and they shall name him Emmanuel," which means "God is with us."*

My human heart is not yet fully satisfied with seeing, reading and hearing that my God as Emmanuel had lived 2000 years back. I long to possess Him as my intimate Friend. I crave for His nearness with no limit of age and place and time. That wish also has been granted when Jesus, the Son of God, sent his Spirit after his resurrection to stay with us permanently as our guide, counselor and power.

Such a heartfelt gratification I enjoy when I think of my praiseworthy belief in Triune God. In the words of St. Athanasius the God, I worship, '*is above all things as Father, for he is principle and source; he is through all things through the Word; and he is in all things in the Holy Spirit.*'

My wild Imagination becoming True Reality

God is a verbal strategy of humans to explain their thoughts and ideas about their biggest dream: The Fullness of Life that is complete, total, wholistic and never-ending. God I worship is the Totality and Wholeness of my soul's dream of self-fulfillment. He is the personification of my eternal dream: Of possessing stability, constancy and steelheartedness; of being a lover that loves wholeheartedly, fully and fruitfully; of acting very wise, prudent, reasonable and scientific; of being always mindful and grateful of what I receive; of behaving a non-comprising honest, truthful and sincere person; of becoming too powerful to be not intimidated, not low-esteemed, not failed but always a winning person; of living as a most chivalrous person who endures patiently, forgiving heroically and influencing as many people as I can; and of myself everliving and being self-actualized. The whole and total package of all the above-mentioned dreams is verbalized as 'GOD.'

My belief in the triune dimension of God helps me to conduct my day today life in a very positive, meaningful and fruitful way. This holding may seem for many as mere human imagination. But as for me it turns out to be the most sensible and practical reality. Instead of imagining and debating about God as Father I imagine myself as if I am in the image of God the Father and make the best use of the opportunities in my efforts at generation, creation and maintenance. All I do to awaken, support and cherish life, all I do to design and build, to grow and manufacture and every kind of my creative artistic and technological attempts reflect my likeness to God, my Parent and Creator. Similarly, every act of my healing, outreach of forgiveness, sacrifice of self for the sake of others; my every embrace of the unwashed and the unwanted; my every word of truth spoken fearlessly against injustice, hypocrisy, greed and violence; all these actions witness to my likeness to God, the Son and my Brother. This sort of my reality-journey with the Triune God takes my likeness to the Spirit being shown in my every burst of inspiration and imagination, in every advance in knowledge and wisdom, in every invention and innovation, as well as in every word and work of love.

The Triune God of my Realreligion is communitarian. God is primarily relational. Father, Son and Spirit are who they are by doing what they do: relate to each other. Then, God creates outside beings to relate to. God relates to rocks and maples and tigers and humans according to their capacity to respond. Absolutely nothing can exist outside of some direct relationship with God. The relationship with humankind took a definitive step when God promised Abraham that his descendants would have a special covenant with God; and when God revealed himself in the humanity of Jesus. God's future was forever linked with the destiny of humans. God's life is henceforth incomplete without humankind; God's happiness now depends on the happiness of humanity. That means that God is intensely involved in each person's life. While God watches over the unfolding evolution and the decline of whole civilizations, he also keeps his eye on every individual. God takes responsibility for every single thing that He has created. In the case of humans, God assumed personal responsibility for each one. It's hard to believe that God cares so much about us. But that is the amazing factual truth.

Faith in Triune God as applied in my life

God in my Realreligion is not a bogus figure but a real person. He is Alpha & Omega of Realreligion. God to me is ground of being, a whole of those existing, and a total of my aspirations and dreams. This Being is Supreme, the Beyond, unreachable but searchable, unapproachable sensually but connectible spiritually. I hold within me only a spark or a tiny speck of this Being's existence and life. I cannot be full and complete until I join into this Whole and Fullness of Life. I possess a potentiality, plus a craving too to connect myself to this Being. My spirit is craving to join to this Whole Being by using the available resources I am endowed with by birth, namely my intellect, my senses and body. I can try to communicate with this Being and I too can be a receiver to the Divine Communications.

My Realreligion esteems that God as a Ground of Being and a Wholeness of Existence. I firmly believe I can relate to that God in an interpersonal communication level. Since my God is all-in-all and Total of Totality I won't address God as any gender form; due to linguistic restrictions in all my addresses or references of my God I would love to use my own newly coined terms such as 'HESHE', 'HISHER', 'HIMHER'. This Being is Supreme, the Beyond, unreachable but searchable, unapproachable sensually but connectible spiritually. I hold within me only a spark or a tiny speck of this Being's existence and life. I cannot be full and complete until I join into this Whole and Fullness of Life. I possess the ability and longing to connect myself to this Being. My spirit is craving to join to this Whole Being by using the available resources I am endowed with by birth, namely my intellect, my senses and body. I can try to communicate with this Being and I too can be a receiver to the Divine Communications.

Very unfortunately many in Realreligion including myself complain sometimes about the Silence, Distance and even Absence of God. One of my retreat preachers enlightened me in this matter with a short story: One day a man approached a holy monk, and asked if the monk would give him spiritual direction. To impress the monk, the man gave a lengthy recital of all his accomplishments—his several degrees, his importance in the business world, his many volunteer activities in the community. As the man talked, the monk began to fill a teacup with water. The water reached the rim of the cup, and the monk kept pouring, until the water spilled onto the table. The man said, "Stop, the cup will hold no more water!" The monk answered, "Neither can I teach you anything. You are too full of yourself now. Come back when you have some room for God." The preacher added: 'Isn't that also our problem? No room for God. No time to listen to God. Not that we don't want to listen to God. But, from every side, we are bombarded by various worldly temptations and physical needs. Our attention is drawn this way and that. We are full of ourselves. Our soul is so much filled to the brim with all those distractions that we don't offer God a place in it.'

From the very beginning of creation God desired to hold an eternal and uninterrupted dialogue with human beings. While majority of God's children never cared to listen to God, many listened attentively to God in a personal dialogue, which is called prayer. Many heard Him but did not listen to Him. Namely they knew what he was talking to them and what he willed for them. But they did not obey His will most of the time. Heroes in Scriptures, we read, continuously lived in communion with this Being, listened to whatever He demanded of them and obeyed Him faithfully.

I consider my life is a precarious journey from womb to tomb, a journey travelled through both light and darkness, day and night, ups and downs. I change as I move from one stage of my life to the next. This happens in every human's life: Being happy kid at home at the laps of parents and siblings, going to different grades of education; after higher studies finding a soul-satisfying job and if need be, getting hold of a lifepartner; having children and raising them, or people like me, going to a seminary, becoming a priest, becoming a pastor; and getting toward the sunset of life, we go through an unwanted period when society no longer considers us young, planning on retirement, finally retiring, being slowed down by our bodies, living our last days in a peaceful acceptance of our limitations, this whole process of life is a journey. In this ominous travelling I personally ascertain that I need this religious upholding of a God Figure. My relationship with God develops with each stage of the journey. My faith life is called upon. It is true, my faith life is challenged; sickness, sadness, and death come into my life; and I too cry out: "Lord, where are you?"

As a matter of fact, I firmly hold that the calling upon the Lord in my struggles is truly nothing but an integral dimension of my journey of faith. Many times I am called to make my journey of life in a new track. I have witnessed this happening in most of my religious friends; it can be from well-built body to disabled one; from walking by walking by two legs to three or in wheel chair; from clear eyesight to blindness; or moving for job opportunities from north to south or like me from further East to the West. During all these changes of life the only thing I do is just listening to my Supreme Being attentively and connect him into my life which is bleeding sometimes, and in its weeping and depressed times.

There is a story in Hindu Scriptures about the creator God. It seems He had two sons. He planned to offer the fruit of eternal life to one of his sons. So the Lord conducted a competition for both. He told them whoever goes round the earth and comes back first receives the wonderful fruit. One of his sons very faithfully began rounding the earth. The second instead started rounding his father the creator God. While he finished rounding his father in no minute, the first son took few more minutes rounding the earth. When both came to their father for the reward, the second son demanded the reward that he was the first in competition. The father wanted an explanation. The son said, 'Father, you as God, are the source of everything including the earth. You contain the world within you. So, the one who rounds you rounds the earth too. This is why I should get the reward.' The story tells that the second smart kid got the reward of the fruit of eternal life from his father. This story emphasizes the truth that the giver is greater than the gifts.

My Guru Jesus therefore said, *'seek first the kingdom of God, and all else will be added to you'*. In the Bible there are many heroes and heroines seeking only God. It is like King Solomon who was the luckiest guy in the world to be blessed by God for what he prayed. Solomon wanted nothing but Wisdom, namely God himself. Paul insists that *"all things work for good for those who love God, who are called according to his purpose."* (Rom. 8: 28) This means if I possess God as everything in my life, then all things that happen to me, even if they seem bad, they turn to be good to me.

If I approach any financial advisor for the best advice, in investing my savings in dark days of Wall Street, I would never think, he would advise me as my realreligion. Surely the financial adviser would discourage me to invest all of my resources in one place. Rather, he would say that it is important to spread my investments out, and not to put everything I have in one place. According to my religion the best way of dealing my resources is to invest them on one thing and that one thing is God. This may sound imprudent and impractical because God for many is a questionable, not even probable being.

However I notice and read millions of people in this planet who were and still are crazy to invest everything on this God. I asked myself 'what is the reason for such idiotic and wild behavior?' Many of my colleagues in realreligion say it is because of humans' absolute need for having a goal in life. Human person needs to have a clear-cut goal to be achieved in order to enjoy and celebrate one's life daily. Even the very heart, which I think, is beating spontaneously, has its own goal either to beat or to stop. It is right therefore to say that 'where the treasure is there my heart is'. It is impossible to survive in this world, without any motif, without any aim or goal. Everyone should uphold a goal as a treasure and make one's life a search, a hunt for it.

There are so many things, life offers me, to achieve as goal: For example, money, relationship, popularity, power, pleasure, entertainment, sleep, restfulness, love, sex, and so on. I want all things I possess to be invested in God and thus behave prudent and smart as King Solomon. I try to be wise and very picky about my choices. I want that one thing, not be short lived or short experienced. I keep my goal to be eternal, forever, and it must stay with me even after my death. Therefore I do not spend my lifetime just in pursuit of physical pleasure, happiness, and emotional satisfaction, which are very temporal, transient and many times turn to be source of hurt and pain. Some call this 'eternal goal' or 'Summum Bonum' (the greatest good); others name it 'eternal bliss'; but most of them call it 'God'. They prefer God to his creation, the Giver to the gifts, the whole to its part and the creator to his creatures.

My Guru Jesus instructs me to be obsessed and impudent not only when I am in pursuit of the treasure but also in possessing and maintaining it once I got it. He wants me to connect this world pursuit to the other world. Mere fluctuation, flirting, wavering, irresolute, vacillating will do no good in life pursuit of this treasurehunt. It needs strong will and smartness with certain impudence, faith, trust, madness, blindness, deafness, dumbness. This pursuit of the eternal treasure is what life is all about. It is indeed a very risky business. My religion directs me to take the risk in possessing God as my one and only treasure. The eternal invitation of Jesus is to sell everything that are temporary, material, earthly and physical in order to achieve God the Giver of gifts as the greatest valuable treasure of my life.

People of reelreligion are afraid to respond to this unpleasant invitation; they like to wait until all their material possessions are dwindled and shrunk. Some of them play the game of in and out in this treasurehunt. I have observed in my life time so many of my realreligion dispose their savings, their talents and their time for the sake of achieving the greatest treasure they want to possess, namely the God and his eternal bliss. They may look dumb and crazy. But they are the greatest in the eyes of the Supreme Being. They are the true pillars on which our communities stand, survive and keeping up their good standard. Truly, only by such crazy people of my realreligion of Jesus, the earth rotates, the world survives, the community flourishes, and the families thrive. Not only have they lived happily but also make others live in happiness. They grow in prosperity, health and peace. It is all because 'whoever seeks first the Giver, the gifts also will be added to them.'

Handling creations by laws of abundance and recycling

The God of Realreligion has been using two laws in his creative action: One, the Law of Abundance and two, the Law of recycling. The law of Abundance means to create something from nothing; to create more from less; to create greater good from lesser evil. This is the story of God's creative power working in the universe. In this regard he manages to use his creatures, both animate and inanimate beings to bring about his creative abundance. He uses them as they are and with what they have. With the available resources and talents found in those beings he creates abundantly. With limited quantity or even restricted and perverted quality presented to him by his creatures, especially human beings, God is abundantly blessing his universe.

Followers of reelreligion feel that it is they who are after God for his abundance. They are accustomed to think they are the only people who are in search of God. But on the other hand they forget that it is God who is seeking them and pursuing them like a hound as the well-known poem of Francis Thompson, 'The Hound of Heaven,' describes. Realreligion esteems always its God being after his children and wants them to be as they are and hand over to him just what they are already blessed with. Even it may be too little, nothing in comparison with the richness found around them.

My God in realreligion expects from me to present to him not more than what I possess and never be afraid of exposing my limitations and constraints. Friends in the Scriptures fretted over as I do sometimes asking God: "How can I set this before a hundred people?" But God asked them to give the available little food to his people. The disciples of Jesus asked Jesus the same question as they were asked to give food to a large crowd: "Two hundred days' wages worth of food would not be enough for each of them to have a little." "There is a boy here who has five barley loaves and two fish; but what good are these for so many?" But Jesus answered them: "You give them something to eat!" (Matthew 14:16). Jesus was not asking his disciples to perform miracles. Rather he told them to do what they could. To place in common and share what each one had. In arithmetic, multiplication and division are two opposite operations, but in this case they are the same. There is no "multiplication" without "partition" (or sharing)!

My God seeks first my limited resources before he does a miracle out of it. God's creative power of abundance is always from less to more, from smaller to greater. He makes me abundant in my richness and other undertakings only with those little and limited things, talents, and treasures I possess but always at his disposal. As Fred Rogers in his famous children's show said, "God loves you just the way you are, but God never leaves you the way you are, because God loves you."

I live in a society where waste is habitual. So much natural resources and artificial products are being thrown to trash heap daily in millions and millions of ton. My realreligion also teaches me about God's second law of creative recycling power. Nothing he creates or created go waste. Everything and every creature, found in this universe, are recycled by God for his creative abundance. He never likes anything in his creation to be wasted because all that he had created, as he found, was good. Therefore after Jesus had done the miracle of multiplication of loaves he instructed his disciples saying: "Gather up the fragments left over, that nothing may be lost." This is God's law of recycling. Nothing that he shared with me and nothing I have created, on behalf of and with God, should not be dumped as trash.

I should never feel that the surplus money or property I have saved or procured over the years are to be spent on my self-gratification, unlimited bodily pleasure and leisure, because I think all I have earned by my own ability and IQ, all I have saved by my prudence are not my own. It belongs to God and even to some extent belongs to others around who assisted me. The God of my realreligion reminds me of the law of recycling in his management of the universe and wants me to use my abundance or surplus to go toward the poor, the orphans, the weaklings of the society. Thus I intend to implement my God's law of abundance equally in this world.

Imitating my God

I am a grownup adult who wants to preserve my originality rather than being an imitation of somebody. I prize highly my own originality. I am born out of a civilization which sings chorus with the Latin poet Horace who denounced imitation saying, "O imitators, you slavish herd." I have learned how importance it is to be original and thus respecting my personal freedom. However my realreligion advises me to be an imitator of God. I approve of its suggestion because I don't lose my personal dignity or glory by imitating God. In Scriptures I am confirmed that God created me in his likeness and image. That is my originality. I am originally a God's child, God's replica. I am divine born human. So when my religion invites me to be an imitator of God it truly wants me to be original as God's image.

My realreligion and my personal experience as well prove that I lost good part of my originality by the human sinfulness as it is handed down to me by birth, formation and culture. Now I am told by my Realreligion to get back my originality by imitating once again God, my Source of being. Religion means to be retied, rebound, renovated, redeemed, renovated and remodeled in God's image and likeness. I should never think 'imitating God' means playing God as some of my friends in reelreligions do in the field of politics, religion and science and medicine. Some others imitate their celebrities and other Hollywood and Halloween images and are satisfied saying that they are truly imitating God. All these performances are fake and sinful many times. Imitation of God includes as Jesus wants, 'to be perfect as my God is perfect; to be compassionate as my God is; to be eternally patient as my God is; to be an amazing grace to my fellowmen as my God is. To imitate God suggests that all bitterness, fury, anger, shouting, and reviling must be removed from me, along with all malice.

I am fully aware of the fact that to imitate God is not an easy thing though it is my originality. It takes my lifetime. It is a hectic journey to reach God's perfection. In this journey of imitating God I frequently have to suffer for want of strength and power to regain my divine originality. I notice many of the members of reelreligions make recourse to the support of pills and prescriptions. Many times they prefer to go into an unconscious state or ecstasy through drugs, alcohol and other perversions and entertainment to forget or to withdraw from those obstacles. I will not join with them. Instead my realreligion recommends to me to nourish myself with the resources being provided by my God, the Bread of Heaven as the Scriptures labels it.

I notice this heavenly supply of God in the lives of His messengers and people of realreligion till this day. For example in the Scriptures I notice Elijah, the OT prophet, feeling so desperate and tried to flee from the cruel hands of the king who planned to murder him for his godly prophecies. In that tension-filled trip he went a day's journey into the desert, until he came to a broom tree and sat beneath it. He was so depressed that he prayed for death saying: "This is enough, O LORD! Take my life, for I am no better than my fathers." He lay down and fell asleep under the broom tree. However God loved him so much that he sent his angel with a hearth cake and a jug of water. I am sure he did not feel eating due to the heaviness of heart. So again God insisted that he should continue to eat and drink what he was offering to him. And Elijah got up, ate, and drank; then strengthened by that food, he walked forty days and forty nights to the mountain of God, Horeb.

This means God is with me at every phase of my life-project to imitate him and he is there offering the source of power and strength whenever I need. He is the source of my spiritual and physical energy like the bread and water to my body. I observe in Scriptures that God's support in my efforts of imitating him is mentioned as food and drink. There is a meaning to it. Food is a basic human need that sustains every human since birth. I know very well I am what I eat and drink. Most of my personality, creativeness, IQ, productiveness, alertness, smartness, dumbness and behavior are all influenced by what I eat and drink. I turn out to be what I eat. So to become God I should eat and drink what he himself provides for my soul. When I eat and drink what God offers to me I become like unto God. This is the biblical logic and indeed a truthful and believable logic.

My relationship with God is very personal and resolute

Martin Buber wrote in his book 'I and Thou' that a real relationship can only exist when one person admits the second into his or her life as a person, not as an object. If someone treats another just as a he or she, a him or her, then that other person is an object of the first person's consideration. True relationships are between one who fully relates to another as a person. Buber went on to say that this is the type of relationship that God has with each of us. The I and Thou relationship is at its strongest when the Thou is the Eternal Thou. Now Jesus taught that God has a personal love and care for each of us. Jesus taught that God enters the life of all who are open to his love. Consequently I esteem God a Person deeply caring for me. With Psalmist I glorify Him daily: *"You are my rock, who trains my arms for battle, who prepares my hands for war. You are my love, my fortress; you are my stronghold, my savior my shield, my place of refuge. You are the One who brings peoples into my life.* (Ref. Ps. 144)

To many of those who follow reelreligions religion is only an extracurricular activity. It's one like a weekend entertainment. It is for them a patch-up business. Indeed it's fruitless to patch up old cloaks to new ones. Yet, all too often, that's exactly what my friends in reelreligions try to do. But as for me I esteem my realreligion as 24/7 life-business. I do not want to be like Sunday-only Christians, with a private, hidden faith who foolishly think all they need do is sew a patch called Christ onto their daily life. It does not work that way. I am certain my religion becomes useful and fruitful only when the person Jesus Christ who is always new has made me anew and changes me to his likeness every moment of my life. So marvelous would be this change that I can shout on the housetop that 'I live, not I now, but Christ lives in me.'

Consequently I become a love-letter of God, as Paul would say, 'known and read by all, written not in ink but by the Spirit of the living God, not on tablets of stone but on tablets that are hearts of flesh.' My Guru Jesus has been a letter from my God written about me and for me. I can say of Him what Alcibiades said of Socrates, "I hate you, for every time I meet you, you cause me to see who I am." The same way I am a letter written by my God in Jesus. Those who come in contact with me begin to read that letter and come to be aware of God and his messages. It happens by the sacrifices and good things I perform for others and also in those trials and sufferings I undergo including my death expose to others a clear picture and comment on their own lives. This happens consciously or unconsciously. This is why I take my life seriously and responsibly.

As a faithful follower of realreligion metaphorically I can boldly say that I am married to God as his bride. I am well aware of the root meaning of the term 'religion' as a 'rebinding force.' My realreligion has tied and retied me to a Supreme God as my lifepartner. I take this spousal relationship seriously in the light of my Scriptures where God himself proposed it. In the passage from Hosea, the Lord says that he will be husband to his people Israel: "I will espouse you to me forever . . . in love and in mercy . . . in fidelity, and you will know the Lord" (2:21-22). Portraying God as the husband in a marriage-covenant with his bride, the people Israel, is an astonishing image which runs like a golden thread throughout the Old Testament (Hosea, Jeremiah, Isaiah, Ezekiel, Song of Songs) and continues in the New.) Jesus refers to it and telling me the life I lead in this world is a wedded life with God. At the time of Jesus, the expectation was that the complete realization of the marriage-covenant with

God would come with the final age. In his response to the question about fasting, Jesus proclaimed that the long-awaited messianic age had arrived. He claimed himself as the bridegroom who brings the promised future reality into the present. The new reality was a marriage feast, a time for celebration not a time for fasting.

Experiencing God rather than debating

I have been in the past accustomed so much to memorizing and reciting definitions of God that I forgot our sacred writers are much more into experiencing than naming. The author of Proverbs, for example, encourages his readers to develop that innate quality that all humans share: the drive to experience God in God's creation. Calling this attribute "the Wisdom of God," the author presumes its presence at the very beginning of creation. "From of old," Wisdom announces, "I was poured forth, at the first, before the earth . . . . When God established the heavens I was there, when God marked out the vault over the face of the deep . . . then was I beside God as God's craftsman" (Pro. 8:22-23, 27, 30).

I should not test my God

Scriptures describes to me that there were so many servants and children of God being tested by Evil force permitted by Yahweh: like Abraham was tested his worth to sacrifice his beloved son Isaac; like Job tested by Satan who got special permission from God for doing this; and like Jesus who was tested by His Father in everything except sin. With all these tests of men, I notice in the same Scriptures another long list of tests humans conducted against God himself. Humans indeed tested and tempted God in their own way. There are hundreds of references in OT which depict how much God is sad to see his own people testing him. God's own people have been putting the Lord their God to the test. In Psalms I read: "they tested God in their hearts, demanding the food they craved"; "again and again they tested God and provoked the Holy One of Israel; they tested, rebelled against God Most High, his decrees they did not observe."

The same thing was true when people dealt with Jesus the Son of God. As Scriptural scholars say the Gospel story of temptation is simply a summary or forward for the entire life of Jesus. His entire human life was warfare between himself the Good and Satan the

Evil. Mel Gibson's 'Passion' is a dramatic and filmic painting of such terrible horrible warfare and its climax at the final hours of Jesus. St. John's passion narrative clearly refers to this fight between evil and the good, the darkness and light. So during his public life Jesus met his enemy Satan in many forms. He was in the form of certain group of Jews, some of his own disciples, his relatives, his apostles especially Judas and Peter. Judas, as John says, was possessed by Satan. On the night Jesus was betrayed Satan entered into the heart of Judas. When Peter rebuked Jesus not to go to Jerusalem Jesus remarked: 'Behind me Satan.' Jesus as God was tested by humanity in three ways: the craving passions of humanity is preoccupied with one's own self and forgets all the deeds of God; it demands and cries for more and more of worldly pleasures and possessions; it longs to covet the power from God and to stand alone independently of God running the whole show of life.

My realreligion proves thus God is tested by human beings until they are away from God's territory. But once they enter into a deep relationship with God, with Jesus they also will be tested by the same Satan. But God would use this testing time for their glorification as he did to Jesus. Therefore my religion reminds me often that I will be going on complaining against God and blaming him for everything and allowing the devil to use me to test God himself. Surprisingly God is truly blessing me. I have what I need. Yet my sinful craving for more blinds my eyes to see the goodness of the Lord and of my own responsibility to share my resources with other needy people. God has offered me good health, good fortune, young and energetic mind and heart, wonderful creative talents, shrewd political diplomacy, and other opportunities. He gave all this to me so that I can be a steward and minister to other people who are deprived of all these gifts. But I feel myself guilty of being silent, inactive, insensitive, cold, and stony hearted. My religion questions me: Are you not then testing the Lord in this?

My realreligion reports that God always speaks in silence. I agree with it hundred percent. The only best language God uses is His silence, his stillness. God who acts by justice and compassion is there in still, looking at His own people how they blame each other, cheating themselves and killing each other. Jesus my Guru has shown by his own silence in many events of his life that God holds his eternal patience and hope-filled silence and does not do anything in hasty performances and corrections. In his parable on the 'wheat and the weeds' he indicated this fact. God is a lenient and patient teacher who allows time for repentance to take root and bring about graced growth. God is ever hopeful that the children who have been created to be good will find their center in God and remain rooted in the divine goodness. Always merciful and gracious, always slow to anger and abounding in kindness, always good and forgiving. God, the only true gardener, is willing to forego the prerogative to root out the unworthy and the unresponsive. Always kind to those who may call out for mercy, God listens and waits; at the very slightest movement in the right direction, God responds, lavishing grace and fostering growth. I understand very well that God never uses his veto power or the magical 'be gone' button to erase me from the map of his house even if he finds me as a weed in his garden. God provides me ample room and opportunity for growth to take place. God's policy of letting weeds and wheat grow together until harvest time precludes the use of a "be gone" prerogative that might cut short the opportunity for weeds to become wheat by a thoroughgoing transformation of mind and heart.

I avoid worshipping 'molten calves'

The true God, whom I worship, is a God of love, compassion, forgiveness, goodness, justice and peace. He is a God of life. As Pope John Paul II said, when God gives life, He creates it for eternity. *"The Lord relented in the punishment he had threatened to inflict on his people." "The grace of our Lord has been abundant, along with the faith and love that are in Christ Jesus. Christ Jesus came into the world to save sinners." "I tell you, there will be more joy in heaven over one sinner who repents than over ninety-nine righteous people who have no need of repentance."* In reelreligions people worship their own gods, in Scriptural term I can name them as molten calves. Molten calf was the idol made of gold and silver by the Israelites in the desert while they lost their patience in waiting for Moses who went up to the Mountain of God to commune with Him. The Israelites disobeying God began worshipping their own creation as their god and displeased their Creator and redeemer. This molten calf became later a simile for any human attempts worshipping god of their own whims and fancies. In this modern world we discover many such molten calves which can be categorized as:

A god of fanaticism of any kind. It can be religious, social, and racial. Paul confesses all the atrocities he performed, even as staunch religious, against Christians came out of his ignorance in unbelief. Human history including the church history tells us in the past even today many of those atrocities we inflict on others have been coming out of our ignorance of belief. Ignorance is always blissful. But many times this ignorance joins with fanaticism and arrogance. There comes the tragedy. We have to stamp out such god of fanaticism.

A god of terrorism, violence, and injustice. Wherever the sources of violence, terrorism are found in the form of training spots, funding agencies, they must be thoroughly eliminated from the earth. Here we also must add one of those subtle sources of violence and hatred: the Modern Media. TV, Movies, radio, Music that encourage or endorse hatred, violence, and terrorism must be purged out. They may be just a play, an imagination, a game or an art. But they too play a pernicious role as the tool of the molten calf.

A god of hatred, retaliation, and vengeance. Whenever we wage war against evil forces, surely god approves it and even He continues to join with us in the battle. However we have to be very careful in planning our strategies and purify our motivations. Tit for tat, tooth for a tooth is not in the dictionary of Jesus. At the same time we know God uses his humans as his instruments to eradicate evil from this world. So before we do anything in this regard, we have to first listen to Him and get wisdom and act through.

A god of secularism, materialism, licentiousness, worldliness and immorality. Almost all religious leaders are shouting out this truth. Before waging war against evil forces outside let us humbly submit to the Supremacy of our God of love and fight against the god of immorality. Let us start discipline ourselves in accordance with the commandments of the Lord. The future of the world, as Pope Pius XII said after World War II, will be in the hands of those who love life.

God in my earthly choices

As my clothes are textured by the horizontal and vertical running of threads and as my body is composed of veins and cells, so is my life made of thousands and millions of choices and decisions I make in my daily life. In my realreligion there are millions of saints. These were the people who decided to be cheerful when it was difficult to be cheerful; decided to be patient when they found it hard to be patient; they pushed on, when they would have stood still; they kept silent when they could have talked; they were agreeable when there was a chance to be disagreeable; they loved when they had a desire to hate. The best of them all is that they made these choices on the inner drive to please and glorify their only Master, and on their childlike attitude toward life.

My realreligion teaches me that the secret of success in making my choices in life consists in the priority I give to God in my decision-making process. All the Bible heroes got their final victory only by deciding for God and taking sides with God. Joshua, for example, before he went to fight against Amorites, did not try to make best choices of arms and ammunitions. Rather, he told his people: "Decide today whom you will serve: the Lord whom myself and my family serve or the gods beyond the River or the gods of the Amorites?" In life I get innumerable chances to make serious decisions. The decisions may be on employment, on the choice of marriage partner, on sex-dealings, child-bearing, birth and death of human lives, and other social and political issues as abortion, crime bill, health care, social welfare and so on. Every decision of mine, however the small and private it be, brings the best and worst out of me. Many times it can become an instrument of hurting, killing other people. Especially when I make choices in dealing with my relationship with my neighbors I need the God of love and wisdom as my counselor.

I consider the choice I have made to follow a realreligion is the greatest of all other decisions I make in my life. While my parents, teachers and other elders in the community paved the way to choose a religion that was mostly theirs one day I stood on my own ground and made my own personal decision toward my realreligion. Thus I was bold enough to differentiate myself from others, especially those who follow the reelreligions. I too picked out a God of my own and Jesus as my Guru. I took a strong decision to follow very strictly my Guru's policy of managing life and my relationships. Many around me placed lot of hurdles and barriers to keep up to such choices; I too have been disturbed and confused in the past noticing many around me leaving my realreligion, its God and my Guru and his principles. This is a perennial factor in the history of humanity. Even while Jesus was alive, many of his followers abandoned him, making a bad remark that "Jesus' saying is hard; who can accept it?" And many returned to their former way of life and no longer accompanied him. However I continue to hold on to my realreligion.

My Surrender to God's continuous Call

In my realreligion I am directed to believe that God invites me on regular basis to have home with Him but in many ways: As Samuel the prophet while he was young was called directly and personally I shall be called in my dreams, during my sleep or when I am awake and surely while I pray. Moreover I will be called by God in my life's situations and events. Many times I may be called by the Lord through the advice, directions, and public witnesses of certain authors, preachers and socio-religious leaders as Jesus my Guru called many persons in his lifetime to be his disciples. It is also true sometimes as John was called by Jesus through his brother Andrew to be his apostle I may be invited through my relatives and friends. Above all, the Lord invites me to his intimate relationship through my own physicality with its beauty, and ugliness, sensual and emotional urges, sickness and health, and other body clock ringing because as the Scriptures notes my body is the temple of God's Spirit. When my body is diagnosed with certain sickness or disability God is calling me to suffer with him smilingly. He is calling me when the body gets tired and weary because of old age. Age call, though very difficult to digest, is a unique one which invites me to salute the sovereignty of God and my limitations. He too calls me through every event that happens around my life, such as accidents, natural disasters, physical sicknesses of my loved ones, above all, the sudden demise of my near and dear ones.

When God invites me in any one of the above-mentioned ways as it pleases him I am told by my religion as Eli advised young Samuel, 'if you are called, reply, 'Speak, LORD, for your servant is listening.' I am supposed to be attentive to the voice of God while I encounter him. Also, I should respond to him with my full heart and mind. I should be willing to obey what he tells me to do. If he says for example 'leave everything and follow,' I must do so as the apostles did to the call of Jesus. God always invites me to cooperate with him to create, to redeem and to maintain what he is shouldering as his work, namely to bring every human being closer to him to make everything anew, and to make everybody joyful. As Jesus told his apostles about the reason why he called them God tells me he calls me to be with him and to go out and perform what he entrusted to me as my life's duties. He calls me when I hear or see my neighbors crying for help and support in their miseries. He is calling me in the prick of my conscience, the good human spirit to avoid certain bad habits and sinful ways.

Once I submit myself to the call of God I should become morally good. Since God is holy he would expect me who tries to be in his encounter to be holy and he would command me therefore 'avoid immorality.' This leads me to glorify God continuously in my physical environment in all possible ways and never abuse my bodily life for my own gratifications. It is to take up with him completely and to dedicate my whole life to following him wholeheartedly. It means spending a lot of time with him in prayer each day, it means studying the scriptures, it means going the extra mile, it means loving till it hurts, it means avoiding all forms of evil, and it means helping to carry his cross. Most of all it means dying and rising with him. If I respond to God's call in this way, then the Lord will be always with me as the Scriptures say about Samuel: "Samuel grew up, and the LORD was with him, not permitting any word of his to be without effect." I will be empowered by him. I will be raised with his strength to accomplish unthinkable deeds. As an immediate result change will come into my entire personality as Jesus changed his apostles and saints.

Unfortunately most of my friends who follow their reelreligions are not attuned to his voice. They listen and obey the voice of the bad spirit. They forget many times that from all their life situations those supernatural bad spirits talk to them and they misunderstand them as if coming from God. They do not possess the ability of the discernment of the spirit. Therefore my realreligion advises me to be careful in discerning the call. It may come from either the devil or from my own spirit of pride and arrogance, spirit of selfishness and self-gratification. This is why in Scriptures I read: *Beloved, do not believe every spirit, but test the spirits to see whether they are from*

God. (1 Jn. 4: 1) How do I discern God's call? My Realreligion prompts me first to use my reasoning powers to evaluate what I think God calls me to do then I check with my feelings to see if it feels right for me. I should use my head to see if it makes sense, then I follow my heart, to hear God's unique call for me.

Chapter-3:
Jesus Christ in my Realreligion

"I believe in one Lord Jesus Christ, the Only Begotten Son of God . . ." (Nicene Creed)

My ever-growing faith in risen Jesus

My childhood Religion made me recite frequently as one of the elements of my belief about Jesus: *I believe in one Lord Jesus Christ, the Only Begotten Son of God, born of the before all ages, God from God, Light from Light, true God from true God, begotten, not made, consubstantial with the Father; through him all things were made. For us men and for our salvation he came down from heaven, and by the Holy Spirit was incarnate of the Virgin Mary, and became man. For our sake he was crucified under Pontius Pilate, he suffered death and was buried, and rose again on the third day in accordance with the Scriptures. He ascended into heaven and seated at the right hand of the Father. He will come to judge the living and the dead and his kingdom will have no end.* This descriptive faith holding about Jesus of Nazareth has been formulated over the centuries in my Mother Religion from two sources: The Sacred Books of the New Testament and the Traditional belief handed down from the Apostles through the centuries. As years passed I tried to analyze and ponder over on this element of belief about Jesus of Nazareth, I came to appreciate and appropriate it in the following way in my own Realreligion:

As Oswald Chambers stated, to believe is to commit. In the program of mental belief I commit myself, and abandon all that is not related to that commitment. In personal belief I commit myself morally to this way of confidence and refuse to compromise with any other; and in particular belief I commit myself spiritually to Jesus Christ, and determine in that thing to be dominated by the Lord alone.

From my experience I can say that my faith in Jesus of Nazareth as Living God takes its full shape only after so many encounters with him in daily life. I had been like Martha whose faith-travel is being exposed by John (Chapter 11) in his Gospel narration about Lazarus' resurrection. I read Martha believing in the power of Jesus Christ, she believed that if He had been present He could have healed her brother; she also believed that Jesus had a peculiar intimacy with God and that whatever He asked of God, God would do; but she missed a very important dimension of her belief, a closer personal intimacy with Jesus. Jesus led her on until her belief became a personal possession and then slowly her faith grows real and true which she proclaims saying: *"Yes, Lord, I believe that you are the Christ."* And that is how my faith in Jesus Christ is developed and continues to be so till my death.

Who is Jesus now to me?

In all three synoptic Gospels the evangelists narrate a dialogue held between Jesus of Nazareth and his disciples (Matt. 16: 13-16; Mk. 8: 27-29; Lk. 9: 18-20) in which Jesus first wanted to know from them what the public think about him and they duly presented various ideas about him floating around; and then he proposed the same question to the disciples: *"Who do you say that I am?"* Today if my risen Lord comes to the world and inquires about what the world thinks of him I will be answering him the same way as Peter did: *"You are the Messiah, the Son of the living God."* (Matt. 16: 16); *"You are the Messiah."* (Mk. 8: 29); *"The Messiah of God."* (Lk. 9: 20) Or in some other occasion when Jesus asked the disciples, 'do you also go away from me as the others do?' Simon Peter answered him, *"Master, to whom shall we go? You have the words of eternal life. We have come to believe and are convinced that you are the Holy One of God."* (Jn. 6: 68-69)

Jesus proved himself as Emmanuel, God with us by his sense of solidarity with the common man. Describing this truthful fact about Jesus Pope Francis preached in one of his homilies: *"Jesus is in the midst of the people. He welcomes them; talks to them; heals them. He shows them God's mercy. In their midst, He chooses the twelve Apostles to be with him and, like him, to immerse themselves in the concrete situations of the world. The people follow him and listen to him because Jesus speaks and acts in a new way, with the authority of someone who is authentic and consistent; someone who speaks and acts truthfully; someone who gives the hope that comes from God; one who is revelation of the face of the God who is love. And the people joyfully bless God."* (Taken from Vatican Website)

Every moment I stand before the risen Lord in my prayers and other social and religious rituals and actions I perform in his name, I feel hearing the same question raised by him in my inner chamber. More than the past, now not like a parrot, but with full will and rationality I offer him my sincere answer as I have been gradually enlightened and strengthened by my Realreligion. Here is that answer:

Jesus Christ is the beginning, process and end of my Realreligion. Though I don't find any specific words he has said of starting a new religion different than Judaism which he practiced in his whole life, I have valid reasons to believe that he was the founder of my Realreligion. The newness of his own religion consists in that he is its center. He clearly states: *"I am the way, the truth, and the life." "No one comes to the Father except through me." "Whoever believes in me will possess the eternal life."* Also I too firmly believe as an important part of my faith that *"I am ransomed from my futile conduct, handed on by my ancestors, not with perishable things like silver or gold but with the precious blood of Christ as of a spotless unblemished lamb."* (1Pet. 1: 17-21)

He has asserted that his religion is not as other religions as Judaism and so on for the fact that previous religions' dream and vision of the establishment of God's Kingdom in this world has been already done by him and his religion: "the kingdom of God is in your midst"; the kingdom of heaven is among you." He too said, 'I didn't come to abolish the old Law but to enhance it,' meaning his religion is a new offshoot of his birth-religion of Judaism. As an efficient Commando of his new religion he promulgated a new commandment *'love one another as I have loved you.'* He has spelt out very clearly his new religion's policies and guidelines in his Sermon on the Mount which Matthew and Luke have engraved in their Gospels. Jesus has shown his prudent and efficient leadership of his religion by delegating his leadership to others to run his religion in his physical absence. *"And so I say to you, you are Peter, and upon this rock I will build my church, and the gates of the netherworld shall not prevail against it. I will give you the keys to the kingdom of heaven. Whatever you bind on earth shall be bound in heaven; and whatever you loose on earth shall be loosed in heaven."* (Matt. 16: 18-19)

Jesus Christ is all-in-all of my Realreligion

While I join with other religions in proclaiming every day that 'there is God who made the world and all that is in it, the Lord of heaven and earth, does not dwell in sanctuaries made by human hands, nor is he served by human hands because he needs anything. Rather it is he who gives to everyone life and breath and everything. He made from one the whole human race to dwell on the entire surface of the earth, and he fixed the ordered seasons and the boundaries of their regions, so that people might seek God, even perhaps grope for him and find him, though indeed he is not far from any one of us.' I too contend that 'in the same God I live and move and have my being, and I too am his offspring.' (Acts 17: 24-28) In addition to it, I also confess daily that 'in Jesus, through Jesus and with Jesus I continue to live and praise my God the Creator and Redeemer and Sanctifier'. It is because I trust that all the promises, that were offered to me by my God, are being shared, poured, experienced and fulfilled in me when I encounter the risen Lord Jesus today. I agree absolutely with Paul that all revelations from heaven have become complete, total and wholistic only in my risen Lord Jesus. *"In him we have redemption by his blood, the forgiveness of transgressions, in accord with the riches of his grace that he lavished upon us. In all wisdom and insight, he has made known to us the mystery of his will in accord with his favor that he set forth in him as a plan for the fullness of times, to sum up all things in Christ, in heaven and on earth."* (Eph. 1:7-10)

In England there is a traditional custom of shouting 'Long live the king!' or 'Long live the queen!' whenever the king or queen appear in front of the public. This has been made to be practiced among the people in British colonies. We understand the meaning of it. But the same greeting has to be performed even when the king or queen is dead. You know why? People believe that the individual kings or queens may disappear but the kingship or queenship stays with no interruption because there is always somebody to inherit that position as their sons or daughters or even adopted ones. Realreligion's members also greet the risen Jesus 'Long live the King of kings!' We relate to him as our life's all in all about which John heard in his vision: *"I am the Alpha and Omega, the one who is and who was and who is to come, the almighty."* (Rev. 22: 13)

My Jesus is human and divine

I assert my Jesus in Realreligion is Mary's Son as well as a Product of the Holy Spirit. Jesus of Nazareth continuously asks me and my friends in the Realreligion whether we know well about his true identity as he did during his life with his disciples in Palestine. *'Who do you say that I am?'* Immediately I respond to him like Peter that 'he is Christ, Son of the Living God.'

According to the Bible and Tradition as human he was a typical Jewish Galilean in all his culture, race, language and religion; he lived a life of 33 years out of which thirty years seem to be spent by him in low profile and hidden manner and the rest of three years he lived as a vagabond travelling Palestine with a few of his wellwishers expending much of his time in teaching people many invaluable truths about God and human life and performing good deeds for the needy and spending many hours of day and night in communing with God his heavenly Father. Very sadly as any other chivalrous and truth-speaking persons in history, he underwent slanderous opposition from his enemies; after undergoing unbearable sufferings, he was murdered and buried.

While he was alive in his body he proved to be a beloved child of God, a loving obedient son to his mother and a Jewish Teacher very faithful to his Jewish religion. Thus my Jesus verified himself as fully human like us born of woman. The Author of the Letter to the Hebrews three times emphasizes this truth about Jesus the human. *"He had to become like his brothers in every way . . . he himself was tested through what he suffered."* (2: 17-18) *". . . one who has similarly been tested in every way, yet without sin."* (4: 15) *". . . he himself is beset by weakness."* (5: 2)

My Jesus's identity didn't end there. He was also fully divine. Traditionally I am told in my birth-Religion that this kind of Jesus' identity is unique which can be called theologically the *'incarnation'*, meaning that Jesus of Nazareth was *God in flesh*. While Jesus was playing in the streets of Nazareth with kids or working as a young carpenter in his village or during his public life most of his contemporaries couldn't see through his other side as God in flesh; even when he explained sometimes about his divine origin to his intimate friends they couldn't grasp his claim fully. Seeing his performance of wonderful miracles people acclaimed and praised him only as a great prophet and not the real Son of God. According to the testimony of his Apostles and disciples only after he rose from the tomb and appeared alive to his friends they understood the double identity of my Jesus. Followed by their sincere authentications, human history witnessed from the days of Apostles to this day so many miraculous encounters and experiences with the risen Lord Jesus alive. Hence I firmly uphold the Jesus of Nazareth is both human as well as divine; God and Man.

Jesus is my Savior and Christ, the Anointed One

Out of such formidable faith in Jesus Christ I retain certain considerations about him and his relationship with me. First of all, as the name Jesus means in Hebrew 'God saves' I absolutely ascertain he is the Savior of the universe; Israelites expected a deliverance from bondage of slavery under Roman empire; they expected a Savior; many came forward in the name of Jesus in those days and tried to work for their political liberation; but my Jesus of Nazareth promised a twofold salvation: social and spiritual; a deliverance from sin and death; this He gave by his sacrifice on the cross. Secondly, I esteem Jesus as Christ, the title that has been bestowed on him by Biblical writers and Jesus' disciples, meaning 'the anointed one'; consecrated and set apart for God's service; he has been chosen by God exclusively for His service. I contend also my Jesus is Lord as Israelites used this term only to refer to God. It is because I believe that Jesus is God Himself; therefore I am bold to attribute to him the power, honor, and glory of God. I believe that he is the key, the center and the purpose of the whole human history.

From dictionaries and different authors we come to know that the term *Christ, (Christós,* in ancient Greek) means 'anointed'. As a matter of fact, Jesus claimed that he was an anointed one: *"He was handed a scroll of the prophet Isaiah. He unrolled the scroll and found the passage where it was written: "The Spirit of the Lord is upon me, because he has anointed me . . . Rolling up the scroll, he handed it back to the attendant and sat down, and the eyes of all in the synagogue looked intently at him. He said to them, "Today this scripture passage is fulfilled in your hearing."* (Lk. 4: 17-21) Then his Apostles identified him in their preaching and witnessing not merely as Jesus of Nazareth but as Jesus Christ.

Being anointed by God was esteemed in Judaism of Jesus' time to designate a person as either a Prophet, or as a King or most surprisingly as a Messiah. There are many incidents where Jesus proved himself worthy of possessing these three titles with their anointed power. He was truly regal when he calmed the sea and commanded the winds. His power was obvious when he fed the multitudes with bread and fish. His authority over the demons that were thought to cause every kind of human malady was incomparable. When he debated with the religious authorities, his superior wisdom was nothing short of kingly.

My risen Jesus possesses supreme power and authority

Realreligion, following the Apostolic Tradition as handed down to the world through Scriptures and Dogmas, proclaims uninterruptedly the risen Lord's kingly supremacy and Messianic identity. Before discussing about the super power and authority of my Jesus Christ, let me clarify what I mean here by those terms: Power is an inner ability of a person to carry out an exterior action and authority is an external exposure of human inner power over influencing and assisting other people. "Power" is considered by some as the "the ability to do or act; capability of doing something." By definition, power has to do with one's personal ability to do something. "Authority" is defined as the "the power to determine or settle issues; the right to control; persuasive force." To have authority has nothing to do with our ability or our capabilities. To have authority means that the "power" has been bestowed upon me; in this it is irrelevant whether we have the ability or not. For example, power is often identified by people who hold a particular office or position like the leaders of nations or states. In many situations, especially like in democratic form of governments, even a leader may be esteemed as a very powerful person, usually he/she doesn't have the authority to do as he or she wishes. Legislation cannot be passed by him/her just because he or she wants it passed. That is a prime example of one of the differences between power and authority. From the above-quoted definitions of others, I personally consider that power means certain ability possessed by human person within-physical, emotional, intellectual or spiritual; but authority refers to a person's external capacity to control, influence or move others either for better or for worse results.

Only God, who is believed by all religions as the Supreme Sovereign, possesses both power and authority: He is all powerful within and all authoritative outside over His creatures. When such a rare-blend of power and authority is claimed by any creature it is considered as an abnormal, unwanted and very dangerous dictatorship. However even the almighty and all powerful God has shown Himself in Christian Scriptures as very relenting, compassionate and merciful One who eternally respects especially the freedom of humans.

Jesus is shown in the Bible revealing himself possessing both very peculiar power within and authority outside that were shared from his Father God. Referring the prediction of Daniel (7: 14) Jesus claimed that *"all power in heaven and on earth has been given to me"* (Mt.28:18). He repeatedly ascertained about his Father's magnanimous offering to him: *"Father, you gave him (Jesus) authority over all people"* (Jn. 17: 2); *"The Father loves the Son and has given everything over to him"* (Jn. 3: 35); *"All things have been handed over to me by my Father."* (Lk. 10: 22) John testifies also that Jesus was in full knowledge of this fact. *"He was fully aware that the Father had put everything into his power."* (Jn. 13: 3)

This is why the people and higher authorities at His time were wondering about the authority with which He spoke and did miracles. His disciples witnessed within those three years marvelous power and authority in Him as He preached and performed wonders. We also notice how the disciples of Jesus encountered Jesus' power and authority after His resurrection. In one event Jesus asks "Children have you caught anything to eat?" They answered "Not a thing" "Cast your net off the starboard side," He suggested, "and you will find something." And they got it, not just what they wanted but more than what they expected. We read John in his Book of Revelation portraying that both above in heaven and below on earth all the living creatures of the universe with one accord acknowledged the power and authority of this Jesus Alive: *"To the One seated on the throne, and to the Lamb, be praise and honor, glory and might, forever and ever!"* (Rev. 5:13)

Paul, being astounded observing the great deed of God accomplished in Jesus Christ, writes: *"What is the surpassing greatness of his power for us who believe, in accord with the exercise of his great might, which he worked in Christ, raising him from the dead and seating him at his right hand in the heavens, far above every principality, authority, power, and dominion, and every name that is named not only in this age but also in the one to come. And he put all things beneath his feet and gave him as head over all things to the church, which is his body, the fullness of the one who fills all things in every way.'* (Eph. 1: 19-23)

Undoubtedly my risen Jesus' authority in Realreligion is consisted of three kingly characteristics. First, he is entitled for domination becoming the center, focus in his disciples' lives as his citizens: *"He received dominion, splendor, and kingship; all nations, peoples and tongues will serve him."* (Dan. 7: 14a) Secondly he is endowed with richness, namely depot of spiritual resources, treasury of heavenly kingdom's riches along with stock of all earthly properties; due to this belief I hold great trust in God as Paul writes: *"My God will fully supply whatever you need, in accord with his glorious riches in Christ Jesus."* (Phi. 4: 19) I too eagerly await with Paul for my final enrichment that is geared by my King Jesus: *"In him you were enriched in every way, with all discourse and all knowledge, as the testimony to Christ was confirmed among you, so that you are not lacking in any spiritual gift as you wait for the revelation of our Lord Jesus Christ. He will keep you firm to the end, irreproachable on the day of our Lord Jesus [Christ]. God is faithful, and by him you were called to fellowship with his Son, Jesus Christ our Lord"* (1 Cor. 1: 5-9).

Thirdly, more than anything else, Jesus seems to be coveting victorious crown at every combat's final round; he has been always a winner as Daniel prophesied: *"His dominion is an everlasting dominion that shall not pass away, his kingship, one that shall not be destroyed."* (Dan. 7: 14b) Paul clearly picturizes how my King complete his rule on earth: *". . . then comes the end, when he (Christ) hands over the kingdom to his God and Father, when he has destroyed every sovereignty and every authority and power. For, he must reign until he has put all his enemies under his feet. The last enemy to be destroyed is death."* (1 Cor. 15: 23-26) My Realreligion's vision and dream is the same as that of John which is nothing but to witness the final victory of Christ the mighty King: *"Behold, he is coming amid the clouds, and every eye will see him, even those who pierced him. All the peoples of the earth will lament him. Yes. Amen. "I am the Alpha and the Omega," says the Lord God, "the one who is and who was and who is to come, the almighty."* (Rev. 1: 7-8)

My Realreligion claims therefore that my Jesus in his resurrected status is King of kings and Lord of lords. Usually a leader of a nation or community emerges from the people, sometimes elected and chosen by people but always for the people. We can observe this in both past and present history of humanity. Jesus is honored in Realreligion by the same way David was elevated to covet his Kingly power and authority for four reasons: First, Jesus is of our flesh and blood, a person of the human crowd as David who was chosen by the people (Ref. 2 Sam. 5: 1) because as he was their kith and kin, namely in blood and flesh of their race and culture, son of the soil. Secondly, as Israel recognized the valor of David in their past *("In times past, when Saul was king over us, it was you that led out and brought in Israel."* 2 Sam. 5: 2), Jesus has been proving his strength, power and worth wonderfully by accomplishing marvelous deeds till this day and brought victory of salvation for us. The third reason is because we are certain that Jesus has been anointed by our God and abides in him as Israel were fully convinced that their God, Yahweh, was with David and anointed him prophesying that *'he shall be shepherd of my people Israel, and he shall be prince over Israel'*. We too heard and believe that God spoke to Jesus many times and proclaimed also to us that he is His beloved Son and we should obey him.

We, in Realreligion, are convinced with Paul and other Apostles that Jesus has inherited this stupendous divine power and authority from his heavenly Father: *He has delivered us from the dominion of darkness and transferred us to the kingdom of his beloved Son, in whom we have redemption, the forgiveness of sins. He is the image of the invisible God, the first-born of all creation; for in him all things were created, in heaven and on earth, visible and invisible, whether thrones or dominions or principalities or authorities—all things were created through him and for him. He is before all things, and in him all things hold together. He is the head of the body, the Church; he is the beginning, the first-born from the dead, that in everything he might be pre-eminent. For in him all the fullness of God was pleased to dwell, and through him to reconcile to himself all things, whether on earth or in heaven."* (Col. 1: 12-20)

Realreligion's Portrayal of Jesus Christ

By my cradle-religion I was led into certain devotion toward Jesus venerating the icon of Infant Jesus dressed in regality; the pictures and statues of the Sacred Heart; the Divine Mercy and so on. The above-mentioned descriptions given to me and others by artists, and other creative and inspired saints might have in some situations made many turned their back on the Church but held on to their love of the Master. Their company would include world-class poets, artists, and philosophers. As for me and for my friends who follow the Realreligion these historical efforts don't dissipate our belief in the real Jesus Christ. As one preacher said, we contend that anybody can call Him anything they want: Christ the Sultan, Christ the President, Christ the Pharaoh and so on. It matters not at all to my risen Lord. He is what He is: the Son of God and the Second Person in the Trinity. He turned history, as the Acts of the Apostles tell us, upside down by His resurrection and He continues to do so to this day. Encountering Jesus Christ through Scriptures, tradition and personal experience as a Messiah crowned by Kingly power and amazing authority, I personally cherish him in my Realreligion with some metaphoric illustrations:

Risen Jesus is my Shepherd

Prophet Ezekiel in his Book, by quoting God's own words, brings home to us that God is our Shepherd who gives to us life as well as he saves it when it is being hurt or destroyed. *"For thus says the Lord GOD: Look! I myself will search for my sheep and examine them. As a shepherd examines his flock while he himself is among his scattered sheep, so will I examine my sheep. I will deliver them from every place where they were scattered on the day of dark clouds. I will lead them out from among the peoples and gather them from the lands; I will bring them back to their own country and pasture them upon the mountains of Israel, in the ravines and every inhabited place in the land. In good pastures I will pasture them; on the mountain heights of Israel will be their grazing land. There they will lie down on good grazing ground; in rich pastures they will be pastured on the mountains of Israel. I myself will pasture my sheep; I myself will give them rest—oracle of the Lord GOD. The lost I will search out, the strays I will bring back, the injured I will bind up, and the sick I will heal; but the sleek and the strong I will destroy. I will shepherd them in judgment."* (Ez. 34: 11-16) With this same belief David sings out his Psalm 23: *"The LORD is my shepherd; there is nothing I lack. In green pastures he makes me lie down; to still waters he leads me . . ."*

While Jesus was moving among humans he claims that his Father God has entrusted His Shepherdship to him: *"I am the good shepherd, and I know mine and mine know me, just as the Father knows me and I know the Father; and I will lay down my life for the sheep."* (Jn. 10: 14-15) He goes on to affirm that *"My Father, who has given them to me, is greater than all."* (Jn. 10: 29) This is mainly because, as he has been continuously emphasizing, that *"The Father and I are one."* (Jn. 10: 30) This hardcore truth in Realreligion has to be accepted now and forever because that is the basis and source for true Christian discipleship recognized and proclaimed in Scriptures and in Tradition. Paul offers an anchor to this belief when he writes about this interim deal made between the Father and His Son: *"For, he (Jesus) must reign until he has put all his enemies under his feet . . . so that God may be all in all."* (1 Cor. 15: 25-28); *"I have other sheep that do not belong to this fold. These also I must lead, and they will hear my voice, and there will be one flock, one shepherd."* (Jn. 10: 16)

Risen Jesus is my Bridegroom

The imageries of 'bride and bridegroom' and 'husband and wife' are prevalent in most of world religions' Scriptures, especially in our Bible. They are used as similes for portraying the profound and contractual relationship of the Lord God and his people. *"For now your creator will be your husband, his name, the Lord God Almighty; your redeemer will be the Holy One of Israel, he is called the God of the whole earth."* (Is. 54: 5) In the Book of Isaiah we hear God, after asserting that His chosen ones are 'the anointed', the "Priests of the LORD," and the "Ministers of our God", proclaiming some more surprising names for the chosen ones both as individuals and community: *"No more shall you be called "Forsaken," nor your land called "Desolate," But you shall be called "My Delight is in her," and your land "Espoused." For the LORD delights in you, and your land shall be espoused. For as a young man marries a virgin, your Builder shall marry you; And as a bridegroom rejoices in his bride so shall your God rejoice in you."* (Is. 62: 4-5)

In the book of Hosea there is a lengthy description of how God's people behave unfaithful to God as wife to the husband, then how they are repent and come back to Him and on their return how God treats them with fidelity and understanding. He dreams and declares an oracle at the end: *"On that day you shall call me "My husband," and you shall never again call me "My Baal."* (Hos. 2: 18) The entire Book of Song of Songs is a lengthy, dialogical erotic and conjugal love poem sung between Bride and Bridegroom. Both exchange their spousal love and conjugal union with all emotions and feelings. This Poem, later in the time of Church Fathers and Christian mystics had been considered to be a prefiguration for the love of Christ the Bridegroom and Church as his Bride.

On the groundwork laid by the OT Writers, the New Testament Writers present Jesus Christ as the Bridegroom of the new People of God. Paul, who is deemed as the first Apostle who put down the risen Lord's values and dreams regarding his Church, not only used this OT allegory of Bridegroom and Bride but also how such relation between Jesus and his Church-all its members, should be demonstrated in practical life. In his Letter to Ephesians he does this remarkably. He advises Christian couples how their relationship should be maintained as it is seen between Jesus and the Church: *"As the church is subordinate to Christ, so wives should be subordinate to their husbands in everything. Husbands, love your wives, even as Christ loved the church and handed himself over for her to sanctify her, cleansing her by the bath of water with the word, that he might present to himself the church in splendor, without spot or wrinkle or any such thing, that she might be holy and without blemish . . . This is a great mystery, but I speak in reference to Christ and the church. In any case, each one of you should love his wife as himself, and the wife should respect her husband."* (Eph. 5: 21-32) Paul, being a mystic, uses that very same imagery to highlight the mystical union we have with risen Lord as our Bridegroom: *"For I am jealous of you with the jealousy of God, since I betrothed you to one husband to present you as a chaste virgin to Christ."* (II Cor. 11: 2)

Another mystic Apostle John in his Book of Revelation describes vividly the risen Lord's status as Bridegroom at present in heaven and on earth. He is waiting there to take his Bride the Church into his wedding Chamber and enjoy the eternal heavenly banquet. *"Let us rejoice and be glad and give him glory. For the wedding day of the Lamb has come, his bride has made herself ready. She was allowed to wear a bright, clean linen garment."* Then the angel said to me, *"Write this: Blessed are those who have been called to the wedding feast of the Lamb."* And he said to me, *"These words are true; they come from God."* (Rev. 19: 7-8) John observes the Church as the holy city, cleansed, purified and adorned by Jesus the Bridegroom: *"One of the seven angels who held the seven bowls filled with the seven last plagues came and said to me, "Come here. I will show you the bride, the wife of the Lamb." He took me in spirit to a great, high mountain and showed me the holy city Jerusalem coming down out of heaven from God."* (Rev. 21: 9-10)

In the Gospel of John we come across John the Baptist as the first person making testimonial to this breathtaking identity of Jesus as the Bridegroom. In his preaching on the banks of the Jordan, telling that he was not the Messiah, John declared: *"The one who has the bride is the bridegroom; the best man, who stands and listens for him, rejoices greatly at the bridegroom's voice. So this joy of mine has been made complete."* (Jn. 3: 29) What he would have meant was: "I'm the best man. I'm the bridegroom's first attendant. I'm the one who comes with him, who leads him in, who presents him to the people, but I am not the bridegroom myself. I am not the Christ. I have been sent before him. He who has the bride is the bridegroom. The friend of the bridegroom who stands by and hears him rejoices greatly at the bridegroom's voice. Therefore this joy of mine is now full. He must increase; I must decrease." Thus John the Baptist professed Jesus is the Bridegroom, because he's the one who has the bride, the Church.

Many church fathers take John's narration of Marriage at Cana (Jn. 2: 1-11) and interpret it as a sign of projecting Jesus as the Church's Bridegroom. Quoting from the Gospel of John: *"Jesus did this as the beginning of his signs in Cana in Galilee and so revealed his glory, and his disciples began to believe in him"* (Jn. 2:11), late Pope John Paul II, during his catechesis on this topic in one of his general audiences, said: *The words "did this" state that the bridegroom was already at work. At his side the figure of the bride of the new covenant was already beginning to take shape: the Church, present in Mary and those disciples at the wedding feast.*

There is an incident narrated in all three synoptic Gospels (Matt. 9: 14-15; Mk. 2: 18-20; Lk. 5: 33-35) where Jesus is identifying himself as the Bridegroom. And he says, "If I am the Bridegroom and the disciples are with me, well, they're going to rejoice with me. But then the day is going to come when the Bridegroom is going to be taken away, and when the Bridegroom is taken away, then they will definitely fast." And, of course, we, his disciples of Jesus today do fast, because our Bridegroom, Jesus, has been taken away, but we're waiting for him to return again. In the same Gospels we read Jesus' parables portraying our eternal life in heaven as Wedding Banquet. One of those parables illustrates how the wise and the foolish virgins are waiting for the Bridegroom Jesus to come, and very sadly how the foolish ones missed chance of entering into the Bridegroom's chamber. I love this parable that instigates me to be always ready for my Bridegroom Christ to come, and watch and pray because I don't know the hour when he is coming.

St. John Chrysostom in his [second] homily on Eutropius, said, "The Son of God loves us like a young man madly in love with a whore, madly in love with a prostitute." He loves us like Hosea's supposed to love his unfaithful wife, to the total end, never being faithless, never being betraying. Thérèse of Lisieux, a famous Catholic saint, said, "The Cross is the bed on which God consummates his love affair with his creaturely bride."

Risen Jesus is my King and Judge

It is my Realreligion's belief that the risen Jesus, who is my King, Master and Proprietor, will be also my judge to go through my endeavors and accomplishments in this earthly life and either reward or punish according to his findings. One of my Realreligion's beliefs is *Jesus will come to judge the living and the dead.* Christ Jesus has been made King to rule me and my fellowhumans until the end of the world. At the end of his kingly ruling of the world he will exercise his authority to judge his citizens and he will either reward or punish according to their love-in-action. God who is the supreme Judge has entrusted this judging duty to him because Jesus has already committed himself to human life and has become part and parcel of human drudgery. He said: *'I am with you till the end of this universe.'* And *'whatsoever you do to my little ones you do it to me.'* So Jesus knows my in-and-out activities and all my personal agendas and ulterior motivations behind my accomplishment. So he is the apt person to judge me. He walks with me, he weeps with me, he laughs with me, and he fails or succeeds with me. It is also true, as he stated, he is present in every human being, especially in the time of their needs.

Realreligion's members observe Christ being present in their families as they pray together at home before meals or at bedtime; also present in their spouses who need spousal support when he or she has had a bad day; he is present in their children whose needs drain the parents;, when they get up at midnight to nurse their infants, they see Christ in them; a toddler, getting into everything and making a mess quicker than their parents can clean up after him or her is considered as Christ; to them a child not understanding mathematics is Christ; a teenager needing both wings and protection is Christ. My friends in Realreligion meet the same Christ in those people who are prayerful, spiritual, and charismatic; and they are convinced he is also present in those, who may not even recognize his presence in their own lives. They are totally persuaded by their inner spirit to help Christ in needy people struggling to make ends meet.

The existence of evil and injustice in the world is certainly a mystery and a scandal, but without faith in a final judgment, it would be infinitely more absurd and more tragic. For many millennia of life on earth, man has become accustomed to everything; he has adapted to every climate, become immune to every disease. But there is one thing that he has not gotten used to: injustice. He continues to feel it intolerable. And it is to this thirst for justice that the universal judgment will respond. Realreligion's faith about final judgment responds to this most universal of human hopes about justice to be served. French poet Paul Claudel wrote very beautifully: *"On the day of the universal judgment, it will not only be the Judge who will descend from heaven but the whole earth will rush to the meeting."*

My hope in the risen Lord's Final Judgment assures me that injustice and evil will not have the last word and at the same time it calls on me to live in such a way that justice is not a condemnation for me, but salvation, and I can be one of those to whom Christ will say: *"Come, blessed of my Father, take possession of the kingdom prepared for you from the foundation of the world."*

Risen Jesus is my Master

In John's Gospel we hear Jesus admitting his Mastership. *"You call me 'teacher' and 'master,' and rightly so, for indeed I am."* (Jn. 13: 13) God the Father has entrusted to Jesus is this position of being the Master to the whole humanity, especially to Jesus' disciples. At that same Last Supper Master Jesus says that he prefers to be called by us as our friend for two reasons: One, because we obey sincerely his love-command. *"You are my friends if you do what I command you."* (Jn. 13: 14); two, because of the true knowledge we possess about him. *"I no longer call you slaves, because a slave does not know what his master is doing. I have called you friends, because I have told you everything I have heard from my Father."* (Jn. 13: 15)

I am so pleased to call the risen Jesus as my Master though he wanted us not to call him master but friend because he is not like any other human masters who degrade the humanity of their servants or disciples as some sort of toys or machines to gratify them or like pet dogs who always wag their tails at their masters' voice. My risen Jesus is a loving Master who esteems me as his equal; he behaves like parents, though they are large in stature bow down or kneel down before their tiny little babies to show their love and concern for them. That is why before he called his disciples friends, he demonstrated his love and concern for them by bowing and washing their feet. I feel that the friendly statement of Jesus proclaims only his greatness and magnanimity.

Now I must prove my worth by testifying the truth that Jesus is my loving Master. After his resurrection my Realreligion, with NT Writers and long-standing Christian Tradition, holds a firm belief that the risen Jesus has been granted a delegation of God the Father's power and authority; consequently he has inherited from his Father the role of being the author of life; the source and giver from whom we all receive many natural and supernatural gifts; a Proprietor and surely Master of the whole human race. Throughout his life he instructed us about how to manage and end our lives; he too has pointed out very clearly that we should be fully engaged in using all that heaven has given to us. The primary gifts among them are those sources, he has bestowed on us, his disciples, are some important principle investments in us and he expects us to make the best and fruitful use of them. This investment-package contains heavenly Father, Jesus Christ, the Holy Spirit, the Church, the Bible, the grace of redemption and sanctification plus all the earthly opportunities and material talents and so on.

Jesus revealed in his preaching that his heavenly Father through him offered us his precious gifts. On the natural level, he equips each one of us with unique talents, abilities, and aptitudes; he has shared with us the beauty, health, energy, wealth, business knacks, freedom, knowledge, creative power, arts and skills, love, humor and so on. Absolutely these endowments bestowed by the Master, not in keeping with our worth or interest, rather according to his plan and will. We cannot question his distributive justice; because his justice is unique and always for our good. No one person will ever be exactly like another or have the ability to excel in every discipline. It lies in fully realizing our God-given identity of talents and gifts through a virtuous and generous life. Recognizing and accepting God's plan for each of us is essential for our happiness. C.S. Lewis wisely wrote in The *'Problem of Pain'*: *"When we want to be something other than the thing God wants us to be, we must be wanting what, in fact, will not make us happy."* By the Catechism of the Catholic Church we are taught that: *"On coming into the world, man is not equipped with everything he needs for developing his bodily and spiritual life. He needs others. Differences appear tied to age, physical abilities, commerce, and the distribution of wealth. The 'talents' are not distributed equally."* (CCC 1936)

Realreligion's holders are convinced that every one of us is gifted by God to do our part in building up his Kingdom on earth. God wants us to do the best we can with the particular talents we might have. There are some of us who have the opportunity to determine and influence public policies and provide for the common good; some others are have the skills to bring healing, hope and wisdom to others; many may have the ability to help others understand, affirm and celebrate the humanity we share; but most of us, though, are quiet, ordinary people whose opportunities consist in bringing hope to others through the sincerity, kindness and values we bring to the everyday dimensions of life. Members of reelreligion are like the useless servant found in Jesus' parable who cannot see beyond their own eyes and who squander their talents or who use them irresponsibly for personal profit or self-gratification alone.

When we begin to recognize, accept, develop God's gifts and put them in proper use we should never think everything would turn to be successful and reach our goal. It takes certain amount of risks. Yes I say risk. I do not say this. It is the Lord today tells us that we should be always risk-takers. As an old axiom says, quitters never win and winners never quit. The Lord dislikes those losers and quitters who do not dare to take risks in life. This is why he gave us another beautiful gift along with other natural talents, namely the faith. Faith simply means taking risk. As one author puts it, 'faith is to leap into darkness.' Every step we take in the journey of faith is a risk. We do not fully know where we are going; it is not tangible or visible. But still since we walk by faith and not by sight we do not grope in darkness and we are ready for any challenges of life.

This is how my Master lived and taught. Here is an amazing dimension of my Master. He has been a gambler on his life. As the master is so his disciples are. He encourages us to jump into life and run the risk of growing. Hence in Realreligion mere avoidance of serious sin does not make for good disciples. We use all the gifts God gave us. If we are not moving forward, chances are good we are marching full speed backwards. My Master does not want me to stay in my seclusion but move out into the street. He tells me, *"Launch out into the deep."* (Lk. 5: 4) This means, "You are never more wonderful than when you are taking big chances." His ordering of me to get out echoes a wise saying: *The ship is so beautiful and fresh when it is at the seashore. But it was not made for that. It is to be launched into the salty water, deep into the ocean, become rustic and being worn out of salty air and water."*

In his 'Parable of the Talents' Jesus provokes our mind picturizing what would he do on our Last Judgment.(Matt. 25: 14-30) Sitting in his Father's Throne the risen Lord will judge our greatness not on the basis of what or how many gifts we have got from Him but how we have used those gifts. It's not what we accomplish with them that make us eligible for his rewards but it is what we are and what we become through those gifts is esteemed glorious. In this story Jesus narrates that the Master first praises those who have accomplished remarkably with what he had given them saying: *'Well done, my good and faithful servant. Since you were faithful in small matters, I will give you great responsibilities. Come, share your master's joy."* Then he chides the one who didn't do as he expected of him telling: *"You wicked, lazy servant! So you knew that I harvest where I did not plant and gather where I did not scatter? Should you not then have put my money in the bank so that I could have got it back with interest on my return?"* He too removed from that person all his birth-gifts and even punishes him with literally hell.

Cautioning about the Day of the Lord which is expected in every human's life at their death and at the end of the world, Paul writes: *"For you yourselves know very well that the day of the Lord will come like a thief at night . . . But you, brothers, are not in darkness, for that day to overtake you like a thief. For all of you are children of the light and children of the day. We are not of the night or of darkness. Therefore, let us not sleep as the rest do, but let us stay alert and sober."* (1Thess. 5: 2-6) Paul indicates rightly what my Master Jesus expects of me. Since I am a child of the light and disciple of Jesus, I should not fall asleep and lazy as couch potato. Rather I should stay alert, sober and work hard and take any risk to put in use all the resources God has entrusted at my disposal.

We can sin not only by deed but also by omission. Therefore we recite in our Confiteor, *"I confess what I have done and what I have failed to do."* A mournful line in a John Denver folk song says, *"I am sorry for the things I didn't say and didn't do."* 'To live is to change', says John Henry Newman, 'and to be perfect is to have changed often.' Mark Twain advises that 'the safe thing is to run risks; the risky thing is to play it safe.' There is an old story about a traveler walking down a road who came upon a sparrow lying on its back in the middle of the road. The traveler looked down at the little creature and asked: "Why are you lying down like that?" "I heard that the sky is going to fall today," the little bird replied. The traveler began to laugh. "I suppose you think your spindly little legs are going to hold up the big sky?" The determined little sparrow said simply, "One does what one can." And that is really what myself and my friends in Realreligion do. To gain the approval of God, we must take a chance and do what we can. That the one who will be punished is the one who does nothing. The man with one talent did not lose it. He did not do anything at all with it. If he had tried and failed, he would have met compassion and forgiveness. I heard in one movie a man in his desperate moment meets God and begs Him to make some miracle for him. The Lord immediately smiles and tells him, 'go and be a miracle to others.'

In this regard there are many rolemodels shown in the Scriptures. In the Book of Proverbs (chapter 31) I read about a woman. This Lady Wisdom, as I name her, is gifted and graced by God with many abilities, especially the gift of love. She is given by the limitation of her Jewish culture just only one chance of being a homemaker. She is honestly and responsibly puts all her abilities to use for the sake of family and friends, as well as for the poor and the needy. She is esteemed by God's standard as a worthy person to be valued as precious as and even far beyond pearls. My master, who entrusted to me certain talents and gifts which he expects in this earthly life to be doubled, to be used productively by me and to submit to him when he comes back to reward us.

It is normal for any human being to be recognized and appreciated and rewarded at the end of any accomplishment. At the end of our hard labor we expect an appreciation from our employer in the form of wages or a salary check; at the end of a day any business man would expect lot amount of profits to be deposited in the bank as a reward for his hard work in his business; a student naturally would expect from his/her teacher some appreciation in the form of either words or marks and ranks. The same way if anything best we expect would happen at the end of our life it is to hear from our Creator the same words which the master in Jesus' parable says to his industrious servants.

The final words I hope to utter at my death bed should be as those of Paul: *"I have competed well; I have finished the race; I have kept the faith. From now on the crown of righteousness awaits me, which the Lord, the just judge, will award to me on that day, and not only to me, but to all who have longed for his appearance."* (2 Tim. 4: 7-8) Plus, with most of my friends in Realreligion I yearn for hearing such blessed words from my Master and Judge at the end of my earthly life: *"Well done my good and faithful servant. Since you were faithful in small matters, I will give you great responsibilities. Come and share your Master's joy."*

Jesus' personal demand: Becoming his Possession

The closer I get closer to the risen Jesus the greater becomes his demand. The first demand, my risen Lord places before his Realreligion's members like me, is to allow him freely to be possessed by him. In an intimate climate of two friends, lovers or spouses there is always an inherent desire to possess each other. Bible underlines that the God whom we worship is a jealous One because He considers every human creature as his spouse. Jesus, the replica of God, is also very jealous of us. Therefore, like his Father, he protects us and guards us. *"When I was with them I protected them in your name that you gave me, and I guarded them."* (Jn. 17: 12a) And he never wants to lose us. *"This is the will of the one who sent me that I should not lose anything of what he gave me . . ."* (Jn. 6: 39) *"No one can take them out of my hand. My Father, who has given them to me, is greater than all, and no one can take them out of the Father's hand. The Father and I are one."* (Jn. 10: 28-29)

In one of my marriage counseling sessions I asked a couple about the meaning of 'intimacy'. They again and again repeated that it was 'closeness and nearness' between two spouses. They sounded very realistic and practical. I made them understand intimacy is deeper than mere being closer to each other. There are couples who live many years under the same roof and share the same bed and yet they don't enjoy the true intimacy. This is because the nearness they have is very shallow and external; the closeness of both hearts and minds is the true intimacy. The risen Lord is fully aware of this fact of intimacy and therefore he tries to illustrate his relationship with us is like that of vine and branches. His relationship and union with us is so intimate that it is not just a face-to-face presence but a life-to-life, heart-to-heart ontological connection. Hungering so desperately for spiritual intimacy with humans he insists repetitively: *"I am the true vine, and my Father is the vine grower . . . Remain in me, as I remain in you. Just as a branch cannot bear fruit on its own unless it remains on the vine, so neither can you unless you remain in me. I am the vine, you are the branches. Whoever remains in me and I in him will bear much fruit, because without me you can do nothing."* (Jn. 15: 1-5)

For the same reason my risen Lord revealed his continuous attempt to dine (according to me-to have date) with me: *"Behold, I stand at the door and knock. If anyone hears my voice and opens the door, [then] I will enter his house and dine with him, and he with me."* (Rev. 3: 20)

Jesus' second demand: Accept him as Friend

Secondly risen Jesus craves for being esteemed by me as my dearmost friend. We read Paul telling us that we are no more slaves because of the Spirit's outpouring and he labels us as brothers and sisters of Jesus by calling God 'Abba Father.' (Rom. 8: 15) But John goes little further when he remembers and quotes Jesus saying: *"I no longer call you slaves, because a slave does not know what his master is doing. I have called you friends . . ."* (Jn. 15: 15) It is very interesting to note among all OT heroes like Moses, Joshua, and David who are referred as God's servants only Abraham is called by God as 'His friend'. (Is. 41: 8)

I observe there are many in my Realreligion who have become very intimate friends to the risen Lord. In the past I loved to join the club of Jesus' friends. Gradually I began realizing the real meaning and crucial demand it takes to be intimate friend to Jesus. To be intimate friend to Jesus means to become literally his life-partner and co-creator and co-redeemer in his Kingdom. This would happen only if I follow minutely, sincerely and meticulously his Gospel values in every moment of my life. It calls for the total surrendering to the will of the Father and the Son and the Holy Spirit. Joining with my friend Jesus I have to recite a mantra: *"Let it be done unto me according to your Word."* My friendship with Jesus directs me to accept willingly and very passionately any suffering and pain that come along the way. In addition, it burns a fire within me and urges me to lead a life of justice, love and peace.

I am encircled by many friends of reelreligions who are so materialistic, that it is easy for them to forget what really matters in life. To so many of them happiness depends on possessions. A beautiful house, a luxurious car, the latest in video and sound equipment, a boat, all these things become their goals in life. Then, if one of these items cannot be attained, if a young couple cannot get a mortgage for their dream house, if an older couple cannot retire as they expected to, if the boat a person always wanted sinks, then, for some people, life has taken a terrible turn for the worse, then they become extremely sad. They no longer can have what they really wanted.

Recently an international magazine called 'New Scientist' conducted a worldwide survey in 65 countries on the topic: 'which is the happiest nation on earth today?' that means, which country has got the largest number of happiest people? The findings are very amazing. A general fact was that the happiest people are all living in rural areas because they feel most secure, well protected and get lot of support from closely connected rural community environment.

To become the happiest person possible is the human innate dream from the day the humanity started breathing. Every person on earth tries to employ many strategies to realize such dream. When a young man who was in quest of the source of the happiest and never-ending life approached Jesus one day and asked him to offer some help in this matter. Jesus is quoted saying to him: "Besides observing God's commandments, you do one more thing. Go and sell everything you possess and give to the poor and you will have treasure in heaven; then come follow me."

According to my realreligion, to sell everything, to give it to the poor and to follow Jesus is not an exhortation addressed only to those who are seeking for canonization. Nor it is just as an entrance exam for becoming Jesus' disciples. Rather it is meant for any human person who desires and dreams of becoming the best in God's realm, and of becoming the happiest person in the community and in the world. Following Jesus means to follow a way of life with love. Live and die for love. If God is love and Jesus is the incarnation of that Love, then when Jesus said 'follow me' he indicated that I should follow him in his love, live for his love, and die for his love. So I become the best and the happiest person in the world only when I go out of myself, out of my personal conveniences and comfort that is by selling and disposing of all my personal self-oriented attitudes and possessions for the sake of love for my friends, family, community, Church, nation and the entire humanity.

My friends in reelreligions pray one thing and wish another: When they say in the Lord's prayer 'thy kingdom come' their hearts interiorly wish: 'God, let thy kingdom of money and prosperity come, let your kingdom of control and power come; let your kingdom of pleasures come; let your kingdom of retaliation and punishment of my enemies come; let your kingdom of glory, promotion and prestige come.' My realreligion advises me to pray and wish only one thing, namely, 'Lord let thy kingdom of Love come.'

One evening after CCD class hour, a mother asked her little son, 'How was CCD class today?' He said, 'Oh! all right!' 'Just all right?' mother asked, 'Who was your teacher?' 'Well, I don't know,' the boy replied, 'but she must have been Jesus' grandmother. This is why she was talking all the time about Jesus.' That teacher was right. She cannot do more than because she belonged to realreligion. Her realreligion is a religion of Jesus, for Jesus, and with Jesus. There are hundreds of religions and thousands of cults existing in the world. Some religions are based on doctrines, philosophies, wise teachings, values of life, moral behavior and so on. My realreligion is based on a person. And that is Jesus. If I call my religion as a way of life, then it is Jesus who is that way. My realreligion is a religion of relationship and fellowship which is generated, nourished and fructified by the interpersonal contact I sustain with Jesus, the loving person.

Jesus wants me, if I plan to be a part of his religion, to prefer him to other possessions. Why does Jesus demand this kind of weird behavior? St. Gregory the Great wrote that *'the more we are involved in temporal things, the more that we are insensitive to the spiritual.'*

People of reelreligions find hard entering the Kingdom of God not because they are not concerned with the Kingdom of God but because they are more concerned with the Kingdom of the world. Concern for the kingdom of God means to see things as God sees them; to understand as God understands; to enjoy the fruits of creation as God means them to be enjoyed and to use my talents and gifts and my very works to come closer to God.

Knowledge of God's Laws is good; to go after the wisdom of God is also good; to observe the commandments faithfully and to be very moral is all the more good; to be always a winner in saving wealth, to accumulate material possessions and to pile up too many titles and good names in public is praiseworthy. However to be hundred percent sure of achieving the rewards in the kingdom of God and to be the most perfect human being, my Guru Jesus suggests that I should be ready even to sell what I have and give to the poor and then come and follow him; This means a total renunciation of all that I have or am endowed with, all realities of life such as the entire world, all relations, all accomplishments, all plans and projects, all dreams and visions, all that I saved and procured as my treasures, for the sake of possessing only one and that is the God in Jesus. Nothing is permanent in life; nothing is going to come with me to the grave; I saw in one of the burials in India, people were cutting the finger of a woman because they were unable to remove a ring from her finger. There is a belief that no golden ornaments should be buried with the dead body. So willy-nilly, I will lose everything either one by one gradually or as a wholesale at some natural calamities like Tsunami.

My Realreligion says to me that I should not wait to possess Jesus until I have achieved, performed, earned and saved what I desired. Rather, my Guru Jesus very audibly tells me to begin my projects and efforts with him, continue to run the race with him, whether I fail or succeed at the end, I should hold him in my heart; to smile when I win and to keep head straight in failures. Jesus is not against the rich, opting only for the poor. It is true he runs with those runners even when they are far behind the goal but he settles permanently in the hearts of those winners who got riches, properties, titles, popularities, good names and makes use of them as his proxies or agents to help the runners who are still poor, weak, timid, handicapped, unhealthy and downtrodden.

The endresults of my relationship with Jesus alive

Almost 99 percent of Christians fail in obeying Jesus' demands we hear from him in the Gospels. Too many Christians are afraid to take the risk of being alone in this act of being light and salt. Many know in their hearts there are so many good things left undone or not cared for around their life situation. The greatest sin of a Christian, as one author puts it, is not doing what he/she thinks is good for others. Many of us here try our best to comply with our Master's demand. But many times we fail in it. That is because of either doing too much or doing too little. There are many quitters in Christianity following their reelreligions, who sit back and think they are relaxing and enjoying life while watching and commenting on those very few who are daredevils accomplishing what the Lord demanded them to do. Not all have the good will to obey the Lord to be the light and salt to others' lives. Even among those who have good will, only very few possess strong will to go for it till their last breath. I witness this wherever I am posted as pastor.

The upshot of my friendship with Jesus, if it is sincerely maintained I personally have been experiencing the following: When my days are dark my heart craves for Jesus to be my only light. It can be a time of fear of failure; fear of the unknown; fear of heights; fear of financial disaster; fear of sickness; and certainly fear of death. At those moments I begin to rest on my friend's shadow; he shields me when I take refuge in him. When my life turns out to be useless, being rejected and humiliated by others; when I meet only coldness and ingratitude for what I do for others; when I do not receive any appreciation and even I am left alone to do everything as no one comes to help me, still I feel in the presence of my friend Jesus not losing my energy; not burnt out. I continue to love, share and care and do my best to serve the needy and the poor.

The thoughts and beliefs I hold in my religion make me feel that I am born great in Jesus and make me treat my life fruitfully and successfully. First of all, my religion makes me live patiently, not only enduring the hardship and unfairness of life but also going forward doing, working, witnessing, performing, and accomplishing all that the Lord wills me to do in love. Scriptures instruct me to be patient like a farmer who waits for the precious fruit of the earth. *Be patient, therefore, brothers, until the coming of the Lord. See how the farmer waits for the precious fruit of the earth, being patient with it until it receives the early and the late rains. You too must be patient. Make your hearts firm.* (Jas. 5: 7-8)

I too feel the feeling of anticipation of joy. My dream of fullness of life will come true. I begin to use my prayer as a vehicle for such reason and will not make it a magical enterprise. In the Scriptures I read: *"Have faith in God. Amen I say to you, whoever says to this mountain, 'be lifted up and thrown into the sea,' and does not doubt in his heart but believes that what he says will happen, it shall be done for him. Therefore I tell you, all that you ask for in prayer, believe that you will receive it and it shall be yours.'* (Mk.11/22-24) This is nothing but a command of my Supreme Being to live and pray in anticipated joy, contentment, fulfillment,

My Christ-related religion makes me live a contented life in an anticipated joy and hope. I pray daily with the Psalmist, *'My Whole Fullness of Life I proclaim your total love in the morning, and your unfailing faithfulness in the night.'* (Ps. 95) That is my attitude toward my life. My life's cycle consists of day and night, brightness and darkness, ups and downs, spring and fall, summer and winter. When I face with the bright daytime of life I proclaim God's love and mercy by performing Love-deeds to other people, by sharing the produces, the talents, the savings, and go out of the way, out of the family, out of the self-centric campus and extend our loving hands to the needy to express our love for God. Also when I am encircled by the darkness of life, the night of my soul, I in no way get weary, cold, indifferent and stop performing the love deeds. On those gloomy days I witness to the fidelity of my Supreme Being. In other words, not losing hope or faith I continue to be firm in love-walk and in my expression of love to God through worship and prayer.

I was wondering for long time why my cradle-Religion insisted to add resurrection to death of Christ as the source of human salvation. First I thought it is referring to the Lord's entire Passover enacted in his life not only as cause of my salvation but also as a pattern for my own life in Christ—a passage from darkness to light, from death to life and from sorrows to joy. Later on as I began meditating the words of Paul from his Letters, especially Letter to Romans I have been enlightened to be aware of specific upshot of each event-death and resurrection, in Jesus' life. In Romans 4: 25 Paul writes: *Jesus was handed over for our transgressions and was raised for our justification.* In other words, by his death Jesus brought redemption from our sins and by his resurrection he offered us the justification for all that we endure for his sake. From many meanings attributed to the word justification I personally love to use the meaning 'reason' in this regard. Resurrection was Jesus' ultimate goal not only for his human life-filled with sufferings but also for his disciples' adherence to him despite the hardships they undergo for his name.

Conclusion

I try hard every day to persevere in my intimate relationship with the risen Jesus as that of Fr. Pedro Arrupe, one of Superior Generals of the Society of Jesus. In his journal he wrote, *'for me Jesus Christ is everything. He was and is my ideal. He was and continues to be my way. He was and still is my strength. I don't think it is necessary to explain very much what that means. Take Jesus Christ from my life and everything would collapse, like a human body from which someone removed the skeleton, heart and head'.* I may contend that I am Jesus' friend and possessed by him. I like to add this to it: It is not that easy to get involved with my Jesus alive. It has taken days and nights prayers, fasting, sufferings, and every part of my body! It cost me so much separation, disappointments, even at the risk of losing my very life. Nobody knows, including me how and when He enters in and makes my heart and mind as His throne. Only one thing I hear from people: I am crazy, stubborn, freaky and weird.

Certainly I have a long way to go in fully realizing my dream of being totally possessed by my risen Jesus as well as me possessing him forever. Therefore with the Psalmist I say uninterruptedly to the risen Lord that my soul is thirsting and pining for the Him and as Saint Augustine used to pray, *'our hearts are restless until they rest in the Lord.'*

Chapter-4:
Holy Spirit in my Realreligion

"I believe in the Holy Spirit . . ." (Nicene Creed)

A. True identity of the Holy Spirit

In Nicene Creed we proclaim our belief in the Holy Spirit saying: *"I believe in the Holy Spirit, the Lord, the giver of life, who proceeds from the Father and the Son, who with the Father and the Son is adored and glorified, who has spoken through the prophets."*

Early days of my school life like other students I memorized both the Apostles Creed and the Nicene Creed. It was easier for me and others too to keep in mind the first Creed than the second. Besides the second one is too lengthy, a main reason was some of the terms used for the truths about the Holy Spirit were harder to me to understand, even till this day. After I became aware of the struggles and tensions Church Fathers experienced in deliberating these words about the Spirit's identity I tried to settle down in peace and impudent faith. However my Realreligion never permitted me to be stuck there. It led me to study little deeper the Scriptures and Tradition and also to get acquainted with some Charismatic and Pentecostal groups through whom I began appreciating Holy Spirit's Presence and Activities in humanity.

Holy Spirit is Spiritual Energy

We live by energy, we love energy, and we breathe energy. Our life ends when our internal system of energy ends. When energy crisis comes in, when we feel losing energy or hit at the bottom of energy, what do we do? We go for pills, drinks, and other medication and treatment. All are purchased and drunk in the name of energizing our human bodies and human spirits. Have we ever seen that inner energy any time? Let us closely notice our inner drives. The passion between two lovers that makes them overcome any obstacle to be together, the bond between a mother and her child, the patriotism that moves men to sacrifice their lives for a flag. These are some great powers of our existence. Yet we cannot see them through our physical eyes. There are most powerful forces outside of us too. The gravitational pull of the sun twirls earth like a toy on a string; the earth's gravity does to the moon; the moon's movement around the earth pulls entire oceans into high and low tides; the rise and fall of air pressure, unseen and unfelt by humans, triggers great changes in weather. I don't think such energies as such have been seen by humans. All these powers and energies are invisible. We see where they come from. We feel their results and know where and when they end. But we surely cannot understand their shape, their form, their color, and their dimension. They are unseen powers.

Above all these powers, my Realreligion believes there exists the most powerful and eternal power, namely God. Some religions say He is the one that contains all the other powers. Others say He is the source of those powers. Some others say every power we feel, we notice, whether material, physical or spiritual, is a particle of that Supreme Power. My Realreligion, basing its holdings on the Scriptures and Experiential Tradition, believes that God is the source of all the existing powers but He is a separate person from all these. Holy Spirit is none other than the Energy generated from Trinity. When Jesus of Nazareth introduced Holy Spirit to his disciples at the Last Supper he named Him Counselor, Consoler, and Advocate. But when he became the risen Lord Jesus spoke of the same Spirit as 'Power from on High.' (Lk. 24: 49)

Holy Spirit is Trinity in Action

I cherish the amazing identity of the Holy Spirit as the outward bursting out or flowing of the Trinitarian God's Life, Love, Wisdom and Power. Jesus therefore could exclaim how he was the source of life filling his disciples through the flow of the Holy Spirit in them. *"Let anyone who thirsts come to me and drink. Whoever believes in me, as scripture says: Rivers of living water will flow from within him."* To this John adds: *"He said this in reference to the Spirit that those who came to believe in him were to receive. There was, of course, no Spirit yet, because Jesus had not yet been glorified."* (Jn. 7: 37-39) Jesus too reveals about how his Father and he are resourcefully related to the Holy Spirit: *"I will ask the Father, and he will give you another Advocate to be with you always, the Spirit of truth, which the world cannot accept, because it neither sees nor knows it. But you know it, because it remains with you, and will be in you. The Advocate, the Holy Spirit that the Father will send in my name—he will teach you everything and remind you of all that [I] told you."* (Jn. 14: 16-17, 26)

According to Jesus, Holy Spirit is the outward brightness of God's light exposing the dark sides of humans: *"I tell you the truth, it is better for you that I go. For if I do not go, the Advocate will not come to you. But if I go, I will send him to you. And when he comes he will convict the world in regard to sin and righteousness and condemnation: sin, because they do not believe in me; righteousness, because I am going to the Father and you will no longer see me; condemnation, because the ruler of this world has been condemned."* (Jn. 16: 7-11) Jesus, who testifies that he is the Truth and to this truth he came to witness, identifies the Holy Spirit as Trinitarian Source of Truth being shared with humans: *"When he comes, the Spirit of truth, he will guide you to all truth. He will not speak on his own, but he will speak what he hears, and will declare to you the things that are coming. He will glorify me, because he will take from what is mine and declare it to you. Everything that the Father has is mine; for this reason I told you that he will take from what is mine and declare it to you."* (Jn. 16: 13-15)

Spirit is Risen Jesus alive

Jesus, after his earthly and physical experience of life with all its drudgeries, pain, and suffering and death, rose from the dead and started his resurrected Spirit-life. My realreligion says to me that this resurrected Jesus is alive today and moving in our midst. I believe it strongly because Jesus himself said: "I am with you always, until the end of age." Scriptures and history prove that people encountered the resurrected Jesus in the past and continue to get his glimpse; they see him, they speak with him, they touch him, and they walk with Him as a living and loving friend. These are not just stories like those of Hollywood superman movies; rather they are real and authentic life-experience of millions of Jesus' followers for two millennia. So many things peculiar and sometimes unthinkable they speak and perform with a peculiar authority and power. And they claim this exceptional authority is derived from that Jesus alive.

Jesus Himself promised to His disciples before He ascended into heaven: "You will receive power when the Holy Spirit comes upon you and you will be my witnesses . . ." (Acts1:8) It is this resurrected Jesus befriends me; his Spirit starts integrating with my human spirit and my whole life-perspective, world-view, and attitudes change. I begin to live in a total different realm of life. People around me watch and find out certain uniqueness about my behavior and in how I handle my day-today life.

Once I am with Jesus alive, his spiritual power enters in and dwells in me. I become powerful within. It is from there I get strong determination and authority. I am liberated from my low-esteemed attitudes, inhibitions and complexes. When I am exposed to the reality of life: a life that is haunted by struggles between human authority and divine one; between truth and lie; between pride and innocence; between flesh and Spirit, I am bold enough to stand on my values of Jesus and say: "Better for me to obey God than men!"

My religion is not at all a 'fiction-religion.' It is truly a reality-religion, the realreligion. My religion is Jesus Alive religion. My religion is not based on fictions though most of the events narrated in the Bible are like fictions, things made or formed (the Latin *fictio* means shaped or feigned) they have their foundation in a God, in a Christ whom their authors were willing to die for. Plus the resurrected Jesus is mystically and spiritually alive in the midst of living people today.

B. Characteristics of the Holy Spirit

To grasp this mystery of the Holy Spirit, which is something invisible, infinite, and unfathomable beyond our human understanding, God in the Scriptures, especially in NT, uses different physical descriptions and symbols such as strong wind, burning fire, living water, dove, and breath.

Holy Spirit is like the strong wind

"And suddenly there came from the sky a noise like a strong driving wind and it filled the entire house in which they were." (Acts 2: 2) We experience so many times the force of the wind, in the form of storm, tornado, and cyclone. Any strong wind shatters, shakes, smashes, wrecks, uproots and demolishes throwing overboard anything and any person on its way. This is the powerful result of the coming of the Holy Spirit. He breaks through all barriers, shatters the bondage both inner and outer situation of any person. He breaks our chains asunder. He tears down to pieces the gates of bronze and snaps the bars of iron that are on his way.

He is like Fire

There appeared to them tongues as of fire, which parted and came to rest on each one of them." (Acts 2: 3) Another terrible natural resource is fire that possesses a remarkable and awesome power that is too hard to be contained by ordinary human ability. It will give light as bright as even the eyes can be blinded; it burns anything and anybody on its route; if it touches anyone it is simply a kiss of death. It is also a source of destroying dirt, trash and melting even the iron to its taste. We see here a wonderful symbol of the effects of the Spirit if he enters into our hearts. He ignites within human heart a burning for the love of God; He melts the stony hearts as the Prophet Ezekiel would say, *'I will give you a new heart and place a new spirit within you, taking from your bodies your stony hearts and giving you natural hearts. I will put my spirit within you and make you live by my statutes, careful to observe my decrees.* (Ez. 36: 26-27) He will create within us a broken and humbled heart as pleasing to the eyes of God. We are purified by the fire of the Spirit. In Spirit's light that pierces through into our inner soul shows us all our evil deeds; we cry for forgiveness; He warms our psychological coldness; frees our frozen heart from fear; melts away the masks we wear; kindles the fire love in our hearts; and makes our hardheadedness and hardheartedness very pliable and bending in humility and simplicity.

He is like Breath

In the Gospel John narrates an event when the risen Jesus offers his Spirit to his disciples. *". . . he breathed on them and said to them, 'Receive the holy Spirit. Whose sins you forgive are forgiven them, and whose sins you retain are retained.'"* (Jn. 20: 22-23) Breath is the source of life in our bodies. The breath of God in Jesus enters the second time after our creation and renews it. We begin to possess a renewed life of God. Through this new life two important elements are settled in us permanently: First it is a feeling of Reconciliation. After bestowing the Spirit, this is what the risen Jesus pronounces: *"Whose sins you forgive are forgiven them."* We are reconciled with God; our sins are forgiven and we are enabled to give forgiveness to each other.

He is like Dove

Consequently the true peace of God abides in us. Let us remember how the Spirit at the time of Jesus' Baptism descended upon him in bodily form like a dove. All the Evangelists and John the Baptizer testify to it. Dove is always considered as the symbol of peace. This is why before breathing his Spirit on the disciples the Lord greets them saying: *'Peace be with you.'* An internal peace begins to dwell within us when we are reconciled with God and neighbors through the Spirit.

C. Marvelous Actions of the Holy Spirit

The Triune God's main preoccupation in His life, as our Scriptures reveal, is to share His Self with humanity; namely, His image and likeness, His power, wisdom, love, justice, joy and peace. He continues to do this daily from the time of creation till this day.

Among them the most significant and thought-provoking occasions were a) at the time creation and b) on the day of Pentecost.

His Pervasive Presence and Action

Jesus said to Nicodemus during his discussion with him on his disciples' rebirth in water and Spirit: *"The wind blows where it wills, and you can hear the sound it makes, but you do not know where it comes from or where it goes; so it is with everyone who is born of the Spirit."* (Jn. 3: 8) There is no any boundary or border to the Spirit's action. There is no this and that way through which he moves human beings. He does it mysteriously and very subtly. He has no barrier of any kind to discriminate any human person in the name of race, class, religion, philosophy, theology, culture and nation. He is beyond everything we think as God's choice. Even from stones he can bring out a proclamation of God. From the group of atheists, materialists, agnostics and of the irreligious he can proclaim his good news.

They can be out of the campus of Moses: *"The LORD then came down in the cloud and spoke to him. Taking some of the spirit that was on Moses, he bestowed it on the seventy elders; and as the spirit came to rest on them, they prophesied. Now two men, one named Eldad and the other Medad, had remained in the camp, yet the spirit came to rest on them also. They too had been on the list, but had not gone out to the tent; and so they prophesied in the camp. So, when a young man ran and reported to Moses, "Eldad and Medad are prophesying in the camp," Joshua, son of Nun, who from his youth had been Moses' aide, said, "My lord, Moses, stop them." But Moses answered him, "Are you jealous for my sake? If only all the people of the LORD were prophets! If only the LORD would bestow his spirit on them!"* (Num. 11: 25-29) Or even out of the Realreligion of Jesus; *"John said to him, 'Teacher, we saw someone driving out demons in your name, and we tried to prevent him because he does not follow us.' Jesus replied, 'Do not prevent him. There is no one who performs a mighty deed in my name who can at the same time speak ill of me. For whoever is not against us is for us.'"* (Mk. 9: 38-40) They, then, can be from the non-Pentecostal or non-charismatic groups; from anywhere, at any time, in any way the Spirit works; He moves every one of his children. He is inside of everybody; because we are the temple of the Holy Spirit.

Holy Spirit's Action-1: Bestowing me individual Power

In Genesis we are told God the Father together with His Son and Holy Spirit created the universe and all that in it. At every rite of blessing of Baptismal Water, Church invites us joining her in affirming our belief that the Spirit's Presence in the beginning of creation: *"At the very dawn of creation your Spirit breathed on the waters, making them the wellspring of all holiness."* (Prayer at Easter Vigil Service) John in his Gospel introduces Jesus as the Logos of God existing even during the creative endeavor of God the Father: *"In the beginning was the Word, and the Word was with God, and the Word was God. He was in the beginning with God. All things came to be through him, and without him nothing came to be. What came to be through him was life, and this life was the light of the human race."* (Jn. 1: 1-4)

Moses, the writer of the story of creation exposes to us the glorious status in which the Triune God created all humans. First God shared the power of life by breathing His Spirit into them; thus He created humans 'in His image and after His likeness' (Gen. 1: 26). In addition God delegates to them some of His Power and Dominion. He said to His first man and woman: *"Be fertile and multiply; fill the earth and subdue it. Have dominion over fish of the sea, the birds of the air, and all the living things that move on the earth."* (Gen.1: 28) According to the interpretation of my Realreligion, these words of God clearly point out the fact that He offered us the power of individuality. He gave us natural power to probe into the mysteries and unseen powers of nature. As I mentioned earlier our universe is full of energies; not only outside of us, but much more within ourselves. We possess multifarious powers in the body, in the mind, and in the spirit. History proves that from the day humans came to this earth, they have been working hard to get into the deep and unfathomable energies of nature. Indeed as of today, we encounter we have brought many of those natural powers under our control.

Holy Spirit's action-2: Making me anew

To grasp this mystery of the presence and actions of the Holy Spirit which is something infinite, beyond our human understanding, Scriptures use different physical descriptions such as fire, wind, light, warmth, peace, charism and so on. David Watson, an author of many spiritual books has suggested that we should think of the Holy Spirit, as the early Christian mystics did, namely, He is the *kiss of God*. We frequently use the term 'worship' for all our masses, services in religions. That word 'worship' is a translation for the Greek term *'proskynein'* used in the Scriptures. It is actually derived from a root meaning *'to kiss'*. Generally our ancient civilizations used the act of kiss very rarely for only sacred and holy persons and things. The very act of kissing-provided that kiss is not formal but genuine, indicates that either party is empty or even nothing without the other. There is a tremendous transaction going on between the kisser and the kissed physically, emotionally, psychologically and spiritually. On this background the act of worship therefore in all religions is a time when we kiss God and we are kissed by God.

On the day of Pentecost God released his kiss toward the humanity not as a hush-hush kiss, nor as a flying kiss. God kissed certain persons of his choice very fervently, most intimately, and with great unction. That experience of getting kiss from the Holy was like a strong wind blowing, like drinking very strong wine. It made the receivers exclaim: 'Wow'. When God kisses me, the first effect of Pentecost is the 'kiss-and-makeup'. Namely, a merciful and loving reconciliation is made between God and humans. Secondly there is also something more and deeper happening: I call it 'the kiss-and-tell' of the Spirit, namely, a bright enlightenment and revelation settles in the human hearts and minds. It's a weird experience. By the action of the anointing from the Spirit a total transformation is occurring within the recipients. It can easily be shown from examples both in the OT and NT the Spirit continues to change those in whom He comes to dwell; he so transforms them that they begin to live a completely new kind of life. Saul was told by the prophet Samuel: *"The spirit of the LORD will rush upon you, and you will join them in their prophetic ecstasy and will become a changed man."* (1Sam. 10: 6)

When I come to the risen Jesus, proclaiming him as my savior and Lord, and repenting for my sins, my Realreligion believes with Paul and Church Tradition that the Holy Spirit offers me power to change and stop sinning, which I found hard to do. This process of transformation, my preachers explained, is the action of sanctification. Consequently I become more like Christ. The precious gift of being in the likeness and image of God bestowed in me by my Creator has been damaged and dirtied by my human sinfulness. I drifted away from my original divine image. Now, when I return back to my God as a prodigal son, through His Spirit God purifies me, beautifies me, and renews me to the divine image, as a sort of travel-back to my proper identity as God's child. Paul marvelously states this transformation in a very succinct way: *"All of us, gazing with unveiled face on the glory of the Lord, are being transformed into the same image from glory to glory, as from the Lord who is the Spirit."* (2 Cor. 3:18)

He also explains this transformation occurring in me by the Action of the Spirit relocating myself from old style to new style of life. Talking about the renewal I would be gifted with by Christ's Spirit, Paul writes: *"You should put away the old self of your former way of life, corrupted through deceitful desires, and be renewed in the spirit of your minds, and put on the new self, created in God's way in righteousness and holiness of truth."* (Eph. 22-24) With the Holy Spirit dwelling in us I have power over my old nature, to subdue it and make it subject to my new man. In the Spirit I will be the ultimate winner in the combat I am facing within me between the old lifestyle I wrongly selected in the past and the new one I enjoy by the anointing of the Spirit.

This unbelievable transformation occurring in me shocks me to the very roots, it shakes my foundations. I can never be the same after that experience. It brings a new vision to my life, a new quality. I feel within me a sudden jump from one end to the other, from one bank of the river to the other. I become totally a different person inside. As for outside, to others I may appear the same; I may go through the same routine drudgery of daily life. But as I pass through this ordinary life, in my heart there is tremendous peace, wonderful joy, and unthinkable liberation. From that day of Godly Kiss, I feel free; totally free to do anything as the God, my life-partner wants from me. I am there but nowhere there. I am human but different person. I am weak but I am strong. I am nothing but I am the greatest. I am suffering but I am joyful.

I think all of us are gifted with some creative power offered at our creation. The Lord indeed has kissed us at our conception in the womb of our mothers or test tubes. And we go on performing and accomplishing certain things in life with that creative energy released by the first kiss of God. But there are many who have had the second-kiss from the Lord, namely the experience of Pentecost, oh my God; they are remarkably releasing certain power and energy from them to their neighbors, and to the entire world. I am surprised to find such people not only in our Christian campus but also in other religions, and even in places where the word God seems abominable and absent. I dare say it is only through these powerful human persons who got the second kiss of God the earth survives, the society is safe, the communities are secure and the families are normal.

My friends in reelreligion ask me 'is it all real?' I affirm and say to them: 'Yes, it is really real; that is what we hear from the Acts of the Apostles, from Paul, plus from the two-millennium experience of the Church; I tell them also that, what I testify about the power of the Spirit is indeed unreal as long as they stand at the one side of the bank of the holy river; it may seem a dream as long as you sleep in your cozy and comfortable couch; but it turns to be real only for the persons who are awakened, who have already crossed or jumped to the other side of the river. Whichever community I have been serving as pastor there are inevitably two groups of Christians: One, following a reelreligion; and the other, a Realreligion which I have defined in my introductory pages. The former are the ones who can be labeled as 'nominal Catholics'. In the lives of these out-standing people I discover their ears are opened, but they have received nothing through their hearing; their eyes are wide open but they don't observe anything beyond natural and material; their mouths are somewhat big but they never open their lips to proclaim their faith; their hearts are beating endlessly for seeking nothing but emotional and physical pleasures; surely their hands are energized and active to reach out but only to get and not to give. The same people may recite their regular prayers, attend services, register their vows, and sign their pledges inside a church of their liking, and determine to go through, but unfortunately they don't understand none of these is salvation. Salvation means that we are brought to an in-situation of life-namely a systematized religion where we are able to receive two gratuitous gifts from God on the authority of Jesus Christ and by the power of the Holy Spirit: 1. Remission of sins. 2. Then follows the second mighty work of grace, called the Sanctification. In sanctification the regenerated soul deliberately gives up his right to himself to Jesus Christ, and identifies himself entirely with God's interest in other men.

It is amazing to see thousands of people who lived and live today, I call them 'people of good will', without even having any recourse to any religious systems, are endowed with virtues like faith, hope and love; gifts like wisdom, understanding, counsel, fortitude, knowledge, piety and fear of the Lord; and fruits of charity, joy, peace, patience, benignity, goodness, long-suffering, mildness, faith, modesty, continence and chastity.

My point is all the above-mentioned virtues and qualities are already the Creator has shared with humans. The real difference between reelreligion and Realreligion is how they are redeemed and used. Let us take Jesus of Nazareth. Like any human, he was as cute as his mother Mary; he was skillful and hard worker to earn his livelihood as his father Joseph; he was as intelligent as any other Scribes and Pharisees of his time; for his survival he was very diplomatic to join certain network of race, subgroups like Essences and he conducted himself as Nazarene-a prestigious label in his home land of Galilee; he cherished as his pride to belong to a supreme race of Jews; he could attract through his unimaginable charisma thousands of followers, especially women; he made himself a celebrity of his neighborhood and in his land; he could perform lots of miracles; he was wise enough to interpret his Scriptures with authority and could shut the mouth of his enemies; he too created lots of enemies out of his popularity and integrity.

All these can be recorded as natural qualities and talents and endowments of a leader like Jesus. Many can claim them as the typical fruits of Jewish racial DNA. But Jesus always claimed the other way. He proclaimed that every gift he possessed came from his Father. The Spirit of God was the true and only source of all that he owned and accomplished. From the day of his conception to his elevation as the risen Lord he professed that God's Spirit possessed him and empowered him. He was conceived by the Holy Spirit; he was anointed by the Holy Spirit at Baptism; he was led by the Spirit in every step of his journey of faith; many a time he cried out with joy of the Holy Spirit; he filled others with the same Spirit; he promised he would give the same Spirit even when he was absenting himself; history proves he did it as he promised.

Like Jesus we are natural born weak as well as strong, poor as well as rich and wise as well as ignorant. We too own our personal 'survival kits' for our daily survival. We join in hands with others and call it unity, but actually these are all our survival strategies. We come together using our diplomacy and intelligence on the basis of race, caste, creed, subgroups and associations. There is nothing wrong in these natural talents and gifts. Unfortunately these natural gifts are maintained as mere natural and not been elevated as the gifts of the Holy Spirit. With Paul the members of Realreligion esteem in faith that these natural human endowments have been transformed in our First and Second Baptism into Holy Spirit's virtues, gifts and fruits: Virtues of faith, hope and love; gifts of wisdom, understanding, counsel, fortitude, knowledge, piety and fear of the Lord; and fruits of charity, joy, peace, patience, benignity, goodness, long-suffering, mildness, faith, modesty, continence and chastity. Our natural power has been consecrated to the Trinity through the outpouring of His Spirit.

By natural power many humans even in reelreligion come together when they want to kill others for the sake their hidden agenda but not for building up the kingdom of God that proclaims peace, joy, eternal life and justice. Many use their talents and charisma for bringing more divisions rifts and confusion in the community. Some misuse these natural qualities for taking vengeance, retaliation and for one's own gratification. All these atrocious and pernicious activities are being done because they don't make these gifts being anointed by the Holy Spirit. On the other hand, in Realreligion my friends and myself first become aware of all our talents and gifts coming from the Creator; and get the anointing of the Spirit at an hour designated by the Trinity and start using them for the upliftment of our friends, our relatives, our children and the entire human race.

One thing myself and my friends in Realreligion are convinced as an absolute truth and that is whenever we, the disciples of the risen Lord lose the Holy Spirit within us, we have to meet horrible results: as Saul in OT was possessed by evil spirit; or in NT as Jesus points out, we who have been already cleansed by Baptism, will become shelters of too many unclean spirits if we fail to conform to our relationship with the Triune God: *"When an unclean spirit goes out of someone, it roams through arid regions searching for rest but, finding none, it says, 'I shall return to my home from which I came.'*

93

But upon returning, it finds it swept clean and put in order. Then it goes and brings back seven other spirits more wicked than itself who move in and dwell there, and the last condition of that person is worse than the first. " (Lk. 11: 24-26) This is why Psalmist would sing to the Lord fervently: *You hide your face, they are dismayed; you take back your spirit, they die, returning to the dust from which they came. You send forth your spirit, they are created; and you renew the face of the earth. (Ps. 104)*

Holy Spirit's Action-3: He builds up Unity

The second occasion when the Lord of the universe shared His power was the day of Pentecost. Realreligion strongly upholds that God offered on that day to the human beings the power of community; the energy to be together, a power to be united in diversities. This is what happened on the day of Pentecost. Book of Acts indicates that as the risen Jesus directed, the disciples were together with blessed Mother Mary as one family praying for the power from on high as he promised. When they got it, their spirit of unity energized all the people of different races, of different languages and of different cultures hearing everything the disciples spoke in their own tongues. Undoubtedly the Spirit has enhanced, face-lifted and enlarged the entire human individual powers the Apostles and disciples had been given in their creation-their birth. However those gifts of Power were bestowed to them only with the purpose of deploying all of them to build up god's community.

It is indeed hard for a natural man to be together with other people. We are natural born individuals. Individually we are gifted by natural human birth to dominate, to control, and to possess. But there is the other side of God's power. He is both individual and community. He wanted His man too not to be a loner. An individual person cannot be full and whole unless he/she becomes a community person. This is why God poured down His power from on high to energize men and women to become a community. Traditionally the Church feels this is the day she was born. The Church's main goal to be here on earth is to be a sign of that second creation, second shower of God's power of community. The church also remains as the source and environment of that power from on High. It is simply an upper room where you and I can receive the power of community from on High.

That is the Holy Spirit, the Power from on High. St. Paul beautifully states how the Holy Spirit becomes the center and core of making us live together. Without Him it's impossible for us to be together. However smart you may be, however diplomatic or politically correct you may behave, you will not arrive at a genuine unity or togetherness of humans, without the power of the Holy Spirit. As Irenaeus put it, we are like dry flour, which cannot become one lump of dough, one loaf of bread, without moisture. We who are many cannot become one in Christ Jesus, however much serious efforts are taken, without the living water, namely the Holy Spirit.

Paul brings to our attention three issues in which the power and presence of the Holy Spirit is a must. He affirms that no one can confess Jesus as Lord except in the Holy Spirit. This means, any effort to build up a community on the basis of confessing Jesus as the Lord, cannot be possible or genuine if it does not start, continue and ends in the Spirit. Paul tells us also that all the gifts, Charisms, ministries and talents come from the same one Spirit, from one God, and for the one Church. The individual manifestation, achievement is given for the sake of common good. No one can claim any gift or fruit he/she has received as his/her own or for his/her welfare. They are all for the community. In addition, Paul reminds us it is by and in the Spirit we are one body of Christ. Oneness comes by the presence of the Spirit.

These days it is very hard to bring people together, not only the secular and the religious, not just different religious people, but much worse those disciples who say they confess Jesus as their Lord, those who claim they have Charisms from the Spirit, and those who are convinced they are the members of the true Body of Christ. I am sad to find these members unknowingly follow the reelreligion. I see them in my life behaving very individually and being injurious to the unity of the Church. I can very easily identify those enemies of Christ. In my formation period one of my mentors cautioned me, *'Son, if you see certain person always claiming his right, living an isolated life or not interested or hateful to community life, be careful with him/her; a mini-antichrist is there; he or she is the agent of that notorious Devil who sneaked into the Garden of Eden and snatched away the first parents from God.'*

D. Criterions to know we are anointed by the Spirit

Definitely as Peter and Paul preached and proclaimed, acknowledging that Jesus is the Lord, repenting for sins, and being baptized in the name of Trinity are the primary benchmarks of being anointed by the Holy Spirit. Besides those three, the same Apostles enlisted some more yardsticks to find out the amazing outpouring of the Spirit in a person's life: After the Pentecostal Event, when people who noticed the sudden startling change in the behavior of the disciples they were wondering, "What does this mean?" Peter preached and proclaimed to them: *"You who are Jews, indeed all of you staying in Jerusalem. Let this be known to you, and listen to my words. These people are not drunk, as you suppose, for it is only nine o'clock in the morning. No, this is what was spoken through the prophet Joel: 'It will come to pass in the last days,' God says, 'that I will pour out a portion of my spirit upon all flesh. Your sons and your daughters shall prophesy, your young men shall see visions, your old men shall dream dreams. Indeed, upon my servants and my handmaids I will pour out a portion of my spirit in those days, and they shall prophesy."* (Acts 2: 12-18)

According to Scriptures, due to the coming down of the Holy Spirit, there were five changes taking place in the life of every disciple of Jesus: Fear was replaced by joy; Disturbance was replaced by peace; Loneliness was replaced by the presence of the Holy Spirit; Passivity was replaced by a sense of Mission; and Vengeance was replaced by Forgiveness. Paul too enumerates clearly in all his Letters, especially in First Letter to Corinthians (chapter 12) and Ephesians (chapter 12), some more standards of proving the Spirit's possessing of the individual. To what Peter highlights as the gifts of prophesying and seeing visions, Paul adds ability of teaching, performing mighty deeds, expressing wisdom, knowledge and faith, capacity of healing, speaking in tongues and interpreting and discerning the visions, dreams and tongues.

If browse the pages of the Gospels, we detect the weakness and limitation of twelve Apostles as well as other followers of Jesus while they were closely connected to him; while he was alive physically they were not true disciples of Jesus as they should be. True, they followed Jesus wherever he went; they ate with him, they listened to him, they helped him in all his daily ministries; they even worked certain healings when they were sent out two by two to preach the Gospel. Yet, that crowd of disciples included very sadly a betrayer, a disowner, some half-hearted disciples and many quitters, all abandoning Jesus, most of them being timid and living in closed door. So we can say they were not hundred percent true to their call to be disciples of Jesus. Very surprisingly only on the day of Outpouring of the Holy Spirit they became the true followers of Jesus. All was due to the power of the oly HolHHoly Spirit. When the power from on High came down upon these nominally-registered or acquainted or related to the team of Jesus of Nazareth they turned out to be genuine Disciples of Christ. Not only their sins were forgiven but also they were sanctified by the Spirit.

In the light of this God's revelation about the Spirit's Actions in our midst, and from the experiential expositions of Spirit-filled preachers and authors, I like to identify a few more visible and tangible criterions that indicate in day today life whether an individual or any particular parish or church has been anointed by Jesus' Spirit:

Unity

First is the gift of unity. Only the devil from hell uses the tactics of 'divide and rule' and his main ammunition in his battle with Jesus and his Spirit is disunity and dissension. Everyone who, either consciously or unconsciously become the source of in-fight, dissension and disunity, is an enemy to the Spirit. These persons bring damnation first to themselves and to the entire community and the Church. On the contrary the Realreligion's members are peacelovers and therefore always act as peacemakers and peacegivers. They long for togetherness of even strangers.

Sharing

Secondly the Spirit-filled people will always share theirs and themselves with others. Sharing and caring is the greatest gift from the Holy Spirit through which not only a person witnesses Christ to the world but also he/she gets into heavenly mansions. These three gifts of stability, unity and sharing are the outward signs of the Spirit's presence and action in individuals and the community as well.

Stability

Stability is the third greatest gift of the Spirit. This special gift of the Spirit initiates the receivers to be consistent and persistent in following the values of Jesus. People who quit from performing their duties in the church and those who run from one parish to another because of some petty, silly and self-centered motivations cannot be called as Spirit-filled Christians. Those parishioners who are unstable and label themselves as 'Cafeteria Catholics' choosing what they like and leave other elements of Catholic faith cannot be respected as the Spirit-anointed ones.

I discover in every Catholic parish, wherever I was serving as pastor, these three signs of the Spirit are found in the ones whom I fondly call the Realreligion's members. They are stable and content on what they handle as faith values. They keep up their goodness as godliness with no break. Despite all the scandals discovered around them and hurts done to them they still hold on to their faith in the Church and its Traditions. They continue to stay in their local parish stable and sound even though they personally don't like certain things happening, and certain parishioners who hurt and wound them. In Realreligion I see many couples are stable more than many decades in their marriage commitment; many members are stable in serving the community, stable in contributing toward running their local and universal Church. Such kind of stability of mind and heart toward Christian faith and life is a magnificent witnessing of the Spirit's presence and influence in the world.

I also find out so many in Realreligion are longing to be united as one family of God even though they are divided by race, culture, language, customs and opinions. They keep up to their oneness as one Body of Christ. They join together many times for different reasons as one community for example, for the restoration project of their churches, for conducting and celebrating certain festivals and important religious and social occasions. To solve any impending problem of their parish they are there as one family. Even though there are some, among those who are nominally registered to their parish but belonging to their own reelreligion, who always like to see some negative and divisive events occurring in their parish, the faithful members of Realreligion act as peacemakers and as unifying sources. This is absolutely another great evidence for the Spirit of God being present among us and possessing us.

The same members of Realreligion in the parishes, as Paul indicates, (1 Cor. Chapters 12 &13) show a still more excellent way of witnessing to the Spirit's actions. They, endowed with generous hearts, always open their life, time, treasure and talent to be shared with the community. This sharing is continued in parishes for years, even more than a century in some, in building up monumental churches and maintaining and managing beautiful lively parishes. Sharing has become a part of their monthly budget and portion of their family fulfillment; many widows and family couples have donated millions of dollars to their church community; Especially, I personally observe even those homebound, bedridden and lonely seniors regularly sharing their tithes from their limited resources like that of their social security check, pensions and savings. Such a sacrificial sharing cannot be found in a natural human being unless he/she is possessed by the Holy Spirit.

The above-listed actions of the Holy Spirit mold us, shape us and groom us as newly-born again persons for one purpose which is spelt out in the Acts 2: 4: *"They were all filled with the Holy Spirit and began to speak in different tongues, as the Spirit enabled them to proclaim,"* meaning that he Spirit inspired them to witness Christ and to proclaim his Gospel to every creature. The spirit increases our ability to proclaim the powerful deeds of God happened in the past, present and in coming future. The people who heard the Apostles preaching soon after the descent of the Spirit, they exclaimed: *"We hear them speaking in our own languages of the mighty acts of God."* (Acts 2: 11) The Apostles were not speaking about their problems, difficulties, etc. With the help of the Holy Spirit we too begin to see what we, others, our children, our family and parish members, people of other religions have and magnify God for 'His greatness' in us. This is what our Mother Mary proclaimed in her *'Magnificat'*: *My soul magnifies the Lord. I am an ordinary woman. He has done mighty things in my life. Holy is His name.*

According to my Realreligion, when the Spirit fills me he rests upon me and consecrates me. Then he bids me go forth to proclaim his peace and joy; he sends me forth to witness the kingdom of Christ among all the nations; to proclaim the good news of Christ to the poor; to console the hearts overcome with great sorrow; thus to reveal Christ's glory among all the people.

The power of the Spirit is not needed to open our mouth and move our tongues to utter words as we want. However we need his power for opening our mouth to proclaim God's deeds in and around us, and that too to proclaim to all the peoples, however much they are different, be they Parthians, Medes, and Elamites, inhabitants of Mesopotamia, Judea and Cappadocia, Pontus and Asia, Phrygia and Pamphylia, Egypt and the districts of Libya near Cyrene, as well as travelers from Rome, both Jews and converts to Judaism, Cretans and Arabs, in addition, White, Black, Brown, Yellow, Okies and Irish and so on. The Spirit gave the disciples the ability to speak in the language of every nation. God used this symbolic miracle of speaking and hearing in different languages to indicate to us that everyone who receives His Spirit will be understood if they are fully empowered by the love of God.

Love is the universal and perennial language that can be easily, attractively understood by any human person, including the animals and birds. Such love-language is poured out in our hearts by the Spirit. Thus he topples down the babel towers humans build by their whims and fancies. The Spirit came down on the disciples at Pentecost with power to open the gates of life to all nations and to make known to them the new covenant. So it was that men of every language joined in singing one song of praise to God, and scattered tribes, restored to unity by the Spirit, were offered to the Father as the first-fruits of all the nations.

The Spirit of the Lord makes flexible what is rigid, kindles what is frigid, and straightens what is wayward. The Holy Spirit who shatters the proud and stony hearts does also heal and strengthen the hearts that are shattered by fear and natural and social evils; The One who offers each one of us our individuality and self-identity and consequently enjoys seeing the uncountable differences in his especially human creations also enables us to unify everything together as one body, one church, one nation and one globe under one God, Abba Father. As we know well with our human power we cannot even think about true unity and peace. We are born individuals and divided. Only the Spirit's coming down in us and empowering us we can think about it, desire for it, hunger for it, plan some strategies for it and realize it.

Chapter-5:
Church according to my Realreligion

"I believe in one, holy, catholic, and apostolic Church."
(Nicene Creed)

I am vexed to find large number of Catholics drifting away from the Catholic Church which Jesus Christ found and initiated and maintains it with His Spirit up to this day due to their discovery of many flaws in the Church-teachings and practices. This exodus of Catholics is seen worldwide. As one of my parish friends observed, *'the world is crowded with Catholics as number one World Religion'*, he added 'but with difference: Among those Catholics minority are traditionally practicing Catholics; majority are non-practicing Catholics and the drifted-away Catholics.' (He meant our Protestant Brethren of all non-Catholic denominations.) He is absolutely correct in his assessment. Being human, yes, as many contend, Catholic Church is sinful and as all human institutions it is filled with religious, political and social imperfections. When my friends tried to persuade me to join with them in this critical exodus I always told them that if every Catholic in the world was wrong, I would still never leave my Mother Church of Jesus Christ because now I fully believe that is the Realreligion. With unction I continue to recite daily, especially with my congregation during Mass: *"I believe in one, holy, catholic, and apostolic Church"* as part of my faith-package inherited from my forebears. Why?

Expounding this faith-statement my new Church Catechism instructs me that: *The Church is one*: She acknowledges one Lord, confesses one faith, is born of one Baptism, forms only one Body, is given life by the one Spirit, for the sake of one hope (cf. *Eph.* 4:3-5), at whose fulfillment all divisions will be overcome. *The Church is holy*: The Most Holy God is her author; Christ, her bridegroom, gave himself up to make her holy; the Spirit of holiness gives her life. Since she still includes sinners, she is "the sinless one made up of sinners." Her holiness shines in the saints; in Mary she is already all-holy. *The Church is catholic*: She proclaims the fullness of the faith. She bears in herself and administers the totality of the means of salvation. She is sent out to all peoples. She speaks to all men. She encompasses all times. She is "missionary of her very nature" (*AG* 2). And *the Church is apostolic*: She is built on a lasting foundation: "the twelve apostles of the Lamb" (Rev 21:14). She is indestructible (cf. Mt 16:18). She is upheld infallibly in the truth: Christ governs her through Peter and the other apostles, who are present in their successors, the Pope and the college of bishops. (CCC 866-869)

The Catechism also adds at the end another solid truth as enlightened by Vatican II (*LG* 8): "The sole Church of Christ which in the Creed we profess to be one, holy, catholic, and apostolic, . . . subsists in the Catholic Church, which is governed by the successor of Peter and by the bishops in communion with him. Nevertheless, many elements of sanctification and of truth are found outside its visible confines. (CCC 870)

Church according to its Founder

In the midst of multifarious efforts of humans in the form of religions to search, to worship and to obey the Supreme Being, Jesus Christ created a Way of Life not entirely new but certainly a totally-renewed One which later his disciples till this day label as Christianity, Church and so on. This Jesus' historical renewal of old system of religion is very amazing as we spell out with the Church in one of the Psalter prayer: *"Lord, you have renewed the face of the earth. Your Church throughout the world sings you a new song, announcing your wonders to all. Through a virgin, you have brought forth a new birth in our world; through your miracles, a new power; through your suffering, a new patience; in your resurrection, a new hope, and in your ascension, new majesty."* (Morning Prayer in the Psalter for ordinary Mondays)

Realreligion never holds the disconcerting popular theology and rhetoric lately used by reelreligion's members contrasting the Gospel with Church. It goes something like this: "I love Jesus, but not the church." "We just have to get back to Jesus and skip all this religious piety and performance imposed by an institutional church." These reelreligion's members forget the fact that Jesus was really a religious Person and he was the One who planned and dreamt of such Church we see in today's world. I understand from what reason these remarks and attitudes come. Certainly Jesus didn't define Church using the term religion as we use today; neither, except James in his Letter once does, any NT Author refer Church as religion. Besides undoubtedly Jesus used some harshest and sometimes cursing words against those people who belonged to a religion of his time. Indeed he confronted the religion of his day. As one writer explains, Jesus did have a lot to say to people who distort religion for their own purposes and gain. Yet his critique was not so much of their religion as what they had done with it. He called out their motives and their corrupt hearts. His actions and words demonstrate very clearly that he was a religious man, totally committed to his Jewish religion. He spelt out very emphatically his positive mindsetup about his religion: *Do not think that I have come to abolish the Law or the Prophets; I have not come to abolish them but to fulfill them;"* and he too adds the immense necessity and importance of his religion and its values: *"Amen, I say to you, until heaven and earth pass away, not the smallest letter or the smallest part of a letter will pass from the law, until all things have taken place. Therefore, whoever breaks one of the least of these commandments and teaches others to do so will be called least in the kingdom of heaven. But whoever obeys and teaches these commandments will be called greatest in the kingdom of heaven."* (Matt. 5:17-19).

Jesus lived within the Judaism of His day. He was religious through and through. From his early childhood, starting from his Presentation event at the Temple, the Gospels present Jesus' parents raising him in the Jewish religious tradition; he was surely circumcised; his ethnic identity was undoubtedly His religious identity; he was a cradle Jewish; as an adult, he participated in the

Jewish feasts, most notably the Passover; he followed meticulously the structures of Judaism: teaching in synagogues, teaching as a rabbi, calling disciples, etc. Jesus knew the Scriptures of Judaism inside and out; he lived and breathed Judaism.

However, as Man of Truth, Jesus used unsympathetic words against only those religious people who misused and abused their religion. As a preacher says, Jesus took Judaism and made us dig deeper into it. He showed how corrupt hearts misuse religion as a way of establishing one's self before God (legalism) or as a way of establishing one's self before others (moralism). Jesus undoubtedly abhorred this sort of religiosity. He considered the religion they followed was merely a reelreligion, not according to their God. It is also true as the Anointed One from God Jesus saw that all of Judaism was pointing toward himself; and that it found its deepest meaning and purpose in him; he forthrightly would take any religion distorted and broken by humanity as mere reelreligion and turn it into Realreligion. *"I tell you, unless your righteousness surpasses that of the scribes and Pharisees, you will not enter into the kingdom of heaven."* (Matt. 5: 20)

Besides cleaning up the old religious myths and messes, Jesus is seen in the Gospels heading toward a new plan of establishing a system that is fully made of social and spiritual, human and divine elements. He was firmly convinced of a surprising distance between the old religious systems and the new one of his. He expounded this fact through three mini parables: *"No one tears a piece from a new cloak to patch an old one. Otherwise, he will tear the new and the piece from it will not match the old cloak. Likewise, no one pours new wine into old wineskins. Otherwise, the new wine will burst the skins, and it will be spilled, and the skins will be ruined. Rather, new wine must be poured into fresh wineskins. And no one who has been drinking old wine desires new, for he says, 'The old is good.'"*(Lk. 5: 36-39) According to Scriptural scholars, through these parables Jesus clarified his view about how his new System distant itself from the old. Each of those parables speaks of the unsuitability of attempting to combine the old and the new. Jesus' teaching is not a patching up of old religion; or can his concept of religious values be limited to the Old Law. According to the scholars of Biblical interpretation, the saying of Jesus 'the old is gold' would have meant to be ironic; his contention through this statement is that people who are satiated by the old form of religion may begrudge to sampling the new.

Jesus' religious system according to Gospel writers

Personally I think Jesus didn't want to use the term 'religion' to denote his new system because he was very much disgusted by the manner many humans of his time abusing and misusing their religious system. And so were his Apostles and disciples. They all tried to discover from the sayings and life-commitment of their Master some terms that were wholistically descriptive of Jesus' new Order.

First word which came to their mind was *'Kingdom' that is of God, of heaven.'* It had been repeated frequently by their Master. Jesus began his ministry in Palestine with a cordial invitation to the public join in his new religious system. That was his first homily. Mark, who is believed to be the first of the Evangelists, who wrote the gospels, testifies: *". . . Jesus came to Galilee proclaiming the gospel of God: "This is the time of fulfillment. The kingdom of God is at hand. Repent, and believe in the gospel."* (Mk. 1: 14-15) In Luke we read Jesus was preoccupied with his proclamation of his new effort and bringing awareness to the public about his new Order: *"To the other towns also I must proclaim the good news of the kingdom of God, because for this purpose I have been sent."* (Lk. 4: 42) Matthew formulated what Mark's quoting of Jesus' saying: *"Repent, for the kingdom of heaven is at hand."* (Matt. 4: 17) He too tells us that John the Baptizer too testified it with the same statement: *"Repent, for the kingdom of heaven is at hand."* (Matt. 3: 2)

Basically Jesus' contention was every effort he was making belongs to the Heaven; it is God's work; it is spiritually-oriented; and it has an eschatological character of 'already but not yet'. He envisioned his new religious system, *though it is in the world as any human system, yet does not belong to the world*. It is a paraphrase of a passage found in Jn. 17: 13-16) In front of Pilate Jesus witnessed to this truth: *"My kingdom does not belong to this world. If my kingdom did belong to this world, my attendants [would] be fighting to keep me from being handed over to the Jews. But as it is, my kingdom is not here."* (Jn. 18: 36) Hence the new religious system he was creating, according to him, is of his Father, from his Father and for his Father. The uniqueness of Jesus' religious system is simultaneously ritual and spiritual: *"Amen, amen, I say to you, no one can enter the kingdom of God without being born of water and Spirit"* (Jn. 3: 5); it is earthly as well as heavenly: *"Truly I say to you, there are some standing here who will not taste death until they see the kingdom of God."* (Lk. 9: 27) When Jesus was hanging on the cross in his final moment the good thief begged him: *"Jesus, remember me when you come into your kingdom."* To him Jesus replied, *"Amen, I say to you, today you will be with me in Paradise."* (Lk. 23: 42-43)

Secondly the Disciples of Jesus remembered what he was talking with them at the Last Supper. While his disciples were expressing their ignorance of not knowing about both where he was going and what was the way to go there, Jesus told them: *"I am the way and the truth and the life. No one comes to the Father except through me."* (Jn. 14: 4-6) This offered a clue to them to label the new religious system as 'The Way.' In the Book of Acts Luke uses the term 'the Way' to refer to all religious and spiritual practices the early Church was observing, especially using it as a frequent reference of Paul and his conversion. The first reference was in the narration about Saul's conversion becoming Paul: *Saul went to the Sanhedrin and asked the High Priest for letters to the synagogues in Damascus, that, if he should find any men or women who belonged to the Way, he might bring them back to Jerusalem in chains.* (Acts 9: 2) And there are many such references about this 'Way' in passages like Acts 9/ 18/26; 19/9; 22/4; 24/14; 24/22.

Church at its dawn

We discover in the Book of Acts how the Spirit of the risen Jesus led the Apostles and the first Disciples to the clear understanding of his New Religious System. It was indeed slow but steady development. At the start it looked like a group of humans, very closely attached to Jesus of Nazareth. *"Therefore, it is necessary that one of the men who accompanied us the whole time the Lord Jesus came and went among us, beginning from the baptism of John until the day on which he was taken up from us, become with us a witness to his resurrection."* (Acts 1: 21-22) These were, not only the 12 Apostles but also as Luke indicates, 120 disciples, including Jesus' Mother and his brothers. (Acts 1: 14-15) At the second phase of the development of understanding the New Religious System of Jesus the

Holy Spirit brought into the primary team about 3000 persons (Acts 2: 41); and every day the Lord added to their number. At this time the new religious system of Jesus was recognized as a gathering of 'those who were being saved.' (Acts 3: 47)

Then a surprising turning point occurred in the apprehension about the genuine characteristic of Jesus' New Religious System. Jesus' Spirit moved all, belonging to the group of the 'saved' and of 'those who believed', to experience their gathering as a 'community'. This meant there should be a commonality not only in being baptized in water and the Spirit, not only in being devoted to the teaching of the apostles, not only in performing the breaking of the bread and in praying but also in leading a communal life, living together and having all things in common and selling and dividing their property and possessions among all according to each one's need. (Acts 2: 42-46) Jesus' new religious system was recognized as a gathering of believers, gathering of saints, and gathering of Christ's followers (Christians).

We know that in the Bible there is no one word meaning 'community'. The term 'community', as we use today, comes from the Latin *communitas*, which is derived from the root word *communis* or "common". The possible closest word in the New Testament derives from the Greek root word *koin* and its most basic meaning which also means "common". The Greek noun *koinonea* stems from the root *koin* meaning 'fellowship' and also expressing communion, communication, contribution and participation. Though there is no word community as such used by NT writers, there are many examples/models of community found in the Bible as we pointed out earlier about the Common life existing among first Christians. Letters of Paul, Peter and other Apostles are filled with exhortations and models about this Jesus' Community.

Church in its development

Later when Paul and Barnabas took the ministry of preaching the Gospel of Jesus to the gentiles, besides the Jews, we find the word 'Church' to denote the New Religious System of Jesus. Basically keeping up to its identity as the community of Jesus' believers, the word Church represented its other characteristics. Appreciatively I like to enlist some of those characteristics this word 'Church' brought home to the world at the Vat II. My Realreligion lovingly accept what the Catechism of my Mother Religion explicates about the nature and characteristics of the Lord's New Religious System as 'Church. 'Church' is the translation of Latin *Ecclesia and the* Greek *ekkalein,* meaning a 'convocation' or an 'assembly.' We find the term *ekklêsia* frequently used in Greek OT to point out the assembly of the Chosen People in front of the Almighty God. To show the New Religious Order of Jesus as the continuity of this Assembly the first community of Christian believers called it *'Ekklesia'*. Hence the first characteristic of my Realreligion as Church is an assembly of the risen Jesus' followers, believers and disciples. (Ref. CCC 751) *"As the "convocation" of all men for salvation, the Church in her very nature is missionary, sent by Christ to all the nations to make disciples of them."* (CCC 767) Secondly, Church according to my Realreligion is the Sheepfold of the Good Shepherd Jesus. It is the flock of which God himself foretold that he would be the shepherd, and whose sheep, even though governed by human shepherds, are unfailingly nourished and led by Christ himself, the Good Shepherd and Prince of Shepherds, who gave his life for his sheep." (CCC 754)

The Church, the New Religious System of Jesus, seems to be a total mystery, a complex reality, as my Master's Incarnation was. It is human but divine; holy but sinful; universal and local; one but many; visible and invisible; apostolic and missionary. The Church is in history, but at the same time she transcends it. It is only "with the eyes of faith" that one can see her in her visible reality and at the same time in her spiritual reality as bearer of divine life. It exists as any other human social institution, structured with hierarchical organs, at the same time it is the mystical body of Christ; a visible society and a spiritual community; an earthly Church and a spiritual storage of heavenly riches. (Ref. CCC 770-771)

I am in full agreement with the assertion that the Church is Christianity; the Religion of Christ. There is no word as 'Christianity' found in the Bible. However, as somebody wrote in the internet, this term came to common usage in 14th century. It was to differentiate Church from other religious systems existing in the globe. But in the NT period the term 'Christian' has been in vogue as we read in three places in NT: Acts 11: 26; 26: 28; and 1Pet. 4: 16. As many Biblical scholars point out, those instances can be read as outsiders using the name as a reproach. However this term pointed out, as my Realreligion agrees, to someone who was belonging to the crowd of Christ; or very positively and more applicably it was the name of a person who was living in Christ, through Christ, with Christ and for Christ as Paul declares in his Letters. I also feel very sad to admit that in the feudalistic period, since kings and queens and other powerful persons in politics were belonging to the New Religious system of Jesus, the Church, which was getting very popular, they began using it for their political stunt against other existing religions as another competitive form of religion. Consequently the term *'Christ-ianitas'* came to its existence. Very sadly we know in history how such attempt jeopardized the true identity of the New Religious System-the 'Church' as Christ had intended and established.

Church in its growth and Fullness

In the history of Christianity, especially in its beginning stage, there was much that was transitory and exceptional. It was not presented full-grown to the world, but left to develop in accordance with the forces and tendencies that were implanted within it by Jesus, namely His Spirit. The continuous Presence and Inspirational Action of the same Spirit can spectacularly be seen in the subsequent history of the Church. Every Council that was convened by the universal Church over the centuries had its own impact on the Church. In response to a question 'did the Second Vatican Council change any Catholic doctrine?' Vatican said: The Second Vatican Council neither changed nor intended to change any doctrine; rather it developed, deepened and more fully explained it. This was exactly what John XXIII said at the beginning of the Council. Paul VI affirmed it and commented in the act of promulgating the Constitution Lumen Gentium: *"There is no better comment to make than to say that this promulgation really changes nothing of the traditional doctrine. What Christ willed, we also will. What was, still is. What the Church has taught down through the centuries, we also teach. In simple terms that which was assumed, is now explicit; that which was uncertain, is now clarified; that which was meditated upon, discussed and sometimes argued over, is now put together in one clear formulation".* The Bishops repeatedly expressed and fulfilled this intention.

Though there have been many changes in dealing and interpreting the primitive Church activities, the core and cream of the Gospel of Jesus has never been diluted or distorted. Namely as Paul writes: *"Now I am reminding you, brothers, of the gospel I preached to you, which you indeed received and in which you also stand. Through it you are also being saved, if you hold fast to the word I preached to you, For I handed on to you as of first importance what I also received: that Christ died for our sins in accordance with the scriptures; that he was buried; that he was raised on the third day in accordance with the scriptures."* (1 Cor. 15:1-4) Rather, natural causes and the course of events, and human undertakings-even sometimes they might have been disastrous, always under the Divine Spirit's guidance, resulted in Christianity taking on the form which would best secure its permanence and efficiency. This is why I love to encounter the eternal Christ-centered substance in today's Church, despite it has greatly changed in outward appearances during the ages.

St Vincent of Lerins inspirationally and very eruditely describes the genuine form of change that should happen in the Church. According to him, idea of change is not alteration but development. *"Development means that each thing expands to be itself, while alteration means that a thing is changed from one thing into another."* Using the physical body development and growth as metaphor, the same saint writes: *"The religion of souls should follow the law of development of bodies. Though bodies develop and unfold their component parts with the passing of the years, they always remain what they were."*

The Church as of today has grown steadily, as the risen Jesus meant it, to be a religion that is universal, perfect and visibly well-organized. Its universality encompasses both space and time; it has entered into every nook and corner of the globe without distinction of race, language and country as Jesus dreamt. (Matt. 28: 19) As for the extension of its time, its lives today in an eschatological timezone, namely it moves within earthly time but it enjoys within the eternal Kingdom of heaven already. Catechism of the Catholic Church instructs me: *"The Church . . . will receive its perfection only in the glory of heaven,"* at the time of Christ's glorious return. *Until that day, "the Church progresses on her pilgrimage amidst this world's persecutions and God's consolations." Here below she knows that she is in exile far from the Lord, and longs for the full coming of the Kingdom, when she will "be united in glory with her king."* (CCC 769)

Though this Christ's religion is made of both holy as well as sinful members, I admire at its wholistic and total perfection in the fact that its Founder was a Perfect Person and all his teachings and directions are very idealistic. His Values are based on big dreams, big visions and big goals. Probably over the centuries some men and women have misinterpreted those values and consequently deformed them. However, with the guidance of the risen Lord's Spirit, this religion preserved its perfect identity in its volumes of writings as its repeated deliberations and adherence to the perfect teachings of its Perfect Founder. This Church stands visibly as a well-built global organization or institution-I personally call it a 'religion in-situation'. Its external visibility is very imposing as the "House built upon the rock" (Matt. 7: 24), and as the 'City set upon a hill.' (Matt. 5: 14)

This religion of Christ, as a spiritual springboard, is absolutely very personal way for its members to reach heaven; but as its synonymous name 'Church' indicates, it is about a relationship. It is made of individual pilgrims walking on the road to heaven and they are hard-climbers of the Mountain of the Lord to reach its top. Paul envisaged this magnificent uniqueness of the Church: *"You are strangers and aliens no longer. No, you are fellow citizens of the saints and members of the household of God. You form a building which rises on the foundation of the apostles and prophets, with Christ Jesus himself as the capstone. Through him the whole structure is fitted together and takes shape as a holy temple in the Lord; in him you are being built into this temple, to become a dwelling place for God in the Spirit."* (Eph. 2:19-22)

However they are to be together bonded as brothers and sisters by their faith and love of Christ. Truly Jesus insisted each individual must first relate to Jesus 'without whom we cannot enter into eternal Life.' The same Jesus has also said: *"Amen, amen, I say to you, no one can see the kingdom of God without being born from above."* He explained this to Nicodemus: *"Amen, amen, I say to you, no one can enter the kingdom of God without being born of water and Spirit."* (Jn. 3: 3-5) He was referring to one of the most important sacraments of the Church through which those individual Hill-climbers to his heavenly Kingdom start together as one family of Christ.

Institutional Character of Realreligion

Many people who follow their own reelreligions wrongly think that there is nothing but goodness existing in this life as some among feel pessimistically that there is nothing but evil in their lives. They completely misunderstand the Scriptures. The Scriptures of my Realreligion always expose to me that earthly life is a battlefield between the good and the bad spirits. Jesus my Guru in his life and preaching has indicated this truthful fact. The Scriptures says, *"The Spirit drove Jesus out into the desert and tempted by Satan. He was among wild beasts which were the symbols of evil spirits and the angels ministered to him."* Jesus has been torn to pieces by his life's tension, struggle and other evil forces. Like Jesus I too am tempted, tossed around, broken to pieces, wounded, crucified, misunderstood, and diagnosed with different kinds of unheard, brand new diseases; I am struck down by natural calamities and other social and political problems as wars and terrorism.

In order to cope with this life situation, to live in peace and joy in the midst of such problems and temptations and to win my life's battle I try to seek for an ark of safety and security, an ark of power and ammunitions and an ark of protection and cure. Indeed my friends in reelreligions choose the arks according to their whims and fancies; they choose to join a group of their own as safety network, comfort zone, quarantine, and rehabilitation center and call them as tribe, caste, race, color and cult; some among them choose a comfort zone of their own as nightclub or country club; or choose to hide themselves in their own bedroom or sleep tight on their couches; and many others try to escape or to take it easy in this struggle by adhering to alcoholism, drug-addiction, gambling, and so on; even some make recourse to suicidal death.

In all these attempts, I, in the light of my experience, find certain flaw of inconsistency and incapacity. Many times these arks used by my reelreligions' friends adding more harm and become injurious to their security and safety. Hence I am asked by my Realreligion to use my faith as the Ark of safety and security and success. Followers of reelreligions, as in olden days of Christianity or any other world religions, enter into some organized religions in order to protect their identity, to find safety and security from the cruel kings, emperors and unjust regimes. Still today many religions are considered as the ark of security by millions of people who are poor, sick and the weaklings. This is why when people grow high and rich in their possessions, education, knowledge, power and popularity they don't feel the need and necessity of such arks. It does not become their priority or the center of their lives.

Church therefore is the Ark of the Covenant of God and me. According to the Scriptures the ark of safety and security for humanity established by God is not just any human system. He established and built an Ark to save me and to make me feel at home in this vale of tears. The Scriptures call it 'the Ark of the Covenant.' What is it? God first made a covenant with humanity, a covenant that promises that he would love us forever and he would always be a divine healer. In the Scriptural story of the deluge God promised to Noah that He would never permit evil like deluge. But the Israelites continued to be struck by all kinds of evil. So they again searched for the truth and found out as we hear in Deuteronomy God would keep his word if the humans too respond to his covenant. This means, two lovers, namely God and myself, construct the Ark of the Covenant. It is certain God will never violate nor will go against his covenant. It is I who must respond to his call of love and intimacy. It is I who must be always inside of that ark even in the midst of deluge, cyclone, desert-situation, and sickness, in dying, in turmoil, in war, in threats of terrorism.

As he made the rainbow a symbol of his promise, my Realreligion esteems the Church as a symbol of that covenant. If I am baptized into this religion I accept this covenant of love. Then on, my conscience becomes the ark of the covenant of love and justice. This is what Jesus referred to when he proclaimed that the 'Kingdom of God in me'. If such like-minded people of the covenant gather together, we make then the Church the Ark of God. Many of my friends in reelreligions live an unconscious life in that ark and therefore not fully enjoining its safety and security. The people like me who are fully conscious of this fact and act upon it, find strength, power, protection, joy, and success in this vale of tears and the desert of temptations.

Church as Realreligion

There is an incessant debate going on now about the understanding of the difference between spirituality, religion and church. In my realreligion I don't get involved in it; rather I firmly believe the nature and identity of the 'Church', as put forward to me by the Bible and by the Traditional interpretation and exposition of Second Vatican Council, contain very positively all that are spoken about spirituality which is a path, a regimen, a process to reach our ultimate goal the Divine; religion which is not only an institution of beliefs and practices, but much more a living organism which is made of humans, as Dr. Frank Kaufmann put it, who have surrendered their lives to the loving direction of the living, risen Lord Jesus.

As I mentioned in my introduction, religion is being practiced in many ways: Either I can be half-hearted religious or faking religious or one-sided religious or I can be a religious totally involved and surrendered to every iota of the religion I consider the best. The last approach seems to me the true religion, Realreligion and if the mystery of the Church is recognized, digested, lived, experienced and expressed sincerely and truly then that Church I practice is the Realreligion. While most of the reelreligions state that if we obey God, He will love us, the true Church says that it is because God has loved us through Jesus that we can obey. That is how it is esteemed as Realreligion. Since the doctrine of Church proclaims all its efforts and practices are about relationship to the Triune God and neighbors and not merely ritualistic religiosity, it is surely the Realreligion.

So many religions have been founded in human history and too many religious sects even today pop up as mushrooms in modern society. They may be focusing on the Supreme Spiritual Being or mere natural human spirit. My Realreligion, as I indicated earlier, separates itself first of all from those religious attempts taken concentrating only on natural human spirit. Secondly, even among those beliefs founded and continued focusing on God, Realreligion detaches itself from those religious sects which don't hold wholistic and total view about God, Humanity and the relations between the two. Thirdly, though it picks up the Church, Christ's religion as its best choice, it deliberately avoids the reelreligion practiced by the members of various religions, including within Christianity, the Church. Jesus, the Founder, left to the world a remarkable idealistic religion and continues to stay in it and guides it. Very sadly there are too many inside this Church nominally carry the name 'Christians' but practice a religion which is crooked, distorted, perverted and sometimes turn out to be betrayers and disowners of the marvelous ideals of their Leader Jesus. Their religion can be therefore appropriately named as 'Reelreligion'.

The Realreligion I practice within the Church professes that I belong to a flock gathered as one herd; not simply by some registration or enrollment but intrinsically and organically but mystically connected to each of its member. My Realreligion firmly asserts that the Church I am related to is a sacrament of expressing, experiencing and enhancing the intimate union between Jesus Christ and every member of this institution. My realreligion's heartbeat is exactly the same as that of Pope Benedict XVI who spoke on the new understanding of ecclesiology as developed in Vatican II: *"We wanted to say and to understand that the Church is not an organization, not just some structural, legal, or institutional thing? which it also is? but an organism, a living reality that enters into my soul and that I myself, with my very soul, as a believer, am a constitutive element of the Church as such . . . . The Church isn't a structure. We ourselves, Christians together, we are the living Body of the Church. Of course, this is true in the sense that we, the true 'we' of believers, together with the 'I' of Christ, are the Church; each one of us is not 'a we' but a group that calls itself Church."* (From one of his warm and friendly chats with the clergy of Rome; this was held in the Paul VI Hall, in February 2013)

My Realreligion is in one mind with Father José Galindo Rodrigo who wrote a most powerful book *'"The Powerful Saving Force of Christ: A Guide for Christians Given the Present Religious Pluralism,"* saying in one of his interviews that *"Christianity does not belong to Christians, but rather is the property of Christ, "who wills to save everyone."* (Zenit.org) I totally agree with him: *"Present-day religious pluralism exactly as it is often conceived, indeed blurs the saving power of Christ. If one thinks that all religions save, then Christ is diminished. But to equate, when things are not equal, is an injustice and an error."* Undoubtedly several documents of the Church speak about other religions as well as other denominations, as God's instruments of salvation, because having truths and values, they can serve, and in fact serve so that God can save faithful of those religions though always through the merits of Christ, who is the only Savior of all. This offers us a divine mind of Christ to boldly ascertain that any form of absolutism is not correct either in *affirming that only Christianity is right, because the great religions coincide with Christianity in some things-truths and values'.* As Pope Benedict XVI has highlighted, and John Paul II also did, non-Christian and non-Catholic religions must be allies in many important things for the good of humanity. This Godly attitude's one and only motivation is, as Fr. Rodrigo said, that *Christ will be ever more known by very many people who will end by being better followers of his than those of us who now say we are Christians.*

Churches within the Church

St. Cyril of Jerusalem says: *"The Church is called Catholic because she is diffused throughout the whole world from one end of the earth to the other, and because she teaches universally and without curtailment all the truths of faith which ought to be known to men whether they concern visible or invisible things, heavenly things or the things of earth;"* (Cateches., xviii, 23; P.G., XXXIII, 1043).

Pope Francis, in a catechesis during the Wednesday (June, 12, 2013) general audience, discussing about the concept of the 'People of God' which is the true meaning of the Church, is quoted saying: *"To be the People of God first of all means that God doesn't belong to any particular people because He is the one who calls us . . . and this invitation is addressed to all, without distinction, because God's mercy 'wills everyone to be saved'. Jesus doesn't tell the Apostles and us to form an exclusive group of elite members."*

In this One, Catholic, Church which is my Realreligion I am blessed with many churches within One Church. This may sound some pun of words that can lend itself as source of misgivings. Let me clarify how I consider this paradoxical statement. The One church, which is a universal community, is made of thousands of local churches, communities, parishes. As Vat II declared, *"All men are called to belong to the new people of God. Wherefore this people, while remaining one and only one, is to be spread throughout the whole world . . . scattered as they were, would finally be gathered together as one . . . It follows that though there are many nations there is but one people of God, which takes its citizens from every race, making them citizens of a kingdom which is of a heavenly rather than of an earthly nature. All the faithful, scattered though they be throughout the world, are in communion with each other in the Holy Spirit, and so, he who dwells in Rome knows that the people of India are his members".* (LG 13)

As every person is a church by himself or herself, so every community they form locally as Jesus' disciples is a church; and consequently the microfamily each one constructs is called a domestic church. This is possible only when these individuals and the little local churches they are in must be intrinsically connected first to Jesus, the Lord and Savior, and simultaneously to the Universal Church in Spirit and in Truth. The friends who follow Realreligion inside the Church totally agree and adhere to this factor.

Once upon a time there were two men who day after day worked side by side in brick and mortar. It so happened that a child passed by each day and always stopped a moment to watch the two men work. Day after day the course of bricks grew higher and higher but the child could not tell what the two men were constructing. The child did notice however that while both of the men worked at the same pace and with the same expertise one seemed always sad, the other always happy. So one day the child out of curiosity approached the sad looking man and asked "what are you doing?" The morose-looking fellow said, "Mmm . . . I am laying bricks, that is what." The child then turned to the happy looking man and asked the same question "What are you doing?" The cheerful-looking fellow looked up, beamed a broad smile, pointed a finger to the sky, and exclaimed, "I am building a cathedral. That is what!"

The basic secret of our life's success and failure, happiness and productiveness lies largely not on what we do but how we do, and why we do. The bottomline of every success is the kind of orientation we have developed within our mind set-up regarding the purpose of life. Pope Francis, speaking on the Mystery of the Church during his weekly General Audience (June 26, 2013), emphasized that *'Christ is the living Temple of the Father, and Christ himself builds his "spiritual home", the Church, made not of physical stones but of "living stones", which are us.'* As pope Francis catechized, members who practice Realreligion in local churches enrich themselves with a clear orientation of life that believes that 'after all I am a part of a big enterprise of God, even though I am alone in a small tiny little church community.' We believe unhesitatingly that we are the living stones of God's building, deeply united to Christ, who is the cornerstone, and is also a keystone among us. We are the living Church, the living temple. Therefore we are sure that none of us is useless in the Church. No one is secondary; no one is the most important in the Church; we are all equal in God's eyes; none is anonymous.

Any physical structure they build as 'church' symbolizes their belief in their belonging to the 'Big Edifice', namely the universal Church, as its stones. They use their creative talents of architecture, sculpture, painting and so on to symbolize, to inspire the distracted residents in their town or village to meet their God sacramentally; they are fully convinced that the presence of God is in the churches they build and they too believe all that is good belonging to God will flow like living water from those churches to fill their life abundantly. It is more so in their Catholic churches because they contain a tabernacle where the permanent Presence of the risen Lord is encountered in the Eucharist.

Also, Realreligion-friends hold that our individual human nature, our vulnerable human body has turned out to be the dwelling place of the Almighty God through baptism in water and spirit and therefore Paul writes: *"Do you not know that your body is a temple of the Holy Spirit within you, which you have from God, and that you are not your own? For you were bought with a price; therefore glorify God in your body."* (1Cor.6:19-20) Plus, following the footsteps of First Christians, they are connected to the local community as church not just for security, safety and political and social benefits, as any non-Christian tribal community had viewed, but they are united as the local temple of God, an edifice of Christ. They understand fully what Paul writes: *"You form a building which rises on the foundation of the apostles and prophets, with Christ Jesus himself as the capstone."* He also adds: *"In Him you are being built into this temple, to become a dwelling place for God in the Spirit."* (Eph.2:19-22) The main thrust of this 'One-Church-though-many' factor of Catholic Christianity is warmly received and lived by the Realreligion-members because the very term "Catholic" denotes 'universality' which embraces the whole human race with no exception or exemption whatsoever, including the dead 'in communion of saints'. Therefore whenever they gather together as parishioners in a local church, especially within the four walls of a physical church, they experience, develop and express their oneness as the one structure of Jesus. Besides, we also hold on to a truth that we are closely connected as members of the mystical Body of Christ which is being symbolized by the collegiality and papacy of the Roman Catholic Church.

Universality, according to my Realreligion, does not mean uniformity, rather the universal character of the church flows from the Elements: One God, One Christ, One Spirit, One Faith and One Kingdom of God. Every other characteristics or qualities only flow from these main Elements. While the main factors are very spiritual and mystical, what follow are earthly, human and visible. If the First Elements are not found in anything that is done or implemented in the second realm, it is totally perverted and poisonous to the members of the Church. Humans as such don't make the universality; they don't render the Church holy; they don't bring about oneness of it; rather all the above come about only by the belief and adherence they hold firmly to the 'First Elements'. The oneness of the Church as one building was misused in the middle ages to monopolize, to rule, to destroy various cultures, to bring about an egalitarian society, to behave exclusive and esoteric, to build fortress around so that those who were inside led to feel that they are the only elite race and people and thus damaged the real beauty of the oneness of the Church.

In this regard Pope Francis echoes what a genuine church member should uphold. The loving but very stern words he uttered in one of his addresses (June 14, 2013) to writers of the Jesuit journal 'La Civilta Cattolica' are meant to be totally applied in all Realreligion's practioners: *"Your fidelity to the Church still requires that you be hard against hypocrisies, fruit of a closed, sick heart, hard against this sickness. However, your main task is not to build walls but bridges; it is to establish a dialogue with all men, also with those who do not share the Christian faith, but "have the veneration of high human values," and even "with those who oppose the Church and persecute her in various ways (GS 92)."* Recently I read about a community church in Oakford, California, near Sacramento, that calls itself *"The Church without Walls."* It is mainly because the congregation meets most Sundays throughout the year in an open amphitheater. The concept is very interesting. That is the way my Realreligion esteems Jesus' Church to be. It must have both its doors and the hands and hearts of its members always open to any body with no discrimination whatsoever. It is a Church that looks for similarities that unite us but overlooks differences that might divide us from each other. My choice-church must be engaged in building bridges between cultures, nations, races, values, traditions, religions and classes by a common love principle of Jesus, a common baptism, a common faith and a common destiny.

Before the Age of Enlightenment Church has been the center of social life for its members. It has been the center of education, medication, creative cultural arts, and even political and economic dimensions of human life. Even today in many parts of the world, where modernization has not fully entered, we can see such centrality of the church in the communities. In Latin America for example, the Church is not just a worshipping place; rather it is what they call '*Pueblo*', an integral part of the community. They have built a community as plaza where the Church is in the center around which all other activities are performed. When the Spanish people say they '*catolicos*' they do not mean they have been at Mass or the sacraments; they simply mean that they are members of a '*pueblo*' which is catholic. We in this modern world, ignore such community orientation in the church. We prefer to worship alone, individually. This individualistic attitude regarding Church life was all originated from those who practiced reelreligion and still it continues on. It was indeed the result of the misuse of such oneness of the Catholic Church. This cruel and crude experience of the middle ages has brought us to the present church situation where we no more center our life around our Church. We are prejudiced by the past so much that our orientation is dissipated. Many systems and agencies and isms have taken hold of our life-orientation.

My Realreligion teaches that we should go back to the traditional approach to our Church as the One Building. The parish with its church in the center must be a place; but it should in no way repeat the old mistakes; rather it should act as an inspirational center where people of the same faith gather and express their faith, share their joys and sorrows, share and care with their talents, money and time. It should be center of inspiration, higher motivation, and an environment where people celebrate their identity, their closeness with their creator and redeemer. It should be a fireplace where the weary and cold get the fire of the Spirit. It should not be surely a place of conspiracy, or monopoly, or a place of pride. It should be a place for us to meet God in Spirit and in Truth. The money we offer, the talents we pour in, the time we put in, and the energy we share with in a local church must make this church environment a fireplace of the Spirit, an edifice of Jesus from where the Living Water abundantly flows and benefits all who join this community.

A word about my Separated Brethren

Indisputably my Realreligion strongly believes all the explanation on the Church offered by Catechism in the light of Vatican II; I love the Church I belong to; I am totally a committed person to the Church where I am affiliated with from my birth. I am proud to label myself as a cradle catholic. The main reason for such freaky conceit-as many may suspect, is that I belong to a church which has been the Mother of all Christian denominations and sects; despite multifarious oppositions and infights and heresies, she has preserved the Apostolic Tradition which Jesus handed over to the Apostles; while her daughters-denominations, sects and so on, breached out in history for the sake of concentration certain particular holdings or performances, the Mother Church continues to keep intact all of them in a balanced manner but with human sinfulness. Each denomination or sect went out of their Mother's lap only with goodwill of enhancing or enlarging one or another of her own holdings. Hence my Realreligion compels me to amalgamate or consolidate all my separated brethren's historical and chivalrous efforts and try to please my Master by upholding all his Gospel Values in Spirit and in Truth. According to this mindsetup I love to be a devotional and sacramental Catholic; at the same time I am delighted to behave a renovating Protestant; a faithful Evangelical; a mystic Pentecostal; a true Jehovah's Gospel Witness; an alert and ever-praying Adventist; and above all, be rationally and spiritually a Human Person.

Church is my Macro-family

Jesus had his own microfamily which we call the Holy family at Nazareth. He never denied its importance and necessity in this world.

He loved to be its member. But we hear him also that he belonged to some other family which was larger than the microfamily. In sociological studies it is named as 'macrofamily.' When Jesus' mother and relatives came to visit him he took it as an occasion to point out his belongingness to a 'macrofamily'. Looking around at those seated in the circle he said: *"Here are my mother and my brothers. For whoever does the will of God is my brother and sister and mother."* (Mk. 3: 31-35) No man is an island. Our life is a bundle of relationships. We cannot either to get rid of relationships or get away from them. We surely need another or somebody other than us to survive in this world not only when we face trials and calamities such as the hurricane Katarina but also in our ordinary daily life-steps. We are conceived, born, bred, reared, developed, shaped, filled, groomed, used and finally die in families, communities, peer groups, associations, nations and the entire world.

Church, according to my Realreligion, is the most efficacious forum that offers ample environment to nurture relationships among its members and to boost every form of relationships. My Realreligion wants me to consider this Church environment as my home and my macrofamily. It is not only a cradle of belonging but also a table of communion. My relationship with other members in my Realreligion is not one of township or citizenship where I am counted and labeled by ID number or fingerprint but I am intrinsically bonded by being called by God as his adopted children, and as disciples of Jesus. There is only one policy my Guru promulgated to maintain human relationships in my Realreligion. And that is the principle of love. I am told in my Realreligion: *"Owe nothing to anyone, except to love one another; for the one who loves another has fulfilled the law."*

While I apply this principle of love in my relating myself to other members in my Realreligion the greatest problem I face is that I cannot understand well the other person and what is going on inside of the other. Everyone is a mystery to the other. I am most of the time incapable of knowing the motivations behind the other person's dealing and acting. In this mysterious dimension of humanity our God expects from me that I should be responsible to other persons whom I relate to. I can never isolate myself from another and remain cold and indifferent while the other is behaving badly. I cannot tell God as Cain said, "Am I my brother's keeper?" Cain and Abel were blood related brothers of the same family. I too am related to my brethren in my Realreligion more than by blood. In Scriptures God tells me that I have to take care of the conduct of my friends in my Realreligion. He says: *"You, son of man, I have appointed watchman for the house of Israel; when you hear me say anything, you shall warn them for me."* He makes a strong link between us and our neighbors. *"If you do not speak out to dissuade the wicked from his way, the wicked shall die for his guilt, but I will hold you responsible for his death. But if you warn the wicked, trying to turn him from his way, and he refuses to turn from his way, he shall die for his guilt, but you shall save yourself."* A very big responsibility is thrusted by God on me.

Usually in my microfamily situation I really feel the bond, the communion that exists among my family members only at a time when I had done a mistake or big blunder in life, the whole family accepts me, forgives me, corrects me and heals me. It is in the process of healing the family's true color and identity comes to the limelight. The same is true regarding my relationship in my Realreligion. Church becomes true home in its handling of members especially when they commit evil. I should hold that I, as a member of God's family, am responsible for other members. I can never isolate myself from another and remain cold and indifferent while the other is behaving badly. God appoints me as watchman for the house and I will be punished as the wicked brother if I do not correct my brother when he does wrong. Also while I correct my brothers and sisters with the same attitude of family communion and responsibility I should follow an appropriate procedure of correction. My Guru Jesus asks me to hold on to pure love based on God's love while I am correcting. He says to me I should try as much as possible within my ability but never condemn the other. I am advised not to lose my eternal patience and love. In slow process I should try to make my brother understand his mistake. I can use many human resources for this as they are available in the society. Even after all these efforts if that person is callous and stony hearted I still must keep cool and lovable but I must entrust him to the Lord as I do with my reelreligion's members.

My efforts of love, forgiveness, correction and healing toward other members would be successful, my Guru asserts, if my brothers and sisters and I gather together of one mind and one heart, having the same aspiration of love, namely joining in prayer: *"For where two or three are gathered in my name, there am I in the midst of them."* Added to it, he promises, *"If two of you agree on earth about anything for which they are to pray, it shall be granted to them by my heavenly Father."* The relationship found in my Realreligion is therefore so powerful that it brings down heavenly blessings upon the world.

It is very clear from God's revelation that the Church, in which I practice Realreligion, is a home of God in this world. This home is built on faith and love, nourished by prayers and sacraments, corrected and matured by compassion and justice. Members of reelreligion would not believe this is true. Rather, they think that it would be some sort of utopian dream to imagine such thing about a human institution in a world, torn and tarnished by differences, discrimination, conflicts, and in an environment of 'tit for tat', cold war, aggression, and of 'Let us show them our might' attitudes. However for me it is a reality in existence. My Realreligion is truly a mesh of truly-knitted family. Every time I take efforts in the name of Jesus, out of love and in obedience to God's Sovereignty to correct my brothers and sisters, to expose to their conscience their blunders and injustice, to support in realizing certain human dreams and to bring down either blessing or punishment from God to our fellowmen it will be done as Jesus promised. I am certain that the whole world cannot contain the power the Church, my Realreligion, possesses and surely therefore the hell cannot prevail against it.

Here is an uncompromising manifesto of my Realreligion regarding the Church I am affiliated to or registered in:

❖ Jesus is my soul and the Church is my body. Therefore I am the Church, I belong to the Church, I make the Church, I run the Church, consequently I serve the Church and I try to sacrifice my time, talent, treasure and even my very life toward the growth and life of my Church.

❖ Since such is my intrinsic connection to the Church, I have chosen and belonged to a gathering of those Church-oriented people who hold on to the values of Jesus as their blood stream.

❖ That local congregation must have a long-standing and permanent connection to the revelation of Holy God in Jesus, preached and handed over to us through Jesus' apostles and their successors.

❖ That local parish must be universal to go beyond the cultural, human, national, and physical restrictions and embrace the whole universe and its inmates with no prejudices.

❖ That local church of Jesus Alive must be dynamic and moving forward toward a new future and authentically united future as One Shepherd and One Flock. "New heavens and new earth" is the goal of our Savior Jesus both at his first and second coming. He has already started to build up a 'New Age Order of Humanity.' He is continuing his work of renewal through me as my soul works through my body.

❖ In conjunction with this New Age Order plan, Jesus calls me to join in hands with other like-minded people of God to work together as a Church-in-Moving. The members of such Church do not divide sacred from secular, religion from society, political from spiritual. Where my body is there my soul is until I am alive. The same way where I engage myself through my body, intellect and soul, there is Jesus and His New Age Order Plan.

❖ To feel cool, to be successful and useful in my life's pursuit, I take into my intellect and heart anything and everything that is good and purely humane from wherever or whatever source it may come from.

❖ I love that Church, which is always in action, in growth, in moving with right values and toward right destiny.

Chapter-6:
Sources of Revelation
in my Realreligion

"O my God, I firmly believe . . . all the truths which the holy Catholic Church teaches, because you have revealed them, who can neither deceive nor be deceived." (Act of Faith)

The Church where I live, move and practice my Realreligion declares to me the reality of the concept of revelation in her Vatican II Dogmatic Constitution on Divine revelation *"Dei Verbum"* *(2): In His goodness and wisdom God chose to reveal Himself and to make known to us the hidden purpose of His will (see Eph. 1:9) by which through Christ, the Word made flesh, man might in the Holy Spirit have access to the Father and come to share in the divine nature (see Eph. 2:18; 2 Peter 1:4). This plan of revelation is realized by deeds and words having an inner unity: the deeds wrought by God in the history of salvation manifest and confirm the teaching and realities signified by the words, while the words proclaim the deeds and clarify the mystery contained in them.*

Sources of God's revelation about Himself

Though God is unfathomable and beyond all our limited knowledge, for two millennia we, the Realreligion's members, have been calling our God as Father, Son and Holy Spirit. This description about God, though started with limited explanation, over the years it has been developed into a dogma more or less acceptable to our reason and hence we notice numerous research findings continue to fill the libraries of the world-both religious and secular. This is due to the intelligent humans' insatiable thirst for grasping the inexhaustible truth of God and His spiritual realm.

As a matter of fact, due to our human limitation, God has been trying to reveal Himself to us slowly but steadily. In the Gospel we hear Jesus telling us the limitation of our hearts and minds. Hence his plan has been to teach us in heavenly truths gradually, slowly but always under the guidance of his Spirit. John, in his exposition of Jesus' farewell address at Last Supper, includes some amazing words of Jesus to his disciples: *"I have much more to tell you but you cannot bear it now. But when he comes, the Spirit of truth, he will guide you to all truth. He will not speak on his own, but he will speak what he hears, and will declare to you the things that are coming."* In other words, according to Biblical Scholars and interpreters, in John's theology, revelation isn't a one-time event. It's an ongoing process. Just as the historical Jesus took a period of time, perhaps three years, to convey his message, so the risen Jesus, through the Spirit, takes us beyond the period of his earthly ministry.

We patiently but willingly accept this slow revelation of divine mysteries about God and His salvific plans, dreams and deeds saying to Him constantly: *'I do . . . I believe'*. We may not fully understand all those mysteries but we are not either dumb to say 'I believe them.' We encounter it in our daily lives if we are spiritual humans. We know undoubtedly that to recognize and accept God's mysteries is possible only by those who try to become spiritual humans. Paul points out this very splendidly: *"The natural man does not accept what is taught by the Spirit of God. For him, that is absurdity. He cannot come to know such teaching because it must be appraised in a spiritual way. The spiritual man, on the other hand, can appraise everything, though he himself can be appraised by no one. For, "Who has known the mind of the Lord so as to instruct him?" But we have the mind of Christ."* (1 Cor. *2:1-16*)

God's Revelation in Nature

It is very interesting to discover in human history that our God has been revealing to us Himself, His Triune Personality, His characteristics and continuous deeds in our midst, mainly through two of His own creations. First is Nature: It includes its beauty, its power, and its order. The entire Bible is filled with passages that highlight how nature reveals God's power, wisdom and beauty. In many OT Psalms and Canticles we hear God inviting us to see Him in heavens, in waters above the heavens, in all planets like sun and moon and stars, in the mother earth, in mountains and hills, in every shower and dew, in winds, fire and heat, in cold and chill and frost, dew and rain, in ice and snow, nights and days, night and darkness, lightnings and clouds, in springs, seas and rivers, in all water creatures like dolphins, in birds of the air, in wild and tame beasts. (Ref. Daniel 3; Ps. 8; Ps. 104; Ps. 94/95) Some reveal His beauty; some others His meticulous design; and many others his power and love. As Poet Tagore wrote in one of his poems, *"Flowers are the love-letters of God."*

There is also another beautiful hymn, composed by Stuart Hine in 19s, which all Christians love to sing and hear frequently. It echoes melodiously what our OT writers proclaimed:

O Lord my God! When I in awesome wonder
Consider all the worlds Thy hands have made,
I see the stars, I hear the mighty thunder,
Thy power throughout the universe displayed:
How great Thou art, how great Thou art!

Once when Paul was at Athens, as he walked around looking carefully at the pagan shrines of Greeks, he discovered an altar inscribed, 'To an Unknown God.' Then and there he preached about how God revealed Himself even to those pagans through nature: *"The God who made the world and all that is in it, the Lord of heaven and earth, does not dwell in sanctuaries made by human hands, nor is he served by human hands because he needs anything. Rather it is he who gives to everyone life and breath and everything. He made from one the whole human race to dwell on the entire surface of the earth, and he fixed the ordered seasons and the boundaries of their regions, so that people might seek God, even perhaps grope for him and find him, though indeed he is not far from any one of us. For 'In him we live and move and have our being,' as even some of your poets have said, 'For we too are his offspring.'"* (Acts 17: 24-28)

God reveals through humanity

Second source of God's revelation is the humanity: That means, God has been revealing Himself in and through the strength and weakness of human beings: In Psalm 8 David sings about the dignity of humans in God's creation. *"You have made him little less than the angels (a god), and crowned him with glory and honor. You have given him rule over the works of your hands, putting all things under his feet".* Humans possess power of intelligence and will. God has been using them as his resources for describing and expounding His Personality and His Values. It is through them He brought out so many Scriptures which we are now enjoying. Scriptures expound a lot about God as Father, Son and the Spirit. Along with Scriptures, God too used human Traditions, namely their cultural, social and religious and spiritual interpretations, doctrines and practices. It is amazing to notice how God has been engaging his humans as His careers, interpreters and messengers; it is through them He formed many religions; promulgated His own Commandments and Laws; it is through their creative, scientific and technological power He testifies His Power, Beauty and Wisdom. Above all, His revelation about Himself reached its fullness in His only begotten Son, Jesus Christ. As the author of the Hebrews would write, Jesus was typically human like us except sin. Both his human strength and weakness brought to the world the Trinity as God's identity, amazing love, compassion, spiritual beauty, justice, power and holiness. His disciples, committed to walk in the footsteps of their Master, continued to contribute to this God's revelation.

God's Revelation through Human Weakness

Very sadly there is another dimension of humanity that is shadowing and marooning God's Justice and Holiness and that is human weaknesses. Many humans, out of their vain glory and pride and even because of our twisted and limited intelligence, have been forming their own idols in the place of the true God. As I have pointed out earlier, human weakness has degraded God's glory and

His beyondness. This is why, the Lord placed a commandment as the primary one: *"You shall not carve idols for yourselves in the shape of anything in the sky above or on the earth below or in the waters beneath the earth; you shall not bow down before them or worship them"* (Deut. 5: 8).

Factually evil enters into the 'revealing project' of the Triune God and it is being maintained and managed by his own human creatures. However as history proves, God is the ultimate Winner. Very surprisingly His revelation continues uninterruptedly even through human weakness. After describing his strengths of receiving many revelations from God, Paul adds a testimony of his own weakness about which shockingly he boasts: *"If I must boast, I will boast of the things that show my weakness."* (2 Cor. 11: 30) His reason for such incongruous boast is that he had a revelation from God on this issue: *"Therefore, that I might not become too elated, a thorn in the flesh was given to me, an angel of Satan, to beat me, to keep me from being too elated. Three times I begged the Lord about this, that it might leave me, but he said to me, "My grace is sufficient for you, for power is made perfect in weakness." I will rather boast most gladly of my weaknesses, in order that the power of Christ may dwell with me. Therefore, I am content with weaknesses, insults, hardships, persecutions, and constraints, for the sake of Christ; for when I am weak, then I am strong."* (2 Cor. 12: 7-10)

God, through His beloved Son Jesus Christ, has been pouring out mercy and compassion to bring the lost sheep into his family. As we hear from the Book of Proverbs, Jesus, the Wisdom of God states: *"I was beside him as artisan; I was his delight day by day, playing before him all the while, Playing over the whole of his earth, having my delight with human beings."* (Pro. 8: 30-31) Before Jesus left this earth that is what he emphasized. *He will be with the humans until the end of this world as God's Spirit of Wisdom through whom God will declare to us the things that are coming.* Paul is certain about the deeds of God's Spirit among us as our guide and Lover: *"The love of God has been poured out into our hearts through the Holy Spirit that has been given to us."*

Sometimes God takes the evil deeds of humans very seriously and seeing their callousness, stubbornness, hardheadedness he tries to bring them back to their original sense by showing His tremendous power. For this again he uses his creations: nature and humanity. He brings punishment through natural calamities and through the wicked people's wrong choices and twisted and perverted acts. Realreligion is convinced that the Holy God can never bear unholiness, injustice, and other evils that come out of His human children. Therefore He uses His own power given to Nature, plus the destructive power that pops out from wicked and weak humans both as chastisement and purification: *"The Lord chastises those who are close to him in order to admonish them."* (Judith 8:27b) The Author of Hebrews instructs us on this saying: *"My son, do not disdain the discipline of the Lord or lose heart when reproved by him; for whom the Lord loves, he disciplines; he scourges every son he acknowledges."* (Heb. 12: 5-6) He too warns all those disobedient to the Lord reminding them their defilement will be punished because *"for our God is a consuming fire."* (12: 29) Therefore Realreligion's members regard their own sufferings as the affectionate correction of the Lord, who loves them as a father loves his children. At the same time for fear and love of their Triune God they are cautious not defile themselves.

Human Words blended with Divine

Any ordinary words of humans usually communicate what is inside of his spirit-blessing, challenging and even sometimes destroying. If so, what about those words of humans who are intimately overpowered by God's Spirit? Those are the words we possess in our hands in the form of our Bible. Scriptures had and still have tremendous power and influence and impact on human beings despite their controversial debates: Scriptural passages are all good tidings, good news to the poor, to the weak, to the prisoners, to the afflicted, to the blind, the oppressed, the captives; those who read and reflect those words are uplifted in spirit, healed in emotions, weep for sins, change of heart and behavior; through the words found in Scriptures I can have a link between God the Creator and the Redeemer Jesus who claimed himself as the fulfillment and summit of the Creator's re-creative work of redemption; besides all these, the Scriptures I accept as sources of practical guide for me to build up relationship among one another and managing it very fruitfully.

Of all the battles that have been waged over the Scriptures I follow, probably ninety-nine percent of them have been based on a misunderstanding of what kind of books they are. There are innumerable versions, editions and translations of my Scriptures. Among them, I don't give much importance to search for the "real" Bible. The problem is that the Bible was not originally written in English, but in Hebrew, Aramaic, and Greek. All of the Bibles in the bookstore are translations. No two people translate any text in exactly the same way, and this is why there are many versions of the Bible. Some of my friends in reelreligions claim that the language of the Bible is without error and should be interpreted literally. They say: "The Bible is none other than the voice of him that sits upon the throne. Every book of it, every chapter of it, every verse of it, every word of it . . . is the direct utterance of the Most High." Some others are those who claim no divine inspiration for the Bible at all. Between these two extremes are many different understandings of what kind of book the Bible is.

In Realreligion I am very clear about the identity of these Scriptures: I believe in God and his Son Jesus not because of the Scriptures, rather I believe in Scriptures because I believe and love God and Jesus. All the revelations God offered to those writers of Scriptures only when they started believing in God and loving him. So everything I hear from the Scriptures was written from the main source of human beings, namely their belief and love of God. The same is true also about their effects. Only to those who believe and love God and his Son the Scriptures will be useful and fruitful and not to those who read it for curiosity, for finding fault with it and write some new controversial and ear-itching interpretations to it. There are people who keep the Bible as their pillow on their bed telling others they are keeping it that way so that they can find more contradictions in it. Nor it is going to be very handy to those people who intend to use it for apologetics, claiming that their personal convictions are the truthful and genuine ones while others are bad and untrue. So I don't base my faith and love in God only on the Scriptures. I believe and love the Scriptures because I believe and love God.

My Realreligion proclaims all that are written in the Scriptures are the manifesto or the mission statement of God and his Son Jesus. Added to it is the job description of his children and of the disciples of Jesus. The Scriptures nourish my belief and love of God. They give me light and guide to my path of life. My individual life becomes a

Bible of love and belief. Many would ask why a man like me living in this 21st century with all blossoming of human reason into science and technology should always be leaning on to that powerful word of God. With Paul I should say: *"We know that all creation is groaning in labor pains even until now; and not only that, but we ourselves also groan within ourselves as we wait for adoption, the redemption of our bodies."* Yes. I am truly weak and fragile; eventhough I want to do good, I am unable to do; I want not to do bad but I do it. I long to see a life of peace, prosperity, justice, love and joy while I am alive but I am incapable of getting it. I know it; I try it and struggle for it. In such tension-filled life I obviously need some hold and guide to lift me up and take me to my destiny. Surely my natural power, both physical and intellectual can support me in this matter; but they too one day desert me or become powerless. If I join them with the word of God I find a wonderful combination that supports me through my life. There is a remarkable efficacy of the words I read in Scriptures. God says through the prophet: *The word that goes forth from my mouth shall not return to me void, but shall do my will and achieving the end for which I sent it."*

Being strengthened and nourished by the powerful word of God Jesus demanded from his disciples to carry on the conversation that he began, speaking the words that will effect hope and healing, forgiveness and peace, justice and integrity in human hearts. In other words, he wanted me to become his word alive in this world. Paul wrote about me in one of his letters: "You are the letter from God." So my Realreligion urges me to go out into the field of God and sow God's words through my life, actions and then words of consolation, peace, love, justice and truth. Good words, bold words, challenging and chastising words, words of support, words of solidarity, words of compassion and caring must continue to be spoken and to set the agenda for service. Words that wish another well and words that work to make it so; these are the words that articulate my faith. I should utter the God's word of peace, that of comfort, the word of strength and courage and perseverance and hope to the hungry and malnourished of this world; to the homeless, to those in prison, to the poor, to the deaf, the blind, the lame, the lost, the lonely, to those elderly ones abandoned by family and friends to the victims of crime, to those suffering from untreatable illnesses, to the dying who are fearful and alone.

Human Traditions with Divine Signature

The English word "tradition" translation of the Latin noun *traditio* that derives from the Latin verb *tradere* meaning to transmit, to hand over, to give for safekeeping. The concept of tradition mostly refers to beliefs, objects or customs performed or believed in the past, originating in it, transmitted through time by being taught by one generation to the next, and are performed in daily chores.

Undeniably any man-made institution is very much dependent on its specific traditions for its survival and security. In this way, almost all religions and sects totally have to adhere to each one's traditions. However, there is one important difference between religious traditions and others. While all others are centered and focused on their political and social dimension, religious traditions are commonly originated, based and continued to maintain their spiritual goals and results. Traditions that are endorsed by any Realreligion are basically founded on and maintained for its members' personal connection with God, even their political and social connections with Him. Christianity, as all other religions, for its own survival and maintenance, has its own tradition which contains a package of beliefs, rituals, and social practices bound by laws and regulations.

Realreligion's members don't follow the negative approach of certain people who are very much influenced by the spirit of Age of Enlightenment against Traditions. We never attribute any wrong damaging connotation to 'traditions' by contrasting and counter-posing the concept of modernity with the concept of tradition, in the context of progress. We dislike joining in the tug-of-war carried on between two predominant groups existing in the Church: Traditionalists Vs Modernists or Conservatives Vs Liberals. We perceive both groups are unreasonably intense in fighting with each other because of lack of clear understanding of the in-depth meaning and goal of traditions plus because of some bad encounters with their own traditional environment.

The main reason why the Realreligion's members appreciate the Tradition of the Church is that Jesus, the Founder of Realreligion, recognized its validity and observed his Jewish religious tradition very faithfully and by his preaching he never abolished it, rather polished it or enhanced it according to his Realreligion-Perspective. The same way myself and other observers of Realreligion try to love the Church's Traditions and Observances and faithfully perform them in Christ's Realreligion-perspective.

In this context our Realreligion becomes a religion of simplicity-being simple, no complexity, no complicated views, ideas and practices, plainness, unfussiness; a lack of complexity, complication, embellishment, or difficulty. As John Wesley calls it, it is the "simplicity of intention, and purity of affection," one design in all we speak or do, and one desire ruling all our tempers. Though we are so much complicated in personality, in character, temperament, opinions and practices, most of us want a simplified religion and not a sort of laborious forum of volumes of theological and dogmatic treatises. God is simple and therefore he wants his children to be simple and expects them to observe simple religion, a simple way of relating to him. We read God saying to people in today's first reading: *"In your observance of the commandments of the LORD, your God which I enjoin upon you, you shall not add to what I command you nor subtract from it. Observe them carefully."*

Secondly our Realreligion's identification is portrayed as one of integration. Integration is defined as 'a combining of parts or objects that work together well.' This is the real consequence of our observance of Realreligion in simplicity with no distortion or distraction. What we perform outside must correspond to what we profess; what we say outside must be connected to our heart; our outward appearance should resemble our inner soul. Customs, traditions and practices, especially of our religion, form part of every one's life. Some of them have been handed down to the people and are in practice since many generations. Members of Reelreligion practice these unwritten laws in their lives and society without perhaps ever asking why they practice them at all. They get up, get dressed, go to work, come home, have supper, go to a meeting, go to bed and then repeat the same routine the next day and the next and the next. Because of the unavoidable repetitiveness of their daily actions and responsibilities, they tend to fall into a rut that may be boring but is nevertheless somewhat comfortable in its sameness and predictability. However this repetitive routine never assists them in attaining their ultimate goal of holiness. Prayers become rote and participation at liturgy becomes more of a habit than a commitment. Their piety become superficial, and because it is no more than skin-deep, they sink into that place of disconnectedness that Jesus named as hypocrisy. In Realreligion every element in Church's Tradition is not a practiced and soulless routine but a holiness-motivated source that arises from within a heart that is consciously in love with God.

Chapter-7:
Prayer in my Realreligion

"Prayer enlarges our capacity to receive the Gift God has promised to us." (St. Augustine)

P rayer is powerful. It is very productive. It is fruitful. It pays me back all that I wish as jackpots sometimes; and other times in a reasonable way. Undoubtedly prayer possesses certain power to bring God's hands over my life. As I hear from my Scriptures, it will not go unheard and it does not rest till it reaches its goal, nor will it withdraw till the Most High responds. It sounds like the power God speaks about his own Word. *"So shall my word be that goes from my mouth; it shall not return to me void, but shall do my will, achieving the end for which I sent it."* (Is. 55:11) So, in comparison, the power of a genuine prayer equals that of God's Word! My Realreligion informs me that when I pray for justice to be done to me and uproot injustice oppressing me, God hears my prayer as the cry of the oppressed. 'When the just cry out, the Lord hears them, and from all their distress he rescues them.' Prayer redeems the lives of God's servants. As Paul writes, prayer helps me to run the life's race and complete it successfully, to fight the good fight and finally get the crown of victory. Also, when I am left alone without anyone to defend me and when everyone deserts me, through prayer the Lord will stands by me and give me enough strength as He gave to Paul. Through prayer my dreams and ambitions are enlarged; my entire body and spirit begin to cooperate positively either to work hard to reach my goal or to endure all the disappointments and failures that come along its way. The God's gifts of faith, hope and charity start overflowing.

There are several thousands of books and millions of articles have been written about prayer and its power. In today's internet world there are countless websites and blogs dedicated to highlight the importance and efficacy of prayer. Poor author as I am, I too have included one of my books titled 'Prayerfully YOURS'-Qualityprayer for Qualitylife. Here I want to share with the readers my assessment on my personal approach to prayer as a religious practice. When I describe about the religious dimension I don't exclude the spiritual part of it. In the eyes of my Realreligion prayer is not either spiritual or religious. My Realreligion has imbued in me any prayer, if it is genuine one, is nothing but the outward sign of inner spiritual movement of human person. Any act of prayer includes both religious and spiritual elements. Even if one element of them is missing that prayer is not a prayer at all. Hence in the light of this fact here I judge and describe my prayerlife.

Every act of Prayer is both spiritual and religious

This may sound crazy and may look as an anomaly. But that is the reality of human prayer. As my spirit cannot exclude my body in its effort to communicate or commune with God until I am in this world, so any spiritual act of prayer of mine cannot be without my religion's influence. In other words every spiritual act of prayer is a religious act. The words I utter during my prayer, be it in private or public, alone or with a congregation, such as addressing the Supreme Spiritual Being with whom my spirit communes as my God, my Father, my Lord Jesus, and other labels I use referring God is an outcome of my affiliation to a religion. The bodily gestures, songs, dances and surely many rituals I add to my prayer also in one way or another are generated out of my religious culture and regulation. Thus the proofs for interconnection between spirituality and religiosity of prayer are numerous.

Unquestionably in the Bible I am advised by God in Jesus through His Prophets and His messengers to use in prayer equally both my body and spirit. My interior attitude, commitment, longing, love, contrition and promise must be demonstrated externally through my body in the form of rituals, ceremonies, rites and so on. However due to unnecessary separation of the two elements and by the extreme approach and application of either of the two nullify the validity and efficacy of prayer. It is humans' weakness. Therefore my Realreligion follows exactly what the Master Jesus has suggested on this matter.

Well-balanced use of words and gestures in Prayer

When I pray to God, He does not expect too many words. I remember what Jesus advised regarding prayer: *"In praying, do not babble like the pagans, who think that they will be heard because of their many words."* (Matt. 6: 7) President John F Kennedy invited a bishop to give an invocation. The prayer was endless. Later, a smiling President Kennedy asked a guest, "Did you hear that bishop's speech to God?" We need not preach or advise God or show off our poetic and journalistic talents and skills. God is very clear about it. What Jesus expects from us in our wounded or sick conditions is use of few words but more of heartbeats. He always showed fondness for short prayers. He taught us in his 'Our Father' the pattern of how our prayer to God should be 'short and sweet and concise.' Jesus is e-mailing me in the secrets of my heart every time I stand before my heavenly Father the information that brief prayers bring quick answers. I say few words before God but do for Him, with Him and like Him more as a wounded but healed healer.

Jesus also exhorted me about the style, movements and gestures I should use when I pray. *"When you pray, do not be like the hypocrites, who love to stand and pray in the synagogues and on street corners so that others may see them. Amen, I say to you, they have received their reward. But when you pray, go to your inner room, close the door, and pray to your Father in secret. And your Father who sees in secret will repay you."* (Matt. 6: 5-6) I need not spend long time in prayer only informing God all my needs and dreams. As Jesus said, 'my Father knows what I need before I ask him.' In ancient Greece, Pythagoras advised his students not to pray for themselves because, he said, they could never know what was expedient for them. Xenophon said that Socrates taught his followers simply to pray for good things without attempting to specify them; rather, they should leave it to God to decide what the good things were. Biblical scholar C.H. Dodd put it this way: "We cannot know our own real need; we cannot, with our finite minds, grasp God's plan; in the last analysis, all that we can bring to God is an inarticulate sigh which the Spirit will translate to God for us."

I have been enlightened by Jesus and NT Writers like Paul on why and how I should include my intercessions and petitions in prayer very sparingly. I shorten intercessory time in my prayer, not only because God knows all that I need and even more than I think but also because of two other reasons. First I am fully convinced with Paul about the Lord's immense goodness and His indomitable love and His Covenantal fidelity toward me. *"We know that all things work for good for those who love God, who are called according to his purpose. For those he foreknew he also predestined to be conformed to the image of his Son, so that he might be the firstborn among many brothers. And those he predestined he also called; and those he called he also justified; and those he justified he also glorified. What then shall we say to this? If God is for us, who can be against us? He who did not spare his own Son but handed him over for us all, how will he not also give us everything else along with him?"* (Rom. 8: 28-32)

Also, I believe with Paul again that any genuine prayer I perform is not only mine but it is the activity of God's Spirit. So my only contribution to prayer is just be there in front of Go voluntarily, willfully and with commitment. *". . . the Spirit too comes to the aid of our weakness; for we do not know how to pray as we ought, but the Spirit itself intercedes with inexpressible groanings. And the one who searches hearts knows what is the intention of the Spirit, because it intercedes for the holy ones according to God's will."* (Rom. 8: 26-27) In my acquaintance with many of my friends who practice Reelreligion, I have noticed most of their prayertime often consists wholly of a series of petitions, asking God to care for this person or that and to resolve this problem or that. As for me, I think that while such prayer is good and is an authentic expression of reliance on and hope in God, these petitions are to be restricted.

The main reason for this approach to prayer is that I don't really know who God is; because He is mystery in Himself; hence I cannot talk with God any more than my pet can talk with me. God and I live in different worlds on different wavelengths with no medium of communication. Only God speaks with God. This gives me a clue about prayer. Since the Father and Son and Spirit are all equally God they communicate to each other in the same language and understand one another. Paul is correct when he points out my human inability of praying rightly. In this context with him I uphold that when Jesus ascended to heaven after his resurrection, the Father and Son sent their Spirit to live inside me. The Trinity continues their conversation within me, only now I am graciously included in their conversation. As Paul wrote, it is God's own Spirit who prays within me. I also remember that the Holy Spirit does not pray beside me or instead of me or for me. The Holy Spirit is not my prayer partner, not another person to complicate the conversation. The Holy Spirit and I pray together. The Spirit inspires me to speak and then translates my human words into a divine mode. He enables me to think of God and then translates my stumbling words and my limited, sometimes incongruous, rituals and bodily gestures into divine utterance and godly deeds. In short, the Holy Spirit simply incorporates my humble prayer-efforts into the ongoing communication of the Trinity.

Sincere Commitment to fulfill God's Will

As Paul, I understand that prayer, like everything else, is of God. I know that no purely human effort could possibly justify a person before God. I too understand that human intelligence alone cannot lead a person to perfect prayer. Therefore, in order to validate and to make my prayer efficacious I simply surrender myself, my will, my efforts and my intelligence to Him. I notice how foolishly millions of people in Reelreligion are using prayer as a simple, easy and quick way of getting blessing of jackpot in gambling. My Realreligion expects me to use the practice of prayer only as source of commitment to God and my values.

Many years back I attended a summer course on 'hospital chaplaincy' in Houston. I actually went to that study program in order to get out of this diocesan parish priest job and fully committed to an independent ministry of my own to spread the Gospel of Jesus. It was a good motif. But God's plan was not that still. Therefore during that time I was not happy, content, and peaceful. After a month of my stay there Houston, one day I lost my wallet, my billfold while I went for shopping in the downtown. For nearly a week I prayed, I searched, I groaned, I placed lot of petitions to all saints, especially to St. Anthony. It was all failure. That billfold contained lot of my ID cards without which I could not stay in Houston, not even in the States. One Sunday morning, as I was praying in my room in closed doors, as most of us prefer to do instead of attending a church service, some thought struck my dumb mind. This is how I started to pray: "Lord, if you give me back my billfold today immediately (I put all conditions possible, narrowed it down for my advantage) I will obey you. If I get back my billfold that would be the sign from you that you are not ready to accept my present action plan. Then I promise I will take steps to go back to the diocese and work as you want me to be." As I was praying, by God's truth, I heard my phone ringing. One of my colleagues at Houston Methodist Hospital was on the line informing me that somebody in the town has got my billfold. He gave me his address and asked me to go and pick it up. You don't know what a feeling I had. I jumped up and down. I sang. The greatest fun in my lost and found story is it was not a man who found my lost billfold. It was a dog as his master and himself strolling who picked up my billfold and gave it to his master. Being sincere to my promise of commitment to my God I immediately contacted the diocese for requesting them to take me back to the diocesan priestly ministry.

I found out an interesting irony lying beneath that prayer experience at Houston. When the Lord answered my prayer, it ended up in two results: One, I got what I wanted and the second, He got what He wanted too. The first one was so interesting to me, but the second one! I am still struggling with it. I recommitted myself to Him and to His ministry, which demands from me to accept His sons and daughters with their weakness and shortcomings, my life situations with its limitation and weakness, His plan for His entire world. I am only one among his millions and trillions of stars. My only duty is to shine and celebrate Life with Him and with other stars.

Renovating 'Prayer-Device' for more fruitfulness

The lives and words of holy people, especially in the Scriptures attest to the efficacy of prayer. Jesus' main purpose of his life was to make me convinced of the power of prayer. In his life he emphasized it by telling me, "When I call you answer me". This is the continuous claim, before the Almighty, of all heroes and heroines in Scriptures. It was the conviction of all religious people that as God's word cannot return back without yielding its fruits, so the prayer of a broken heart will never go unheard. It will yield its fruits, as the word of God, to some hundredfold, others fifty, to some others thirty. In order to renovate and make my prayer powerful and efficacious my Realreligion teaches me certain norms to follow while I pray. And those norms are offered by Jesus in his Prayer 'Our Father'.

First quality of an efficacious prayer is it should be very familial and intimate. Jesus instructs me to call God as 'Abba, meaning 'papa, or daddy.' He wants me to approach God as a child in an intimate way. Any of my friends who had experience of the power of prayer have testified to this truth. I too observe it in the Scriptures. Abraham for example at all his prayer times sounds like a crazy but bold child or friend of God. The same way are Jacob, Moses, David, Solomon, Isaiah and other leaders. Jesus too is seen in the Gospels acting and speaking to his God in this familial and intimate way.

Jesus told his followers to persevere in prayer. This is the second condition or the most important quality of Jesus' prayer. Explaining through parables, he declared that even if the relationship between God and myself is not that good, he will get up to give me whatever I need because of my persistence. Jesus uses the term 'chutzpah' meaning 'persistence, relentlessness, or impudence. Faith in God is not a belief in a bulk of dogmas or practice of certain disciplines. Rather, faith is simply persevering in my relationship, in my prayer, in my concentration toward God. Saints became saints by somehow hanging on to the stubborn conviction that things are not as they appear, and that the unseen world is as solid and trustworthy as the visible world around them and they persisted in praying to that invisible, unseen but stable God.

I know well enough now why God makes me wait in perseverance for getting the results of my prayer. I always think I know the best for me. Unfortunately what I ask in prayer may not be quiet good to my life. Who knows? In the place of fish, I might ask for snake; and instead of asking for eggs I may ask for scorpion. But as Jesus said, God knows what is best for me like a parent to their child's needs. So, in persevering prayer, I begin to purify my intentions and supplications or I search for His will and design. This is why Jesus added in all his prayers, 'not my will, let your will be done.' Secondly the intimate connection God expects from me may not be fully there while I start praying. My distraction about worldly ambitions and dreams distort that intimacy and concentration toward God. I am indeed distracted from God's connections horribly. So the effort of persevering in prayer is one of the means to straighten out my connections with God.

There is one more thing my Realreligion indicates; and that is Jesus wants me to put in to my prayer, namely boldness. I should be daring enough to ask God even the situation seems hundred percent hopeless and grim. When I memorized and repeated what the Grand Jewish Teacher, my Master uttered: *'Ask you will receive, seek, you will find, knock, and the door will be opened to you. For everyone who asks receives; and the one who seeks, finds; and to the one who knocks, the door will be opened.'* In my deeper analysis of these words of Jesus I discover that Jesus wants me to enter into prayer first as an infant crying and *asking* in an intimate way. If I have not received what I ask in prayer, then I should *seek* and find out why my Dad, God my Papa, is silent; and I should correct the ways and contents according to His Will. If that too is unsuccessful, the only ultimate strategy is, just I should *knock*. In others words I must pray boldly in fasting, in repetition, and in making loud noise if need be. I must fight it out as Jacob was struggling with the angel of God all night until he got back what he requested.

Why should I be bold? First of all as Paul asserts I have been cleansed by the blood of Jesus. *"He brought you to life along with him, having forgiven all our transgressions; obliterating the bond against us, with its legal claims, which was opposed to us, he also removed it from our midst, nailing it to the cross."* He also adds: *'We have received a Spirit of adoption, through which we cry, Abba, Father'*. Moreover in the Letter to the Hebrews I read, this Jesus, my high priest is sitting at the right hand of God, interceding for me. So all my prayers join with the eternal intercessions of this high priest and I know therefore my prayers will be answered by all means. Jesus has very openly promised me, *'I am going to the Father. And whatever you ask in my name, I will do, so that the Father may be glorified in the Son. If you ask anything of me in my name, I will do it.'* This is the reason why I should be bold in asking, seeking and knocking in my prayer. Through these words-ask, seek and knock,

Jesus emphasizes that I should be in no way disheartened but keep on praying in perseverance.

Reelreligion's followers, being succumbed to the deceptive pride of human self, try to work out their own justification to get even with God. As a matter of fact, the Scriptures in my Realreligion remind me of the need of perseverance and hard work both in worldly and godly deeds as well. My Guru Jesus points out the necessity of praying always and not losing heart. His 'parable of the widow' reminds me how consistent and persistent I should be in my dealings with God. My life journey consists of two parallel lines: My engagements with God; and my dealings with the earthly things and persons. My secular studies and formation taught me that perseverance and hard labor are important tools for success in human efforts. Unfortunately the world and the age of Enlightenment have made most of my friends in Reelreligion forget or ignore to use the same strategy in their successful dealings with God. Many times I hear them say in hospital surroundings: "We have done all they can, the only thing left is prayer." It tells me of their wrong attitude about prayer. They are convinced that 'human efforts are what count; God doesn't make a lot of difference, but they might just as well pray; it certainly won't hurt.' The underlying meaning of these words is that prayer won't do any good. That is not what Moses thought when He told Joshua to line up the troops and march off to war because, he told them, 'I am going to pray, and we will win.' This proclaims the greatest truth about how both human earthly deeds and prayer must go hand in hand. I observe this kind of integration of prayer and earthly endeavors in Jesus' life. On one side he was dealing with God intimately in a persevering prayer, and on another side he was performing all his daily works in sweat and blood. Victory in life can never go to the hands of people who are quitters and lazy bones. I mean my total victory, winning this world and the world to come. The only possible way to succeed is to persevere and put my hard labor on both my human efforts and in prayer efforts.

It is very true that most of my prayers are unanswered and remain in waiting list before the Lord. As my Realreligion exhorts me, I don't stop praying but every day I try to restore and renew the spirit and quality of my prayer in the light of Jesus' teachings. He plainly tells me to fulfill the following conditions as my personal efforts to enhance my prayer. Condition-1: I should abide in Jesus and his words. *"If you remain in me and my words remain in you, ask for whatever you want and it will be done for you."* (Jn. 15: 7) Condition-2: I must pray only in his name-in his presence, in his milieu, in his love etc. *"And whatever you ask in my name, I will do, so that the Father may be glorified in the Son. If you ask anything of me in my name, I will do it."* (Jn. 14: 13-14) Condition-3: I should pray according to his drams and wishes. *"And we have this confidence in him that if we ask anything according to his will, he hears us."* (1Jn. 5: 14) Condition-4: I have to pray as if I have already possessed all that my heart beats for. *"Amen, I say to you, whoever says to this mountain, 'Be lifted up and thrown into the sea,' and does not doubt in his heart but believes that what he says will happen, it shall be done for him. Therefore I tell you, all that you ask for in prayer, believe that you will receive it and it shall be yours."* (Mk. 11: 23-24) Condition-5: Whether I pray alone or in the group I must make sure I am consciously connecting myself to the entire human family of God. *"Again, [amen,] I say to you, if two of you agree on earth about anything for which they are to pray, it shall be granted to them by my heavenly Father."* (Matt. 18: 19)

A word on the 5th condition: In this modern Age there is a tendency prevalent among people of Reelreligion to ignore the communal method of praying, justifying themselves that they go straight and sit next to God and pray alone with Him. They are satisfied with the Satan's favorite lies such as that since God is everywhere and we can worship Him anywhere and do not need the 'community of believers', the Church family. It is true that God is everywhere and worshiping Him anywhere is wholesome and good; but it is false to believe that the Church is unnecessary. God in every Realreligion asks his good-willed people gather together and despite the differences worship Him as one Family. Since the earliest days of Christianity, communities of believers gathered together on the Lord's Day to celebrate the Mass and to receive our Lord in the Eucharist. Besides the 5th condition of being connected in group to empower my prayer, Jesus demands from me to show visibly and audibly my togetherness with his family through congregational services. Bible is very clear on the subject of Church attendance and on how our submission to its authority is not only good but required. The main

146

reason is that the Church, its leaders and members, are the Mystical Body of Christ here on Earth.

I am delighted to hear my Realreligion proposing to me to pray in small groups such as my micro-family, my association, my club, my class, and other groups of interest. It is important to worship and pray as a family unit. In addition to assisting at the Holy Sacrifice of the Mass as a family unit, the family or small interest-groups should be going to adore the Blessed Sacrament together, praying the Divine Office or the Rosary together, praying devotions to patron saints of the family and family members, and devotional fasting. Worship and prayer together as a family, both in the parish setting, prayer meetings, adoration, and other corporate settings, and in the privacy of the family at home is critical in developing spiritual health for the family and each family member. Such family devotion forms the foundation for all that each family does away from home in the world of school, work, and society.

Chapter-8:
Sacramental Performances
in my Realreligion

The purpose of the sacraments is to sanctify men, to build up the Body of Christ and, finally, to give worship to God. Because they are signs they also instruct. They not only presuppose faith, but by words and objects they also nourish, strengthen, and express it. That is why they are called 'sacraments of faith.' (CCC1123)

In previous chapters I have highlighted the necessity of the bodily performances in any human act of communing and communicating with God the Supreme. While the individual spirit of every disciple tries to relate to the Supreme Spirit and vice versa, both still need the bodily medium to accomplish their ultimate goal. Second Vatican Council beautifully links up God to Jesus, Church and individual Church member by the term *'sacrament'*. In the *Vat II* constitution *'sacrosanctum concilium'*, on the sacred liturgy Church proclaims the above-mentioned historical truth about Jesus: *". . . When the fullness of time had come sent His Son, the Word made flesh, anointed by the Holy Spirit, to preach the gospel to the poor, to heal the contrite of heart, to be a "bodily and spiritual medicine", the Mediator between God and man. For His humanity, united with the person of the Word, was the instrument of our salvation. Therefore in Christ "the perfect achievement of our reconciliation came forth, and the fullness of divine worship was given to us".* (SC para1) In these words Church proclaims that Jesus was born as Incarnate Son of God and of Mary. The same incarnate Person became source of salvation by his death and resurrection. Consequently he is unmistakably the genuine sacrament of God. His humanity is the outward sign or the instrument of his Divinity. It is through his humanity that the life of the Trinity comes to us as grace. In this regard, as Edward Schillebeeckx titled his book, we can say that *'Christ is the Sacrament of the Encounter with God.'*

When Jesus became the resurrected Spirit the Church became as his Mystical Body. While Jesus became the Sacrament of God, his Church became his Sacrament. The Church both contains and communicates God's invisible grace she signifies. It is in this analogical sense, that she is called a "sacrament". In II Vatican Council's documents as well as in her Catechism book we read that Church is like a sacrament—a sign and instrument, that is, of communion with God and of unity among all men. As sacrament, the Church is Christ's instrument. The Church is both visible and spiritual, a hierarchical society and the Mystical Body of Christ. She is one, yet formed of two components, human and divine. The Church in this world is the sacrament of salvation, the sign and the instrument of the communion of God and men; she is also the sacrament of unity of the human race with God.

It is my Realreligion's belief that Jesus gave us his Body the Church to continue the works he performed during his earthly life and as members of his Mystical Body every disciple of Jesus becomes sacrament only through the Sacraments Jesus has established in his Church. It is because Jesus Christ alone who mediates the sacraments to allow grace to flow to mankind. These Sacraments are by the Church *for she is the sacrament of Christ's action at work in her through the mission of the Holy Spirit.* And they also for the Church *in the sense that "the sacraments make the Church," since they manifest and communicate to men, above all in the Eucharist, the mystery of communion with the God who is love, One in three persons.* (CCC 1118)

As the Church, its sacraments are finite, physical, visible mediators of the sacred, and they are the means whereby the sacred becomes present to us. A sacrament, therefore, is nothing but a vehicle or vessel of the sacred; it is an "outward and visible sign" that functions as "a means of grace." Catechism of the Catholic Church teaches that Sacraments are means by which the church receives God's grace. They are tangible expressions of God's presence in the world. Through them humans can catch some glimpse of the reality of God, who is ever near, yet not fully known.

According to the Church's Tradition there are seven sacraments that are very closely connected and related to human life. My Realreligion wholeheartedly accepts all that the Church, in its Vat II's Constitution on the Sacred Liturgy *'Sacrosanctum Concilium',* has deliberated about the nature and action of the seven Sacraments it proposes to me. As a summary of it, the council says: *"The purpose of the sacraments is to sanctify men, to build up the body of Christ, and, finally, to give worship to God; because they are signs they also instruct. They not only presuppose faith, but by words and objects they also nourish, strengthen, and express it; that is why they are called "sacraments of faith." They do indeed impart grace, but, in addition, the very act of celebrating them most effectively disposes the faithful to receive this grace in a fruitful manner, to worship God duly, and to practice charity."* (SC59) The rituals, (the Church calls them *'the sacramental signs'* with words and actions) are to be understood well and participated eagerly by the people of God. Realreligion's members love the priests and deacons who perform those sacraments with unction and devotion, always focused on bringing out the expected results in the participants. Though the validity of the sacraments gratuitously and abundantly exists exclusively and intrinsically in them by the Presence and Action of God, as Church underlines, the ritual celebration of every sacrament gets its greater efficacy and power from the faith-filled involvement of both the celebrants and participants. St. Thomas Aquinas sums up the various aspects of sacramental signs: *"Therefore a sacrament is a sign that commemorates what precedes it—Christ's Passion; demonstrates what is accomplished in us through Christ's Passion—grace; and prefigures what that Passion pledges to us—future glory."* My Realreligion is very attentive to this sacred factor and urges its members to actively take part in all the ritualistic celebrations of the sacraments.

As II Vatican Council spells out there is the possibility of endangering the true meaning of the Sacramental practices. With the passage of time, as the Council states, there have crept into the rites of the sacraments and sacramentals certain features which have rendered their nature and purpose far from clear to the people of today. It is therefore of the highest importance that the faithful should easily understand the 'sacramental signs, and should frequent with great eagerness those sacraments which were instituted to nourish the Christian life. Hence there is a need of revision of the practices and some changes have become necessary to adapt them to the needs of our own times. The sacramentals too have undergone many revisions which take into account the primary principle of enabling the faithful to participate intelligently, actively, and easily; and the circumstances of the present time too call for such revisions. (SC 79)

Throughout the history of the Sacramental ministry in my Mother Church I have noticed so many changes and renovations taken place. And in my short tenure of life I have been watching those practical changes occurring and theologically exploring still the form, function, and potential of the sacraments, as the Church strives to minister more effectively to the pain and needs in human lives and as it continues to receive the insights of various cultures of the world. Consequently I can perceive evidence in recent history (after II Vatican Council) of how our capacity to provide ministry is enlarged when we perceive new possibilities regarding the sacraments even as we remain grounded in foundational principles. My Realreligion does not consider such efforts as a threat to the importance of the sacraments in the life of the church. Rather, it is an emphasis on the central place of the sacraments in church life coupled with a desire to make sure we are not hindering the blessings God is seeking to provide because of any time bound or culturally bound practices.

Undisputedly every sacrament in facto has the power of sanctification; but very surprisingly only some recipients enjoy all the above-mentioned experiential results. Those are the Catholics who practice Realreligion in their life. The main reason for others' failure is they don't take these rituals seriously and pragmatically; they think everything will be ok if we just participate in it passively; or they don't fully believe in these external acts. But Realreligion's members as I am, I esteem those seven sacraments as my life's resources to attain my ultimate goal. My Realreligion can never deny the truthful fact that through the seven Sacraments offered in my Mother Church—baptism, confirmation, Eucharist, Reconciliation, Anointing of the sick, ordination and marriage, the recipients, from their birth till death, enjoy regular encounters with God's love and keep them in closer alignment with God's purposes than they would have realized otherwise.

I can testify, as I look back over my life, that the sacraments, I have been receiving, have served this purpose well. They have been a means for opening my life and relationships to new dimensions of divine grace, strength, and guidance. They have also been a source of needed stability—of keeping my life anchored in the covenants I have made with God that define who I am and who I am becoming. However for such results I must do some personal and homework as well. Definitely I believe that the sacraments act *ex opere operato*, by the very fact of the action being performed, independent of the minister because they are supernaturally instituted by God in Jesus and divinely guarded and distributed by the Church. In Vat II we read: *"The sacrament is not wrought by the righteousness of either the celebrant or the recipient, but by the power of God."* (SC83) Nevertheless, the fruits of the sacraments also depend on the disposition of the one who receives them. In other words, the effect on the person receiving the sacrament (*ex opere operantis*) depends on the interior disposition of the receiver.

In addition to Sacraments, my Realreligion recognizes the validity and importance of the 'sacramentals' which Church has instituted as sacred signs which bear a resemblance to the sacraments such as blessings with Holy Water, anointing with blessed oils, Reciting the Divine Office, and devotions and Novenas, etc. I have admiration for them and choose them as my needs arise with the faith that they signify effects, particularly of a spiritual kind, which are obtained through the Church's intercession. As Church has instructed me, I make the cautious and discreet use of them in as much as I am disposed by them to receive the chief effect of the sacraments, and various occasions in life are rendered holy. (Constitution on Liturgy art.60)

I ascertain myself and my friends in Realreligion to undergo regular adult education on these sacramental signs and practices so that we approach them with good and proper understanding and frequent them with great eagerness. I esteem every sacrament I participate as a kind of my daily life's survival and development project. Any project, which humans undertake in life for our development and success, demands our serious input in all its three important phases: Preparation; Implementation; Feedback. When I conducted many workshops for rural development workers and volunteers on 'communication skills', I always emphasized that in order to achieve maximum results in their development projects they should pay serious attention to those three phases of their development project: The same thing is true with my Sacramental Project in religious life.

First I am told by my Realreligion to prepare properly before I enter into any Sacramental Ritual. In OT we hear how God demanded from His priests and people serious and intense preparation for His Rituals. Let us take Moses' preparation for example before he conducted the Covenantal Ritual in the desert. First Moses prepared himself staying with the Lord on the top of the mountain many days and nights; then he prepares people first by asking them to accept in one voice what the Lord had spoken to him; next he prepares the scroll of all God's ordinances; finally he erects an altar according to God's Will. (Ex. 24: 3-8) Gospels describe the story of the preparation of the place where Jesus and his disciples were to eat the Last Supper. When the Disciples asked Jesus about where and how to prepare for their Passover Ritual, Jesus gave them very meticulous preparation guide. (Mark 14:12-15) Obeying Jesus' orders his disciples prepared themselves and the environment of celebration as well.

In the same manner I have to prepare myself and the environment conducive to the celebration of the Sacramental Performances. Whenever the priest says before starting Eucharistic Mass: *"Dear friends, to prepare ourselves for this sacred mystery let us call to mind our sins and ask God's pardon,"* I am reminded of the obligation of proper preparation for that Sacrament. But I know those few seconds are not sufficient for proper preparation. It starts early at home as I am getting ready to step into the car to drive toward the church. I use my brain, mind and heart reflecting my life and God's presence in and around me. I settle myself within me all those doubts, distractions and distortions frequently disturbing my relationship with God. I sincerely accept God's ultimate and total goodness. I purify my intentions and deliberately say to myself that I am heading toward a unique chance of participating in the ritual through which I will encounter God in Jesus, his touching my heart, my mind, my body and soul. The same kind of preparation I try to do before every Sacramental Practice.

The second phase of my Sacramental Project is its implementation. For this implementing process, I look up again to Moses and his people during the implementation of their rituals. Exodus says: *Moses took half of the blood and put it in large bowls; the other half he splashed on the altar. Taking the book of the covenant, he read it aloud to the people, who answered, "All that the LORD has said, we will heed and do." Then he took the blood and sprinkled it on the people, saying, "This is the blood of the covenant which the LORD has made with you in accordance with all these words of his."* All those people including Moses seem and sound like dumb and freaky. On the contrary everything they were performing was filled with love, affection, fear, and full of life.

The same thing is true in Jesus' and his Disciples performing their Paschal Meal as Last Supper. Mark writes: W*hile they were eating, he took bread, said the blessing, broke it, and gave it to them, and said, "Take it; this is my body." Then he took a cup, gave thanks, and gave it to them, and they all drank from it. He said to them, "This is my blood of the covenant, which will be shed for many. Amen, I say to you, I shall not drink again the fruit of the vine until the day when I drink it new in the kingdom of God." Then, after singing a hymn, they went out to the Mount of Olives*. Doesn't it sound like some sort of contradiction and farfetched connection between what Jesus handled and the words he uttered? However all who were there full of wonder, love and harmony. That is because all present there were applying their heartbeats rather than their rationality. I always advise my development workshop participants that while they prepare for the project formally let them be informal in its implementation. This means during my preparation period I use my mind and reason as much as possible to get even with God but when I am doing the rituals mostly I definitely use my whole heart. Everything I do as ritual-words and gestures is something heart to heart. I apply my emotions, physical talents, arts, communicative abilities but always with loving, tender care.

Finally the secret of success in any project is to gather in the feedback after implementation. After the august moment of my participation in any Sacrament I try to spend some time in deep silence to munch and digest what went on during the rituals. If Jesus has spoken to me and if I had felt some inspiration from his side, I clarify it, stomach it, digest it and mull over it. I make it my own possession and promise myself I will hold on to it in the days to come.

Chapter-9:
Eucharistic Rituals
in my Realreligion

"The celebration of the Eucharist is the center of the whole Christian life. It is also the fount from which all power of the Church flows." (II Vatican Council)

Among the seven Sacraments of the Church my Realreligion offers special attention to the Eucharist which is the "source and summit of the Christian life," as the Vatican Council famously stated. This is why, when respect for the Eucharist diminishes, the other sacraments also decline. After all, baptism and confirmation find their fulfillment in the Eucharist. Penance and Anointing of the Sick exist in order to restore a person to the Eucharistic table. Marriage is sign of the wedding banquet of the Lamb. And of course priesthood takes its meaning from the Eucharist. The drop in vocations can be tied directly to a decreased reverence for the Blessed Sacrament. Therefore Eucharist is the center of every member's life in Realreligion. All the rituals which are performed in the name of this Sacrament are filled with meanings and values.

Mother Theresa once asked a Hindu, 'How do you define a Christian?' He said, 'A Christian is one who gives.' It's true in what he said. His answer was based on the experience he was having from Mother Theresa and her sisters, from their sacrificial giving of their lives, energies, talents and money. But he did not know how this attribute of 'giving' came to exist in those sisters. If you had asked Mother Theresa about this secret of giving, she would tell you that the source and energy of the spirit of giving came from the Eucharist. I have had longstanding acquaintance with Mother Theresa's sisters in my hometown, India. I was fortunate enough to be their chaplain for few years. I know their relationship with the Eucharistic Lord. Early morning 5am they get up, have their morning prayers and Mass. Soon after Mass they conduct daily one hour Eucharistic Adoration and then only go to their daily duties of charity. Mother Theresa found the Eucharist as the source of power and energy for love, sacrifice, happiness and joy.

Eucharist is the Source of Oneness with Risen Jesus

Realreligion acknowledges the Eucharist as the Body and Blood of Jesus alive. This happens not merely during Mass but even after Mass until it is reserved and preserved inside the Tabernacle to be taken for the sick or to be exposed for private and public adoration and benediction. Jesus said, *'whoever eats my flesh and drinks my blood has eternal life.' 'He will remain in me and I in him.'* The Realreligion, practiced in the Catholic Church, always finds the word of Jesus as Truth-based and Life-giving. This is why early Christians regularly participated in the Eucharist. Consuming the Body and Blood of Jesus, in a sacramental way, changes entirely my psychology, my attitudes and my outlook of life.

Before Jesus left from this world he handed down to his disciples this Eucharistic ritual as the secret of our divine and spiritual experience. We become persons of self-giving. The Sacrament of the Eucharist shows how Jesus gives himself, in total love, to be eaten by us. His self-giving was perfected and completed on the cross when he died, shedding the last drop of his blood for our salvation. Jesus, thus, gives himself totally for us. He gives until nothing is left to give. He loves his own as much as to sacrifice everything for his loved ones. Our participation in the Eucharist should make us less selfish and more self-giving, loving, caring, forgiving and compassionate.

Our participation in this ritual energizes us to be life-giving: Jesus' self-giving was life-giving. Eucharist is true food and drink which nourishes us and helps us share in the life of Jesus. *"Amen, amen, I say to you, unless you eat the flesh of the Son of Man and drink his blood, you do not have life within you"* (Jn. 6:53). He communicates his life to his dear ones by sharing his own flesh and blood with them. He becomes one with us so that we may be transformed into his body. St Augustine heard the words of the Lord in his prayer thus: *"You will not change me into yourself as you would food of your flesh; but you will be changed into me."* We become what we eat! The life that the Eucharist gives is, of course, eternal life as Jesus is the eternal Son of God. The writer of the Letter to the Hebrews states today: *"For this reason he is mediator of a new covenant: since a death has taken place for deliverance from transgressions under the first covenant, those who are called may receive the promised eternal inheritance."* This eternal inheritance is nothing but the eternal life every human being is craving for. Our participation of the Eucharist, challenges us to love, to promote, to uphold and to defend life in all its forms, from the moment of conception to natural death. Just as the Lord shares himself in the life-giving sacrament, we need to share our own lives, our talents, time and resources with the needy. This makes our Eucharist more meaningful and transforming.

Eucharist is the Source of Human Togetherness

During mass two acts of Jesus are enacted: One, Jesus' death in which the blood was separated from the body. Two, his resurrection: in which his entire life had been breathed out to the whole humanity. Through Jesus' death and resurrection we got power to be bound together and power to break and separate even our very life for the sake of our friends and needy. This is what happening during Mass and by Mass. Paul, founder of the church in Corinth, reminded his converts that those who eat of the Eucharistic Body of Christ become the ecclesial body of Christ. Participation in the sacramental body and blood of the Lord incorporates us into the body of Christ that is the community of believers and makes us responsible for that community. Therefore, our "Amen" says 'yes' to Jesus' love command as well as to one another.

Most of us are familiar with the centuries-old regulations observed among orthodox Jews that specify certain foods as clean and therefore permissible to eat, or unclean and to be avoided. Because eating together was regarded as a sign of the unity among those at table, one did not eat with people to whom one did not wish to be bound. For example, when Joseph and his brothers who were visiting him in Egypt reclined at table, the "Egyptians would not eat with the Hebrews because that was abhorrent to them" (Gen. 43:32). This practice was continued by the Israelites, who did not eat with strangers or foreigners except to observe the ancient Near Eastern world's obligation to offer hospitality, freely and generously, as Abraham did at Mamre (Gen. 18). The same kind of forbidding others who are not their own has been promulgated as a law in India for centuries. The lowest caste people cannot sit at table together with the high caste people; any vessel they touch would be burned and broken because it is supposed to be contaminated and polluted.

With Paul, I, as a practitioner of Realreligion, firmly hold that all those participate in the Eucharistic Mass, whether they are holy or sinful, young or old, native or foreign, Jews or Greeks, men or women, slaves or free, their sharing in the Blood of Christ and the Body of Christ forges a unity among them like no other sharing. Centuries ago, St. John Chrysostom beautifully said: *"What is the bread actually? The body of Christ. What do communicants become? The body of Christ. Just as bread is the result of many grains and although remaining themselves are not distinguished from one another because they are united, so we too are mutually united with Christ."*

During mass we are together, we sing together, we pray together, we share the body and blood of Jesus from one bread and one cup. These are done sacramentally and liturgically. We get the power to be bound together as one people of God. Though it's hard these days to be together, the sacrament of Eucharist offers us sufficient strength to be united. Every bit of our humanity tempts us to be divided, to be cliquish. But the spiritual power of the Body and blood of Jesus triumphs and wins. Also, the world of today never appreciates any sacrificial life. Giving oneself, or sacrificing something for the sake of others without any reward or compensation is not in the achievement list of modern mind. But the Eucharist would win and energize people to sacrifice for the welfare of the needy. The power to be bound and the power to be broken are impossible with humans but it is possible with God, with the Eucharist, the Body and Blood of Jesus.

The Eucharist strengthens us to be unifying. Eucharist is the sacrament of unity. Jesus gave himself up for us to unify and reconcile humanity with God. Our participation in the Eucharist, which is a sacrament of forgiving love, unity and reconciliation, should make us long for and work for reconciliation peace and harmony in our own families, communities and the world at large. By participating in the Eucharistic Mass we would possess an amazing ability to see dualities—the pros and cons of situations as change approaches—and to quickly and efficiently think them through before making any decisions. We would dare to look deeply into our desires, regenerate self-awareness and recognize psychological ambiguities. This will bring balance into our home and family life. We would pay attention to the details as we bring our inner and outer life into unity and harmony. Surely we will enjoy the changes occurring within us! As you come to terms with ourselves, we would be able to see a more fulfilling purpose in life, and our field of experience broadens. We would focus on matters that affect us most deeply and, like magic, our life will become easier and things will seem to take care of themselves. We will have all the necessary resources and motivation to make tangible changes and achieve results in all our endeavors. We will become unique persons of self-giving, life-giving and surely unifying. In every step of our lives we will develop into a peacemakers and peacelovers. We will be energized to live like a true champion of Eucharistic unity at home, in the community and around the nation.

Adoration and Devotion to the Eucharist

Reelreligion's members have a wrong notion that the devotional rituals, like Holy Hour, Perpetual adoration, benediction, Procession and so on, are some medieval invention, which they can now brush aside and get on with more important matters. Nothing could be further from the truth. These rituals are based on the belief of the real presence of the risen Jesus with his Sacred Body and Holy Blood. St. Paul, who wrote his Letters 50 years after Jesus ascended to heaven, reminds through them that the communion cup we share today is a "participation in the Blood of Christ" and that "the bread we break is a participation in the Body of Christ." (I Cor. 10:16) About fifty years later St. Ignatius, bishop of the great city of Antioch, was defending this teaching, which he had received from the apostles. He warned faithful Christians about those who "do not confess that the Eucharist is the flesh of our Savior, Jesus Christ." Those people, he said, "deny the gift of God," and "are perishing in their disputes"

Catechism of the Catholic Church declares: *"Because God is present in the Sacrament, we have the duty to render all praise, adoration and reverence to Him. The Church has faithfully celebrated the Eucharist from the beginning according to the Lord's command, in particular each Sunday, the day of His Resurrection. As early as the second century we have the witness of St. Justin Martyr for the basic lines of the order of the Eucharistic celebration, when he wrote to a pagan emperor to explain Christian worship, around the year 155. They have stayed the same until our own day."* (CCC1345)

Among those who practice Reelreligion I find various groups who deal with the Sacrament of Eucharist with misunderstanding and fail to get its benefits. First group is of those who started doubting and questioning about faith in the Eucharist but never cared for the right answer or proper discussion and education and therefore finally left the Mother Church; there is second group of people who still attend the Mass but do not fully believe in the truth about Mass and not resolve their qualms about this Sacrament; some of them attend it as a routine Sunday obligation; some others feel mass is a community social gathering; while many others consider the mass as a devotional prayer service in front of the Holy Presence of God in Jesus. They come here to adore the holy Body and the holy Blood of Jesus Christ silently and never incline to participate in it actively as real Banquet of Jesus. I feel they all approach the Eucharist in an extreme way and consequently they ignore or don't care about the other dimensions of Mass. In my Realreligion a mass is an act of both God and man in and through Jesus to offer sacrifice, to celebrate our communion in a sacred meal, plus adoration of God in Jesus by handling in a holiest way the precious Body and Blood of Jesus. When someone forgets or omits even one dimension of the Eucharist he/she will be dishonoring the Lord's Goodness and will.

Besides the participants' wrong attitudes spoiling their true worship at mass there are so many other factors distract them to do so. For example priest's uncontrolled mannerism or habit, altarservers and ministers' shabby and slovenly behaviors, the unbalanced non-liturgical ornaments, decorations, music, environmental climate and many other obstacles distort the holiness of the environment. These obstacles are like what happen very often in an auditorium. When I go to Performing Arts Center, Tulsa to see a play I always make sure I have a proper seat for right visibility and audibility. Once I chose a seat in the center of the auditorium and made sure the seat in front of me was vacant. Unfortunately just couple of minutes before the play started there came a gigantic figure and sat in front me. He hid all possible dimensions the view of what was going on the stage. I was so frustrated and I went into deep sleep, even snoring. My friends near me tried to wake me up. As I sat distractedly behind that gigantic figure I often wondered why everyone was cheering. I asked myself: What had I missed? It is as if a child who asked her mother while I was preaching in one church very vigorously and forcefully, "Mom why does father get angry?"

It can be like that with worship. My Realreligion reminds me and my friends that without a clear view of what really counts, we are quickly distracted by lesser things in life. And when that happens, our worship becomes ritualistic and routine. Worship isn't meant to be a dull experience, but rather an active, ongoing, enthusiastic response to God for His work and worth in our lives. Losing sight of the real game, God's wonderful worth to us, will make you wonder why others are so excited about God and why you are only excited about your own dreams, desires, and possessions. Maybe it's time to look around the obstructions of life to see Jesus clearly again and notice what He is worth to you—personally.

And what would that worship look like? First and foremost it should be a 'living sacrifice'. True worship is a surrender of all that we are and have. Paul told the believers in Rome to "offer your bodies as living sacrifices" (Rom. 12: 1). Our lives are to be placed on the altar as an act of worship as well! Secondly we should feel and imagine and make over the environment where we conduct ritual worship as holy presence of God. My Realreligion directs me for such clear view of God's Presence to go to the Catholic Church. More than the temples of Hindus, more than the Mosques of Muslims, even more than the evangelical and non Catholic churches Catholic Church is the best environment that totally signifies and leads humans to feel the Holy Presence of God. In general where two or three gathered in Jesus' name God is present. That is true. However unlike other holy places, Catholic churches are totally and wholistically become a holiest environment due to not statues, icons or the sweet smell of incense; rather it is mainly because we keep Jesus as Eucharistic Lord in the Tabernacle. Besides, everything we use or everybody who is around the altar is being blessed and consecrated once they are commissioned by the elders and by being blessed by the priest. When we sincerely try to be fully conscious of this holy environment we will try to behave as if we are in God's presence. We should get out from behind the gigantic figures so we can get a fresh glimpse of Jesus. He's the only action worth worshiping in our life!

As Realreligion-practitioner I am called to create sacred space around and within myself. I remember that each and every one of us is sacred ground. Jesus abides in me and I in him. St Thomas Aquinas, expressed beautifully the Eucharistic faith of the Church in the hymn *"Adoro te devote"*, which he composed for the Solemnity of Corpus Christi. Along with him my friends of Realreligion sing often in front of the Eucharistic Lord: '*We cannot know you through seeing or touching or tasting, but we believe in you through hearing what you have said. We believe whatever you have said, for nothing is more true than your word. On the cross only your divinity was hidden, but here in the Eucharist also, your humanity is hidden. But we believe and proclaim both, i.e., that both your divinity and humanity are present in the Eucharist, and we make the same request of you as the penitent thief.*'

Chapter-10:
Sacrament of Reconciliation
in my Realreligion

'I believe in the forgiveness of sins' (Apostles Creed)

Sin and Forgiveness according to my Realreligion

In one parish they conducted the Celebration of the Sacrament of Reconciliation for the CCD students. One young boy, about eight years old, in his confession told the priest: "Bless me father for I've sinned. I forgot when I did my last confession, probably last year. And these are my sins." Then he paused. Father insisted to mention his sins. The boy retorted: "I can't think of anything bad I've done. But when I do, I'll tell you, father." This is what most of the Reelreligion's members feel when they are asked by the Church to confess their sins before God. May be true, as they perceive, they would not have done any sins that are glamorous to be telecasted on CNN or Fox News or grave like murdering, stealing, coveting others' spouses or properties and so on; perhaps they may usually commit very small venial sins like talking back, feeling jealousy, gossiping about others, not praying, as they should. However the Catholic Church where I am affiliated recommends to me that by all means I should confess. It urges me, even as law-binding obligation, to make annual confession and every time I come to the Eucharistic Sacrifice it invites me to confess my sins and sinfulness and ask for God's

164

mercy for me. In my Realreligion I firmly acknowledge the validity of such attitude and practice of the Church by professing as my creed: "I believe in the forgiveness of sins." Why?

My Jesus demands it

The source of this continuous 'I-am-sinful' mindset is what the Founder of Realreligion emphasized: *"I did not come to call the righteous but sinners."* The two little words 'I came' don't mean 'I came round the corner' but 'I came into the world'. Jesus is stating that this is his whole purpose, the very reason he came down from heaven. This is salvation. This is his mission. He knows me and my fellow human beings. Most of us move around masqueraded, covered or mantled by right deeds, right talks, bright smiling and enticing charm. Even it may be true I am not committing sins both mortal and venial sins. But I question myself, what do I know about God's judgment about my interior status of soul? Before his holiness and justice how is my inner sanctuary? I am ignorant of all these. God is the One who is fully in the know of my interior status.

The Psalmist, knowing how hard it is for him to live with the burden of sins and being fully aware of what happens after his confession to the Lord, sings: *"Blessed is the one whose fault is removed, whose sin is forgiven. Blessed is the man to whom the LORD imputes no guilt, in whose spirit is no deceit."* (Ps. 32: 1-2) I am told in the Scriptures that Jesus came to indicate to his fellowmen that they are living in darkness. They are indeed sinful. He wanted them to confess first their sinfulness and sickness and then as a second part of confession the glory and identity of God in Jesus. People who hold on to Reelreligion do not confess that way as the Lord desires but go on leading a life of denial. They try to live in a world of denial, a denial of no to their conscience, to their God's commandments and to His Spirit's promptings. On the contrary I, who practice the Realreligion, agree fully with Jesus' advice because I know I do not look for a doctor unless first I find out through certain symptoms that I am sick. The priority in Jesus' preaching was to make human persons fully aware of their sinfulness. He wants me therefore first to acknowledge my sinfulness and my need to be cured. He will be very much pleased if I confess: "Yes I have sinned. Yes I am sick. Yes I have screwed up my communication. Yes I have failed to be united. Yes I hate each other. Yes I have prejudices against others in the name of race, color, gender, status, theology, and petty holdings and convictions. Yes I am a victim of my pride, jealousy, and selfishness. As I demand from God His 'yeses' to my prayers and petitions God too expects from me certain 'yeses' to his questions: Are you sinful? Are you in need of me? Do you need healing very badly? Are you sick and troubled, living in darkness?' I should answer him yes and stand before him begging his help and support. That is the Realreligion's spirit. I won't act those Reelreligious people, who always say no to God. They want to live in hell throughout their life preferring to live in denial. They are not ready to be diagnosed and find their disability, sickness and other maladies and thus they find no cure, no change and no progress. These people have spiritually died already. Jesus came to indicate to such people that they are living in darkness.

My Awareness of Human Weakness pleads for it

Paul remarkably portrays the human sinfulness when he writes: *". . . but I am carnal, sold into slavery to sin. What I do, I do not understand. For, I do not do what I want, but I do what I hate. Now if I do what I do not want, I concur that the law is good. So now it is no longer I who do it, but sin that dwells in me. For I know that good does not dwell in me, that is, in my flesh. The willing is ready at hand, but doing the good is not. For I do not do the good I want, but I do the evil I do not want. Now if I do what I do not want, it is no longer I who do it, but sin that dwells in me. So, then, I discover the principle that when I want to do right, evil is at hand. For I take delight in the law of God, in my inner self, but I see in my members another principle at war with the law of my mind, taking me captive to the law of sin that dwells in my members. Miserable one that I am! Who will deliver me from this mortal body?"* (Rom. 7: 14-24) Like Paul, everyone in my human family is naturally born weak, incomplete and imperfect. If some turn to be holy, perfect, complete in life, it is either a miracle occurred in the middle of life or they have developed enough to be smart in hiding their weakness to the public or they are proud enough to ignore and not be ready to accept that they are sinful. Henri Nouwen very succinctly wrote: "We are all handicapped; some are more visibly handicapped than others." No one born human in this world can be daring to say that they have no sin and that they do not make any mistake and therefore they do not need any forgiveness from God and others. One thing I am sure and that is, I am a sinner and I need forgiveness from God.

My Sin-Management Theory and Practice

Since sinfulness is part of my life and of others and I have to deal with it as one of the sources of destroying my peace and joy, I lent myself being trained in sin-management by my Mother Church and I love to apply all the sin-management principles in my Realreligion. "To forgive is the highest, most beautiful form of love. In return, you will receive untold peace and happiness." (Robert Muller) Here below are the three of those important action-oriented principles that truly help me to enjoy true serenity and liberation from the burden of sinful conscience.

Getting forgiveness from a personal God

God constantly proclaims to me that he is merciful to all, he does overlook men's sins that they may repent. He loves them because his immortal spirit is in all of them. Therefore he corrects little by little those who trespass, and reminds and warns them of the things wherein they sin, that they may be freed from wickedness and put their trust in him. As the true agent of God my Realreligion in season and out of season announces to me that *'the Lord is kind and full of compassion, slow to anger, abounding in love.'* I hear the same Good News from Paul that though we are sinners our God is ready to make us worthy of his call, and may fulfill every good resolve and work of faith by his power according to the grace of our God and the Lord Jesus Christ. God so loved humans that he sent his only begotten Son. God loves me. He wants to offer me fuller life, eternal life, a satisfactory and peaceful and healthy life. Not simply as a source of that life but as the very life God sent his Son Jesus. He is my eternal life. He is the way, the life and the truth. Every turning point in life happens by a surprise visit of that life-giving Jesus. He is always standing at my door and knocking and waiting for me to invite him to feast with him. At that moment he feeds me with his eternal life.

Both through the lives of others and my own life God is shown to me as a compassionate person who suffers with humans as they are thwarted and victimized by evil spirits through temptation and deceptive enticement. In those sinful environments God behaves as a personal friend to me, as a loving Father and wise Adviser and Guide. He is fully aware of the humans' weakness. He knows that every human being is a sinner. As Jesus told us, He deals with all his human children as a merciful Father both to the good and the bad. *". . . heavenly Father makes his sun rise on the bad and the good, and causes rain to fall on the just and the unjust."* (Matt. 5: 45)

Hide & Seek Play of Sinners

While my merciful God incessantly invites sinners for repentance, namely to return to him from their sinfulness they many times play continuous gimmicks with him. When people commit grievous sins they feel guilty and acute remorse of conscience. They are heavily burdened with shame, regret and uneasiness within themselves. Hence they take some wrong, crooked and twisted ways to resolve their inner conflicts. In this process their fake pride and blindfolded ignorance rule them. First they try to justify their evil acts as some natural phenomenon or as fate or as unnoticed, unpublished, harmless performances done in private. They try to hide themselves and their sins. They do not want the public know their sins and make remarks about them. They do not wish their popularity or authority and power being lost or diminished in the family and in the community. Surely they do not desire to be caught by the police and put in jail. Above all, they do not want the relationship with their spouses or children being spoiled. So they find certain strategy of hiding their sins. They use put-on smile or behave as a champion of safeguarding morality or joining in any one of the extreme positions and ideologies like terrorism, fanaticism, and fundamentalism and so on. They do all these only for hiding their sins and thus leading an under-cover life. Such human gimmicks are discovered in all ages and in all continents from the day humans began breathing. When Adam and Eve, for example, committed the sin of disobedience what did they do? The Book of Genesis 3/8 says: "When they heard the sound of the LORD God moving about in the garden at the breezy time of the day, the man and his wife hid themselves from the LORD God among the trees of the garden." And there are so many examples like this in the Scriptures and Traditions.

There is also another action sinners would perform when they feel guilty. They search for some sources to get relief from this nagging and irritating feeling of remorse. In many movies when a hero or a villain commits any serious sins immediately they are seen at a bar or pop club. So these sinners find asylum in drug addiction, alcoholism, or any other perversions in order to be liberated from the burden of guilt. They know well they are only resorting to some temporary solutions that can be very destructive to their lives.

Where is God when I commit sins?

The climax of all human gimmickry of sin-management efforts is their attempt of doubting about even God's presence and interaction with them. Their pride or shamefulness makes them blame God. They question: Where was God when I committed sin? They behave like the Israelites in the desert who, being vexed by the absence of God and Moses, began worshipping golden idol. Whatever these games sinners play, God stands there sending uninterrupted mercy-messages through many ways. Jesus my Guru played the magnanimous role of calling such sinners for repentance reminding me about God's approach. Once when I visited one of my parish catechism classes some teenagers were asking me lots of questions regarding our religious faith. One of them was a question that is asked continuously by every reasonable human being and that is: If God is all-knowing and therefore knows well earlier that we would commit sins and evils why does he not stop us from those wrong doings?" This question our forefathers had asked; you have asked; and I too have asked from my catechism class teacher. It only made them feel impatient and irritated. There was no satisfactory yet given. Nor did I give a good answer that was satisfying our children. But Jesus has expounded it very clearly through his teachings, especially in his three parables on heavenly Father (Lk. 15)

In his Parable of the Prodigal Son he summarizes the most incredible attitude of forgiveness found in our heavenly Father God toward the sinners and their return to Him. Look at the Father's dealings with his sinful son: As soon as the younger said to him, 'Give me my share of the estate,' immediately he divided his property into two and handed over a portion of it to the younger son. What is amazing here is that Father did nothing to prevent his son nor did he make any attempt to make him realize the choice he was making was horrible. Secondly the younger son certainly would have left the house or the hometown only after some days. During that time atleast Father should have advised his son not to go but he never did anything to stop him.

Thirdly after the younger son left to a foreign land for his future prospectus of pleasure-seeking and became pauper gathered all his belongings and started off for a distant land where he squandered his wealth in loose living. Having spent everything, he was hard pressed when a severe famine broke out in that land. So he hired himself out to a well-to-do citizen of that place and was sent to work on a pig farm. So famished was he that he longed to fill his stomach even with the food given to the pigs, but no one offered him anything. Where was that Father's concern and love? He should have taken some time to go in search of him or atleast sent some of his servants to look for his beloved son? Nothing he did. Only when the son returned of his own accord realizing his mistakes, as he was still a long way off the father caught sight of him. Then the father was so deeply moved with compassion that he ran out to meet him, threw his arms around his neck and kissed him and gave all royal welcome and unforgettable treat. Look again at this father in the parable. While he did not do anything at the insolent and immature behavior of his younger son, he reacts now with his love and wisdom when his elder son misbehaves: The elder son became angry and refused to go in. His father came out and pleaded with him. So again the legitimate question can arise: This father in the parable showed any concern for his son's wrong choice, nothing he did toward stopping him do the wrong thing eventhough he had love, affection, power and strength to stop this atrocious behavior of his son. We may be inclined to ask: Why did he behave this way? Is his fatherly love only a hypocritical and a lie?

If we go deeper into the mystery of God's eternal mercy we get a little glimpse of a truth. Among the three parables Jesus narrated to explain God's forgiving mercy, both in the parable of the lost coin and in that of lost sheep Jesus mentions about the efforts made by the losers of the coin and the sheep. But in the parable of the prodigal son, we find the loser, Father, did not indicate any initiative of stopping or searching for the prodigal son. You know why? Coin is mere inanimate material not having any life; also, the sheep, though it has life, does not possess free thinking, rationality, freedom and independence. But as regards the prodigal son, he is endowed with rationality, freedom and independence. With his reason he is able to make choices for his life.

Many years back, while I was serving in a rural parish of India, a couple came to me for marriage counseling. They had been married more than 15 years. Invariably everyday they were quarreling and fighting. There was no peace and happiness in their home. After listening to their stories in the form of complaints and reports about each other, I asked the husband: "Did you marry her with all your free will? Did you choose her as your life-partner willingly or out of compulsion?" (You should know here that according to the social customs in India most of the marriages are arranged ones. It is parents who choose brides for their sons, and bridegrooms for their daughters.) The husband in this case told me, "Yes father. I chose her freely to be my wife. Because, unfortunately my parents showed me only one picture of a girl and that was this girl's picture. There was no other choice to make." Interestingly his wife retorted him, "Atleast you had my picture to choose. My parents gave me not even that. I never saw you, never met you before I came to the wedding." While I was Chicago I had a chance to counsel an American couple. Their marriage was on rocks. They were about to be separated. They as usual made chain of complaints against each other. They had been 20 years in married life and had three children. I asked the wife, "How many months were you dating this man before your wedding?" She said, "2 years." I asked her again: "Did you not know then this man's bad habits and manners which you are complaining about?" "Yes father I knew them," she replied, "but as I was too young, I overlooked them and accepted him as he was. But now I feel it is too much for me and my children to cope with."

My human life is simply a heap of both good and wrong choices. Though I am influenced 100% by other humans in the process of making choices, ultimately it is I who am responsible for all my choices. I was not born saint or sinner. I am naturally born blank. I was born tabularasa. It is only through every choice I make I turn to be what I am. To make choices is my birthright. It expresses my human dignity. But the worst part of it is when I make the first wrong choice, I continue to live in it and start feeling comfortable with it.

Most of my bad customs and habits have invaded my life in this way. I act exactly like Miss Havisham, an elderly lady in Charles Dickens's story 'Great Expectations.' She could not change the past, so she made the choice to live in it. She sat at a long banquet table, covered with cobwebs, nibbling mice, and rotted food, waiting for her husband-to-be. She wore a yellowed wedding dress as tarnished and torn as her view of life. While she held desperately to the past, the present was not negotiable. She was a hopeless and helpless person.

That is how I build up a center of decision-making and I call it the personality of my own, the culture of my own and the tradition of my own. I always feel proud in saying then, "This is me. This is what I am. This is my personality. Whether you like it or not, that is your problem." Life offers everyday thousand and one moments to make choices. Each decision-making moment is just a split second. I mean every decision—from the diaper through diet to job. But it is so important for eternity. My yes and no in each and every moment of choosing is the cause of either my godly life of joy or my clumsy life of bad habits and unbearable personality.

God is the Giver of that reason and freedom. Therefore by nature He respects his Gifts to humans. He cannot undo humans' highest status in creation. However in the Bible we hear Him proposing to us two options to choose while we are living in this world: *"See, I have today set before you life and good, death and evil. If you obey the commandments of the LORD, your God, which I am giving you today, loving the LORD, your God, and walking in his ways, and keeping his commandments, statutes and ordinances, you will live and grow numerous, and the LORD, your God, will bless you in the land you are entering to possess. If, however, your heart turns away and you do not obey, but are led astray and bow down to other gods and serve them, I tell you today that you will certainly perish; you will not have a long life on the land which you are crossing the Jordan to enter and possess . . . I have set before you life and death, the blessing and the curse. Choose life, then, that you and your descendants may live, by loving the LORD, your God, obeying his voice, and holding fast to him. For, that will mean life for you, a long life for you to live on the land which the LORD swore to your ancestors, to Abraham, Isaac, and Jacob, to give to them."* (Deut. 30: 15-20) Hence I take seriously what God has said word by word and try to choose of my free will all that leads me to blessed life. God loves to see me make right choices independently.

Every human being has to go through three stages of development in our relationship with God: 1. First stage is when we are directed and taught how to make choices. What to choose as the best for our lives. 'Until you are under my umbrella or roof you have to abide or obey certain rules and customs prescribed by me,' we say to our kids. 2. The second stage of our life with God comes when we begin to think, reason out and ask questions on anything and everything. We are excited to make our own choices whether they are good or bad, right or wrong. We get angry if we are not permitted to choose our own. At this period most of us, almost all of us through our wrong choices make blunders as the prodigal son. 3. At the third stage of our life as a grown-up person, with many scars and stains, we begin to be melted. We feel sorry about our wrong choices; sometimes plan to redo the whole thing or other times use the past as our learning process we correct ourselves and attempt to do better in the future.

I think at this third stage God enters to rescue and redeem us. The word of God points out that our merciful God hugs us when we approach him at this stage. He is too happy to remember what happened in our past. Paul confesses of this merciful gesture of God in his life: *"I formerly blasphemed and persecuted and insulted him; but I received mercy because I had acted ignorantly in unbelief, and the grace of our Lord overflowed for me with the faith and love that are in Christ Jesus."* When we sinned even deliberately God was very much upset like a Father and anxious about us and our future. We did not tie his legs or hands to come and stop us from doing evils. Rather he imprisons himself by his love and respect for us. If he does anything otherwise he would act against his own nature. So he waits and waits for human beings to return.

I want to highlight here one more point about God's relationship with us. He is all powerful. He can touch the stone or desert soil. Water can be generated; he can touch the sea; it will divide and offer path to cross it; he can touch clay; man would be created; he can touch the bone; it will turn out to be woman; he can even tough the dead body; it will resurrect. But even if he touches warmly or forcefully any human being, it needs double miracle for making man to do the right thing on God's behalf. The man will say, 'Stop. First knock at my door; stand there waiting for me until I open it for you. Then you enter into my abode. You have no authorization until I say 'welcome.'

After a long struggle and analysis as above-sited finally I accepted the truth about God's silence and inactivity while I was committing sins. Now I see why, though God knows that I would commit sin, he cannot stop me. But He is present there, may be as one author puts it, He is shedding tears over my weakness. I came to my senses in the middle of my life that sin promises me a life of momentary pleasure and excitement, but the end of it all is misery, depression, dissatisfaction and loss of dignity as God's child. There is no use of blaming God if I carelessly waste his blessings; there is no use of blaming God, if I destroy the God-given health by harmful habits. Far from God I acquire the tendency to do evil and neglect my responsibility and my roles in this world. However no matter how deeply I sink into sin I experience there is always my inner voice that invites me to the Father's house where true freedom and dignity is found.

Forgiving oneself

At the repulsive aftermath situation of wrong doings many in this post-modern age make recourse to the act of 'forgiving oneself' with no qualms. They begin to worship their own proud self and begin to forgive themselves. They think of "forgiving oneself" as an alternate means in the place of God's forgiveness for being at peace with what has been done. Unfortunately the result is nil. Therefore in despair they say: 'I know that God forgives me for everything I did but I have great difficulty forgiving myself. Nothing seems to lessen my sense of guilt and no amount of assurance does me any good. It works only while the person, usually the confessor, is speaking, but the next minute I'm as worried as ever.' Their words betray their longing for being freed of this sin-created tension. In my counseling sessions I exhort them saying that it is an unrealistic desire to forgive oneself. It is like trying to pull oneself up by one's own bootstraps. Forgiveness is something we have to receive; it's not something we can give ourselves. Sin is nothing but a human act of hurting God the loving Father. Suppose if we offend one of our friends what do we do? We go straight to the offended friend and beg him/her to forgive us. At that moment we don't perform a separate act of forgiving ourselves. It is meaningless to brood over within ourselves. The same is true in our sin-management when we offend God. We have to accept that 'forgiving oneself' is not another option for getting forgiveness from God.

As a matter of fact the effort of forgiving oneself is a psychological endeavor on the part of the sinner both before after getting forgiveness from God. As soon as I fail God in my doing His Will, since I am a dedicated disciple of Jesus, I start feeling guilty about my sinful act, groaning and mourning in private as David did: *"I know my transgressions; my sin is always before me."* (Ps. 51) At that moment I think of God and His compassion and mercy shown in and through Jesus Christ. I confirm my belief that I will have peace with God and forgiveness through Christ; any genuine peace or warranted acceptance of the past is through the Cross; otherwise it is nothing better than self-deception. I begin to be cautious of the devil's trickeries that may again make me fall into sin by highlighting in my mind and heart a sin-complex or sin-phobia. It will induce me to imbalanced and unrealistic remorse of conscience and make me hurt my very life and even my religious life as it did to Judas who betrayed his Master and finally killed himself out of excessive compunction. Therefore at the very moment of awareness of my acts of sins I start feeling sorry for those sins and immediately I profess my act of faith in what the Lord has done through his Cross for the purification of my sins. Then I do not dwell on the fact that I committed those sins but totally focus on Christ as the mediator on my behalf. I know well it is not good to dwell just on the fact that I have sinned. It will get me no were. I name this process as 'forgiving myself.'

Paul applied this dimension of 'forgiving oneself' in his sin-management as he portrays it in many passages of his Letters: *"I am grateful to him who has strengthened me, Christ Jesus our Lord, because he considered me trustworthy in appointing me to the ministry. I was once a blasphemer and a persecutor and an arrogant man, but I have been mercifully treated because I acted out of ignorance in my unbelief. Indeed, the grace of our Lord has been abundant, along with the faith and love that are in Christ Jesus. This saying is trustworthy and deserves full acceptance: Christ Jesus came into the world to save sinners. Of these I am the foremost. But for that reason I was mercifully treated, so that in me, as the foremost, Christ Jesus might display all his patience as an example for those who would come to believe in him for everlasting life. To the king of ages, incorruptible, invisible, the only God, honor and glory forever and ever. Amen."* (1Tim. 1: 13-17) Personally I feel that this element of 'forgiving myself' is essential for my sin-management. But among the members of Reelreligion there is a tendency to hold themselves more accountable than they do others; also there exists in them a fear that there is a price, some form of life-long penance that they must pay. There was an elderly man in a nursing home where I went frequently to visit my parishioners for administering the Sacraments. Whenever I approached one of them to give the Eucharist he always denied it shouting to me, 'I am a bad boy.' Till his death he repeated the same as he saw me. There are people like him in this world being fixated and burdened with guilty conscience. There are many others in Reelreligion who are so scrupulous that even after confessing their sins before God and the Church either they are unsatisfactory on their performance or they are doubtful about whether God has accepted their human efforts of confessing. Some others are convinced of the Biblical truth that *when God forgives us, He remembers our sins no more* (Jer. 31: 34). But they wrongly interpret it as if our all-knowing Father God forgets every wrong thing they have done. They forget that, because God forgives us, He chooses not to bring up our sin in a negative way.

So in my Realreligion I hold that forgiving myself is not about forgetting what I committed; it is about not bringing the offense up to myself in negative ways. Forgiving myself is to me simply letting go of what I am holding against myself so that I can move on with God. This primary act of forgiving myself in the process of forgiveness of sins does not let me off the hook, it does not justify what I have done, and it is not a sign of weakness. My Realreligion teaches me a never-ending course on sin-management theory. Before I enter into knowing what God offers me I should first know what are the natural tactics I should apply to manage my sinfulness. Sin is some kind of attitude and deed that goes against God's love, against my own human spirit, against the wholistic Truth and against my relationship with other human beings. When I commit sins this way by nature my inner peace is disturbed. I am hurt; and therefore act or react against this situation being unable to manage the sinfulness in a productive way: I develop a scrupulosity of feeling always guilty; or a complacency of feeling insensitive to the sins; or distracting myself by various hurry-burry 'jollyhood' life styles; or drifting away from faith and religion with justifications; developing a stony heart, hard-headedness and throw stones at others and thus soothing their own consciences. But my Realreligion advise me: The more I feel guilty the nearer I should go to God; to think not about my own ugly past but always the marvelous deeds of God; to behave as if I receive a costly grace from God; to start doing something proactively: to confess my sins not mere by words but by some symbolic deeds of sacraments and other religious and social practices; and to remove completely the stones in my spirit and forgive others.

Forgiveness is a choice that takes courage and strength, and it gives me the opportunity to become an overcomer rather than remaining a victim of my own scorn. I cannot restore lives to where they were before the event. However, when I am healed by the act of forgiving myself I can make a difference in the lives of others; I can give back some of what I have taken away by finding a different place to invest my time and compassion. The guilt no longer plagues me if I repent with the faith in the crucified Savior; nonetheless the memory of them lives on, hopefully to fuel thankfulness and joy in Him.

Sacrament of Reconciliation in my sin-management

In order to reach God's forgiveness from which flow abundant grace of mercy and peace my Realreligion binds me to do three things: First is to accept that my liberation or salvation from sins is done only gradually by God and not as a sudden miracle. Therefore every day, even I do not commit any sin deliberately, I have to tell the good Lord: "Lord Jesus Christ, Son of the Living God, have mercy on me, a sinner." And also I should be ready to confess my sins very often to the Lord and receive the Reconciliation to get pardon from Him in a sacramental way. My Realreligion fully accept what the Mother Church taught me: It wants me to confess my sins to priests and esteems it as one of the seven Sacraments and promulgates it as one of its six precepts to be observed: *"To go to Confession at least once a year during the Easter Season."* By the precept of confessing at least once a year is meant that I am obliged, under pain of mortal sin, to go to confession at least once a year during the Easter/Paschal Season. However Church recommends I should confess frequently, if I wish to lead a good life.

I know this mode of confessing my sins to a priest in the form of 'auricular confession' is the later development in the Church's Tradition. Its validity and authorization is based on the words of Jesus quoted in the Gospels of John and Matthew: *"Receive the Holy Spirit. Whose sins you forgive are forgiven them, and whose sins you retain are retained."* (John 20:21-23). *"Amen, I say to you, whatever you bind on earth shall be bound in heaven, and whatever you loose on earth shall be loosed in heaven."* (Matt. 18:18). This means I confess my sins to priests as they are ordained by the Church which is the only source of forgiveness and they are God's duly authorized agents in the world, representing Him in all matters pertaining to the ways and means of attaining eternal salvation. When I confess my sins to a priest I am, in reality, confessing my sins to God, for God hears my confession and it is He who, in the final analysis, does the forgiving. I too know very clearly if my confession is not sincere, and if it is not wholeheartedly directed to my Father in heaven, my sins are not forgiven at all.

I like the label my Protestant brethren apply to the confessors like priests, ministers and others who are involved in this church ministry of reconciliation. They are called the "accountability partners." Many spiritual authors in non-Catholic circle do preach about the need and importance of confession. There is wisdom, as they put it, in presenting oneself to an accountability partner. Personal accountability is upheld, when we confess to another person whom may hold us accountable for our actions. Confessing our sins to one another, they contend, is a powerful way to break the bonds of sin in our lives. It is much harder to confess our sins to one another than to simply say, "Lord, forgive me". While God is forgiving, of course, it is the demands of personal accountability before another human being that brings our confession into grounded reality that strengthens our commitment to turn away from sin in the future. The same preachers also advise that we must be careful when choosing an "accountability partner." Since we will be revealing very private and sensitive information about ourselves, it is critically important to trust whoever we choose as a confidant to be discreet and to keep absolutely confidential the information we tell him.

In this regard I am gifted with a Catholic priest as my confessor because, while other religious ministers, psychologists, counselors, and others including the Deliverance Counselors of our agency, are also bound either by law, ethical codes, or contract with the client to keep private and confidential all that is revealed to them, Catholic priests are sworn to secrecy on the name of God and Church. Consequently they are forbidden to reveal anything that they hear from me during the Sacrament of Confession to anyone, even the Pope. If a priest were to break the "Seal of Confession" (the secrecy of Confession) he is automatically excommunicated and can be "defrocked". I also discover in my habit of going to confession a great psychological comfort in hearing the words, "I forgive you" or the equivalent, "I absolve you of your sins." Those words I feel as if audibly coming from my Father in heaven. God understands this psychological need. Thus, in His great love for me, He provided a way for me to hear those words in His name. It is God who ultimately forgives sins, but God, according to His sovereign authority chose to delegate this authority to His validly ordained priests. Through His priests, when God forgives, the penitent can literally hear the words, "I absolve you . . ." God is great and so loving to understand my need to hear the words and provide a way for me to experience that forgiveness in an audible way.

Besides, in confession I feel a 'Home-Coming.' I came into the world through my biological family, was raised by families, and came to God through the family of His Church. Thus it is natural that when I fall, I return to Him through the family of His Church. The Catholic Church has always believed in what God has taught about the need for confession and has followed the teachings of our Lord in this matter.

Forgiving others' sins wholeheartedly

If I want to get true forgiveness from God, besides confessing my sins before Him through my Church, God expects me I should accept the reality of human life. I am always surrounded by only sinners, though they, most of the time, are masked. I should accept all my relatives and friends, spouses, parents, children, priests and nuns, congregation and the entire humanity with their sinfulness. This means God wants me to extend my sympathy and forgiveness toward them. My past pastoral experiences taught me to hold an attitude, little crazy, but workable, toward those who hate me or give hard time to me or make me lose my peace in my daily life and ministry due to their sinfulness. That means to consider them as truly sick both mentally and spiritually. As a mother does to her physically sick child, so I care for them, pity them and tolerate them plus I pray for them. It was once very hard for me to tolerate any kind of injustice or insincerity around me. But once I got into the shoes offered to me by my religion I began to hold the attitude of tolerating and forgiving evils and sins of others in this sinful world for which the Lord gave his life and shed his blood. My Realreligion enforces that if I need to be forgiven by God I need to fulfill his condition, namely to forgive my neighbors' sins first. "If you bring your gift to the altar, and there recall that your brother has anything against you, leave your gift there at the altar, go first and be reconciled with your brother, and then come and offer your gift." (Matt. 5: 23-24) We must notice here that Jesus emphasizes not 'getting forgiveness from God' as the primary condition to conduct any religious practices, rather only 'getting reconciliation with our neighbors'.

Secondly as my Realreligion instructs me forgiveness of other persons helps me to be healed. It is always a burden to carry grudges and resentment against my neighbors. It kills me first and then others. Mentally I become sick. As many psychiatric studies have proven, most of the sickness and illness in the body generate from the mental and psychological disturbances and hurts. Unless these roots are cleared off, the physical maladies and deceases cannot be cured. Moreover my forgiveness heals others and binds my relationship once again. Forgiveness has been the key element in keeping my relationships intact. I hear loudly Jesus telling me: *"Unless you forgive your brother from your heart my heavenly Father will not forgive you."* I have to pay serious attention to his words: "From your heart." Indeed I have forgiven others number of times. But do I have really forgiven them from my heart? 'From the heart' means: To forgive somebody with human intelligence or reason but out of one's will; to forgive out of sheer love. It also denotes a forgiveness, which is total and not partial; not just once or twice or even seven times but with no count. In the Gospel I read: *Peter approached Jesus and asked him, "Lord, if my brother sins against me, how often must I forgive? As many as seven times?" Jesus answered, "I say to you, not seven times but seventy-seven times."* In the Lord's Prayer Jesus asked me to add this attitude of forgiving others saying: *"Forgive us our trespasses as we forgive those who trespass against us."* In the Book of Sirach I am asked to: *"Forgive your neighbor's injustice; then when you pray, your own sins will be forgiven".* The Book underscores the importance of forgiveness by telling me: "Could anyone refuse mercy to another like himself, can he seek pardon for his own sins?"

One more reason for forgiving others is the fact 'still I am going to die. A day will come I will die and become food for the earth. Before I die I should set right everything before God and others. I read in Scriptures, "Remember your last days, set enmity aside; remember death and decay, and cease from sin!" Therefore let me not carry a heavy burden of hatred and vengeance in my soul. With that burden it is very hard for the soul to fly toward heaven. Therefore it will be half way fall into hell. This remembrance of death calls me to forgive others soon. In one Scriptural passage I read an advice to couples: 'Before the sunset clear of your debts between each other by forgiveness.' This is what my Realreligion places before me as its highest ideal. There is a most compelling reason for me to forgive others. That is the fact that I am a member of Realreligion who believes and follows the exalted Jesus as my Lord and God. My forgiveness of others comes out of my intimate connections with God the Most High. First of all both God and myself have made covenant with each other in Jesus and therefore I have to live up to that promise. As Scriptures says, I have to 'remember the Most High's covenant, and overlook faults." In addition, since I am baptized in Jesus I live, move and have my being through him, with him and in him. All that I do and say should occur in that environment. As Paul says if I live or die I live or die only in Christ. I do not live or die for myself. In other words such deeper love and union with Christ makes me lose my very self, including its fake prestige, respect and glory. Generally I am hurt terribly by others only because they hurt my fake self-prestige, deceptive good name or good life. But as member of Realreligion my entire life and death belongs to Christ. My true glory, my real prestige and my authentic good name come only by my union with Christ. So others' sins or evil deeds against me do not in any way affect me.

The Amazing Results of Sacrament of Penance

The Sacrament of Reconciliation is for me a time of dual confession-confessing of the immense glory and eternal mercy of God and simultaneously confessing of my own limitation and sinfulness. At every time I perform these two confessions I travel from one shore to the other of the Ocean of Life. In religious circle we name it 'conversion'. It is not some movement from one religion to another; it is a very private and personal move from heart to heart: from merciless heart to merciful, from unforgiving to forgiving, from untruthful to truthful, from unjust to just and self-seeking to selfless. That heart, which is merciful, compassionate, moral, pure, forgiving, just, truthful and self-giving, is nothing but God's Heart. We can imagine it as the Home of God. It is the Divine Heart. All human beings are created that way, 'in His image and likeness,' to live and move and have their being in God's Home. But sadly they drift away from that wonderful Home, get out of it, sometimes go far away, other times while staying in that House they do not abide in the heart of God. In both groups of humans their hearts are not beating according to God's rhythm. One day some realize their mistake and blunder. They immediately take 'U' turn and return to their original Home of God, their sweet Home. This is conversion. All other kinds of conversions are simply its followup.

The main outcome of this Sacrament is, I call it, a beautiful paradigm shift that is very important in my Christian spirituality. Paradigm shift is an intrinsic part of the human, social development. As somebody very well said, "the only element that does not change in human life is 'change.'" Change and shifting from one point to another is inevitable for human growth: change of cells, bones, and other organs in human body; change in attitudes and worldviews; change of diet and change of exercises; change in social status and life situation. All these changes in all dimensions of human life, physical, mental, emotional and social, are a must for our happy living. The same thing is true also in our spiritual and moral life. Though we are born for heavenly bliss, little less than god, we are not angels nor born holy. 'We do not do what we want, but do what we hate. We do not do the good we want but we do the evil we do not want.' As Paul says, 'we are sold into slavery to sin.' In the light of the Bible, we are taught that every human being born sinful and the Church calls it 'the Original Sin.' It all started from the 'First Sin' of the 'First Humans' Adam and Eve. As a perennial gift from our First Parents all that we think through our fallible and sinful mind setup, turn out to be evil-oriented. Almost all our first thoughts are born of sinfulness. For example, low esteem about ourselves; fear for strangers, hatred against those who are not of our mind; ill-feeling against people who oppose our ideas; finding fault with others' undertakings and decisions; quitting from relationship, job, and other affiliations due to the first hurt feeling. There is an endless list of such 'first thoughts and moves we are prone to.

Jesus' disciples cannot afford to work under the spell of these first thoughts. We have been saved and bought from slavery of sin by our Lord. So any person who adhere to such faith will not entertain those 'first thoughts' and surely never execute them as acts outside. There should be a 'second thought' that overcomes the first, a thought that pops up in our mind due to the active grace of God and makes us reverse, rewrite or revisit those first thoughts and start performing deeds according to the second thoughts. If my first thought on seeing a stranger suspicious and hateful, I should stop over, wait for a second, think about my life and the other's life and God in between, and thus change my attitude completely, begin to extend my loving hands to those strangers. Thus we can overcome our sinfulness and be pleasing to God. I know the distance between 'first' and 'second' numerically is very short. But in actual thinking process, there exists an unthinkable chasm as there is between hell and heaven. Remember what Abraham said to the rich man who was in hell: "Between us and you a great chasm is established to prevent anyone from crossing who might wish to go from our side to yours or from your side to ours." (Lk. 16: 26) That is how I notice in some people who are proud to call themselves 'the hardheaded.' They do not have any qualms in behaving exactly as their first thought impels them. They do not understand that while they feel as living in heaven they are hell to all around them. There is and will be always a chasm between them and the true disciples of Jesus who always wait patiently and act upon their 'second thoughts.'

Regular Confessions in the Pursuit of Holiness

I have been astounded to read and hear about saints who made regular recourse to the Sacrament of Reconciliation, even some daily. My mentors explained this crazy habit as the result of saints' resolute search for attaining God's holiness. The most intriguing factor in God's economy of Salvation is that while humans are striving for reaching God, God Himself spends his full time in reaching out to humans and in search of the stranded souls. This astonishing scenario can be traced out in every saint like Saul who became Paul who had been unconsciously 'kicking against the goads' (Acts 26: 16) as the Scriptures put it. 'Kicking against the goads' was a common expression found in both Greek and Latin literature—a rural image, which rose from the practice of farmers goading their oxen in the fields. Though unfamiliar to us, everyone in that day understood. Goads were typically made from slender pieces of timber, blunt on one end and pointed on the other. Farmers used the pointed end to urge a stubborn ox into motion. Occasionally, the beast would kick at the goad. The more the ox kicked, the more likely it would stab into the flesh of its leg, causing greater pain. That was what happened in Saul's life. His conversion could appear to us as having been a sudden encounter with Christ. But based on the Lord's expression regarding his kicking back, I believe He'd been working on him for years, prodding and goading him. God goaded and prodded the stubborn pride of that Pharisaic ox, Saul. Day after day he kicked against those goads, until finally he got the message. There would be no more running. No more hiding. The fight was over. As always, God won. C. S. Lewis likened God's conquering work of Saul's rebelling will to a divine chess player systematically, patiently maneuvering his opponent into a corner until finally he concedes. "Checkmate."

Like Saul, I am no match for God. Checkmate is inevitable. It's no game either. God will do whatever it takes to bring me to a point of absolute dependence on Him. He will relentlessly, patiently, faithfully goad until I finally and willingly submit to Him. Until I have surrendered my life to Christ alone, by faith alone, we're as lost as Saul was on the Damascus road. Therefore I always feel journeying on the road to Damascus when I enter into confessional of a Catholic Church. Once I perform properly my part during the Sacrament of Reconciliation, then when I come out of the confessional full of joy, elated and spirited like Saul who became Paul.

Chapter-11:
Charities
according to my Realreligion

"The works of charity that have flowered down the centuries through the efforts of generous faithful" who *"have endeavored to create and promote charitable initiatives and institutions to meet the needs of the poorest, thus giving concrete expression to the close and indissoluble link between love of God and love of others."* (Pope Benedict XVI)

What is Charity?

The word "charity" comes from the Latin *caritas*, which means love. The word 'love' is ordinarily thought to be a feeling or emotion of human person. But if we go deeper into the explanations of different Sages, philosophers, and all religious leaders, we can discover that love is higher than mere feeling. Charity is an outward action that is generated out of humans' inner states-their motives, intentions and dispositions. Charity, in actuality, means performing generous actions or contributing donations to aid the poor, the ill, or those who are unable to help themselves. To the starving, charity is having food. To the naked, charity is being given clothes. To the homeless, a place to sleep, and to the sick, charity is having relief from illness. Charity is opening your heart and giving a hand to someone in need. Charity doesn't necessarily have to be something material. Sometimes just being there can have much greater value than money or worldly goods. Charity which comes from within the heart shows that you care and have compassion for the people around you. Charity is a state of mind and heart of a person to go out of oneself to enrich and enlighten and empower other humans in their human development and in their pursuit of ultimate goal in life.

Originally in Latin the word *caritas* meant preciousness, dearness, high price. From this, in Christian theology, *caritas* became the standard Latin translation for the Greek word meaning an unlimited loving-kindness to all others. This much wider concept is the meaning of the word charity in the Christian triplet "faith, hope and charity".

Christic Charity is *Agape*

Christ and his Church unceasingly preach and teach a unique style of love to be practiced by Christians. Borrowing a term from Teilhard de Chardin, I dare to call this love as *'Christic Charity'*. It is based on and maintained by the Scriptural version to charity, namely *'Agape'*. Greek philosophers at the time of Plato and other ancient authors have used certain forms of this term to denote love of a spouse or family, or affection for a particular activity, in contrast to *philia* (an affection that could denote friendship, brotherhood or generally non-sexual affection) and to *eros*, an affection of a sexual nature. On this background Thomas Jay Oord defined agape as "an intentional response to promote well-being when responding to that which has generated ill-being." NT Writers, when they wanted to describe the covenant love of God for humans, as well as the human reciprocal love for God, found 'agape' as an appropriate term. Consequently this word began representing divine, unconditional, self-sacrificing, active, volitional, and thoughtful love.

Agape, in Christianity, means love as revealed in Jesus, seen as spiritual and selfless and a model for humanity; it also indicates love that is spiritual, not sexual, in its nature; plus 'agape' is meant, from the early Christian Church up to this day, as a religious meal shared as a sign of love and fellowship as 'Eucharistic celebration'. The term *agape* is rarely used in ancient manuscripts, but was used by the early Christians to refer to the self-sacrificing love of God for humanity, which they were committed to reciprocating and practicing towards God and among one another. When John writes in his first

Letter that "God is love," the word *agape* is used to describe God's love. Agape has been expounded on by many Christian writers like C. S. Lewis, who in his book *The Four Loves*, used agape to describe what he believed was the highest level of love known to humanity—a selfless love, a love that was passionately committed to the well-being of the other.

Most of the NT writers have used the Greek word *agape* to refer to both the love of God and the love of neighbors. *"For God so loved* (in Greek ēgapēsen, past tense of *agapaō) the world that he gave his only Son, so that everyone who believes in him might not perish but might have eternal life."* (Jn. 3: 16) When one scholar of the law tested Jesus by asking, "Teacher, which commandment in the law is the greatest?" Matthew quotes Jesus' responding and summarizing God's OT Commandments into two using the Greek term *agape* to mean love. *"You shall love the Lord, your God, with all your heart, with all your soul, and with all your mind. This is the greatest and the first commandment. The second is like it: You shall love your neighbor as yourself. The whole law and the prophets depend on these two commandments."* (Matt. 22: 35-40) Church Fathers have generally described *agape* as a form of love which is both unconditional and voluntary. Tertullian in his 2nd century defense of Christians, remarks how Christian love attracted pagan notice: *"What marks us in the eyes of our enemies is our loving kindness. 'Only look,' they say, 'look how they love one another'* "(Apology 39).

Pope Benedict XVI' encyclical letter *Deus Caritas Est* (God is Love) has an extensive examination of the Christian interpretation of *agape* and the difference between it and its complementary term of *eros*. Pope clearly distinguishes *agape* as love that is selfless from *eros* as love that is possessive, and ascertains that where there is one, there is the other; but he glorifies and identifies *agape* as Christian Love.

Charity toward God is solely because He loved us first and as a consequence we love Him. He too showed us how to love genuinely through His love-deeds as my mother trained me how to kiss her by first kissing me. God has revealed the authentic love by coming out of Himself and sharing His image and likeness with us, making us participate in His creative and even redemptive works; He has handed over to us all natural and spiritual resources available in His Kingdom

188

so that our lives can be fulfilling and joyful. He did one more thing very ravishingly. He affirmed the real nature of true love by sending His Son whose life in action expounded it more understandably. *"He emptied himself, taking the form of a slave, coming in human likeness; and found human in appearance, he humbled himself, becoming obedient to death, even death on a cross."* (Phi. 2: 7-8) All these are for what? Jesus ascertains: *"As the Father loves me, so I also love you."* He too adds: *"No one has greater love than this, to lay down one's life for one's friends."* (Jn. 15: 9, 13)

God didn't stop with that exposition of His love. He commanded us to love Him in reciprocation totally and wholistically, *with all our heart, with all our soul, and with all our mind.* Plus, He too ordered us to love our fellow-humans *'as we love ourselves.'* Jesus, as his part, avowed our wholehearted love for God and added some nuance to the command of loving our neighbors. First he deliberated that we should love other humans as he did and does. *"This is my commandment: love one another as I love you."* (Jn. 15: 12) He loves us as he loves his Father; he loves us going out of himself and out of the way. In the same he orders us to love our neighbors as Good Samaritans, as intimate friends and as our own brothers and sisters belonging to one Family of God. *'Following Jesus'* means, Pope Francis says, *"learning to come out of ourselves . . . in order to meet others, in order to go toward the edges of our existence, to take the first steps towards our brothers and sisters, especially those who are farthest from us, those who are forgotten, those who need understanding, consolation, and assistance."*

The climatic interpretation of his love-command makes us breathless as he portrays our final Judgment Day. It is in this teaching Jesus codifies what he really means by 'Christic Charity': According to Jesus, as the Shepherd and judge, he will divide the entire human race into two groups, of which one group will be rewarded and the other will be punished. (Matt. 25: 31-40) Jesus shocks us when he details the judgment. He identifies himself suffering with poor and the needy of this world, as they are hungry, thirsty, strange, naked, ill and in prison. Those who assisted him in those needy will be blessed and rewarded with eternal joy and those who ignore and care little for him in the poor and downtrodden will be doomed and punished with eternal suffering.

Jesus is very clear about how he is going to judge us; he also spelt out vividly on what ground and with what benchmark he is going to measure each one's life. His judgment will be based on his own personal encounters with each one of us while he and we are together in this world. I am so happy to notice that my judge Jesus is not going to judge me according to what language I speak and how I speak it. The scale, criterion, measure, norm, decisive factor, benchmark, point of reference and yardstick with which he would judge me is nothing but charity. His assessment will consider only those loveable acts and accomplishments I would have done before I die. This is why Peter writes: *"Above all, let your love for one another be intense, because love covers a multitude of sins."* (1 Pet. 4: 8) As Winston Churchill said, *'we make a living by what we get but we make a life by what we give.'* Saving life is as much important as giving life.

This Christic charity toward others, my Realreligion points out, will be properly handled by me only when I unite myself with the risen Lord and see his presence in others as if they are his proxies. Christ is present in every aspect of my life. The saddest possibility in this judgment scenario is to see the members of Reelreligion, even those who claim themselves living in Jesus' Religion, not recognizing him that way. Jesus says that not only the goats, namely the people who don't help others, but also the sheep, those who do help others, say that they don't remember seeing the Lord. They even may see him present in Church, in Scripture and the Eucharist. But they do not recognize him in others.

Almsgiving as Christic Charity

The spirit of Christic Charity urges me to regularly some charitable deeds. Number one in that list is 'Almsgiving'. My Realreligion demands from me, to put it very bluntly, it pricks my conscience ceaselessly to perform such charities in a personal way. In other words it expects me to open my wallet to fill the stomachs and to help the weaklings to help themselves and exclusively spend (waste?) my precious hours to reach out the needy. As recent research exposes, it is very sad to find that in every country the 10% of the population are hoarding and enjoying 90% of national wealth and properties while 90% of the people survive by only 10% of material possessions nationally. Most people of the richest minority are unwilling to open their wallets to help the majority in need. There have been examinations of who gives more to charity. One study conducted in the United States found that, to my surprise, as a percentage of income, charitable giving increased as income decreased. The poorest fifth of Americans, for example, gave away 4.3% of their income, while the wealthiest fifth gave away 2.1%. In absolute terms, this was an average of $453 on an average income of $10,531, compared to $3,326 on an income of $158,388. By God's grace I enjoy all that I need not just for survival but even for convenience and comfort. Therefore my Realreligion is absolutely correct in its demand. I must help the poor and downtrodden.

More than the above-mentioned sociological and humanitarian perspectives, my Realreligion bases its argument on the Scriptures. Prophets in OT cry out the excellence and necessity of helping the needy. We read in a Letter, attributed to the name of St. Barnabas who, referring to God's words from OT, emphasizes the preference of charitable deeds compared to fasting and other religious rituals for our salvation: God has abolished the sacrifices of the old law so that the new law of our Lord Jesus Christ, which does not bind by slavish compulsion, might have an offering not made by man . . ."*God spoke of this once again when he said to them: On such a day you are keeping a fast that will not carry your cry to heaven. Is it that sort of fast that I require, a day of mortification like that? But to us he says: Is it not this that I demand of you as a fast—loose the fetters of injustice, untie the knots of all contracts that involve extortion, set free those who have been crushed, tear up every unjust agreement. Share your food with the starving; when you meet a naked man, give him clothing; welcome the homeless into your house."*

As we indicated earlier how we would be judged on the basis of charitable works, Jesus presented a list of love deeds toward the sick and the needy. Since helping the poor and the needy was one of his priorities in mission he mentioned it in his first public appearance and speech. He said: *"The Spirit of the Lord is upon me, because he has anointed me to bring glad tidings to the poor. He has sent me to proclaim liberty to captives and recovery of sight to the blind, to let the oppressed go free."* (Lk. 4: 18) In his Sermon on the Mount he included almsgiving as one of three primary duties of his Disciples. He endorsed almsgiving it but he too cautioned us in performing it rightly: *"Take care not to perform righteous deeds in order that people may see them; otherwise, you will have no recompense from your heavenly Father. When you give alms, do not blow a trumpet before you, as the hypocrites do in the synagogues and in the streets to win the praise of others. Amen, I say to you, they have received their reward. But when you give alms, do not let your left hand know what your right is doing, so that your almsgiving may be secret. And your Father who sees in secret will repay you."* (Matt. 6: 1-4)

It is true, Paul's use of the term charity (*agape*) in his Letters is more concentrated on the rare blend of divine and human love. Even in one place he prefers agape to almsgiving: *"If I give away everything I own,* (in another translation: *though I feed the poor with all my goods) and if I hand my body over so that I may boast but do not have love, (agape) I gain nothing."* (1 Cor. 13: 3) Nonetheless the Apostle and other NT Writers reinforce the need and necessity of charitable deeds in Christian life to assist the needy with their resources. *"For if the eagerness is there, it is acceptable according to what one has, not according to what one does not have; not that others should have relief while you are burdened, but that as a matter of equality your surplus at the present time should supply their needs, so that their surplus may also supply your needs, that there may be equality. As it is written, "Whoever had much did not have more, and whoever had little did not have less."* (2 Cor. 8: 11-15)

All religions are never tired of speaking about the necessity of almsgiving. In Islam, for example, it is a strong belief that Allaah (God) has enjoined upon the Muslims to give alms: *"Take sadaqah (alms) from their wealth in order to purify them and sanctify them with it, and invoke Allaah for them. Verily, your invocations are a source of security for them."* (al-Tawbah 9: 103) According to Muslim brethren almsgiving purifies and cleanses wealth, and purifies the soul from stinginess and miserliness. It strengthens the love between the rich and poor, takes away hatred, makes security prevail and brings happiness to the devotee happy. Islamic religion too warns its members that withholding alms brings disasters and evils upon them. Those who withhold it will go through a painful torment on the Day of Resurrection.

We must transcend the mostly selfish mindset that comes so naturally and learn to truly care for the happiness and well-being of others (Mk. 12:31).

The fruitful and right way of giving Alms

Almsgiving, my Realreligion directs me, must be one of private charity which must be voluntary. It should come from the heart. It encourages an attitude of altruism by appealing to one's compassion, not in fear or compulsion. Realreligion induces me to give alms in a discreet, respectful and selfless way. Almsgiving is the most obvious expression of the virtue of charity. It must be properly handled. Jesus advises us *not let the left hand know what the right hand is doing.* Giving the recipients the means they need to survive. The impoverished, particularly those widowed or orphaned, and the ailing or injured, are generally regarded as the proper recipients of charity. These people who cannot support themselves and lack outside means of support sometimes become 'beggars', directly soliciting aid from strangers encountered in public. Most forms of almsgiving are concerned with providing basic necessities such as food, water, clothing, healthcare and shelter, but other actions may be performed as charity: visiting the imprisoned or the homebound, ransoming captives, educating orphans, even social movements. Donations to causes that benefit the unfortunate indirectly, such as donations to fund cancer research, are also charity.

Recently I was reading a book written by C.S. Lewis, a great English author. Describing about our life after death he says that if we were to go to heaven we would experience a triple surprise, more than a triple surprise, a triple shock. First, we would be shocked that there were people there we never would have thought would be there. The second surprise would be the shock at realizing there were people we expected to be in heaven who were not there. The third surprise would be that we would be astonished that we were there. C.S. Lewis is right when we hear Jesus talking about the kind of judgment he would be conducting over the whole humanity after we all die. (Matt. 25: 31-40) Realreligion's members are well aware of the fact that kindness and generosity, showing especially to the needy and the poor neglected by the society are contagious. Sending some money to his needy friend Benjamin Franklin to his friend wrote to him: *"I do not pretend to give such a sum; I only lend it to you. When you meet with another honest man in similar distress, you must pay me by lending this sum to him. Enjoin him to discharge the debt by a like operation when he shall be able . . . I hope it may thus go through many hands before it meets with a knave who will stop its progress. This is a trick of mine for doing a great deal of good with a little money."* (Benjamin Webb dated April 22, 1784) He is absolutely right.

Almsgiving is an act of giving of one self and one's own treasure, time and talent without expecting anything in return. The relation of charity to community is that if you give to the community without any expectations the day you require help the community will be in a good position to help you because you made sure to give time and help to does less fortunate. By giving you enabled others to prepare to give back when it is their turn. Asking for and receiving help from others is often beneficial for both giver and receiver in mysterious ways. However there is also some negative side to it. As some of my friends often remark, giving alms to particular needy and poor people likely make them to become dependent and lazy. Indeed there is possibility to such wrong results but we should never deny the fact of life, as Jesus indicated, that poor people will be there always around us; their poverty, their inability to work, their ignorance to manage life and so on are caused by birth, by sickness, by unjust society and criminals. Among them some may pick up very quickly, others gradually and slowly the way of helping themselves. Being aware of the truth that charitably helping the needy requires more than throwing money at the problem, my Realreligion certainly encourages me to help the weak to help themselves; and to uplift them to take responsibility and become self-supporting members of society; but it also exhorts me to assist the needy and the poor as long as they are incapacitated by physical and social evils.

When Pope Francis visited the Cathedral of Rio in July 2013 to greet his Argentine compatriots, he offered an impromptu address. He asserted: *"I want the Church to go out into the streets, to go out from that which is comfortable, from that which is clericalism, and from all that which makes us being closed up in ourselves."* Pope's words reminded me of my stage play on the life of Frederic Osannam who started the charitable association, Vincent De Paul Society. His outcry throughout his life was, *"Church, Come out to streets and take care of the poor and the needy.'* All saints did the same in their lives. The saint, Elizabeth of Hungary, refused to be owned by the trappings of European royalty—she chose instead to dress simply and to share her wealth daily with the poor folks who gathered at the palace gates. Even when she was mistreated and thrown out of the palace after the death of her young husband, she continued to share whatever she had with the poor. St Francis of Assisi did the same following radically what Jesus demanded of the rich young man: *"You are lacking in one thing. Go, sell what you have, and give to (the) poor and you will have treasure in heaven; then come, follow me."* (Mk. 10: 20-23) All of his committed Disciples who follow Realreligion take seriously in their lives what their Master recommended: *"I tell you, make friends for yourselves with dishonest wealth, so that when it fails, you will be welcomed into eternal dwellings."* (Lk. 16: 9)

Myself with friends and benefactors of Green Cross Ministries in Oklahoma absolutely believe the Psalmist words and therefore try our best to share our possessions as much as we can to the uplift and welfare of the poor and the needy around the world: *Oh, the joys of those who are kind to the poor: The LORD rescues them in times of trouble. The LORD protects them and keeps them alive. He gives them prosperity and rescues them from their enemies. The LORD nurses them when they are sick and eases their pain and discomfort."* (Ps. 41: 1-4) Realreligion's members hold some valid reasons for coming out of one self and performing almsgiving. There are many reasons: one is, *to give us, who are favored with enough, an opportunity of showing our love to Jesus.* We show our love to Christ when we sing of Him and when we pray to Him; but if there were no sons of need in the world we should lose the sweet privilege of evidencing our love, by ministering in alms-giving to His poorer brethren; He has ordained that thus we should prove that our love stands not in word only, but in deed and in truth. If we truly love Christ, we shall care for those who are loved by Him. The words of the Lord Jesus are unceasingly ringing in our ears and hearts: *"Inasmuch as you have done it unto one of the least of these my brethren, you have done it unto me."*

The Jews called the poor's box 'the box of righteousness'. It is true, our alms-deeds do not deserve heaven; but it is as true that we cannot go to heaven without them. James bluntly writes, *"Religion that is pure and undefiled before God and the Father is this: to care for orphans and widows in their affliction and to keep oneself unstained by the world."* (James 1: 27)

Pope Benedict XVI very beautifully said: *"For all Christians, and especially for 'charity workers' love of neighbor will no longer be for them a commandment imposed, so to speak, from without, but a consequence deriving from their faith, a faith which becomes active through love. Christians are people who have been conquered by Christ's love and accordingly, under the influence of that love. 'Caritas Christi urget nos'. They are profoundly open to loving their neighbor in concrete ways. This attitude arises primarily from the consciousness of being loved, forgiven, and even served by the Lord, who bends down to was h the feet of the Apostles and offers himself on the Cross to draw humanity into God's love."*

Adhering to Jesus' admonition, my Realreligion persuades me to perform all charitable deeds out of pure love of God, out of docile obedience to my Jesus' New Commandment of love but surely with some Holy Strings Attached: The first string is all for the greater glory of God. *"Hallowed be Thy Name; Thy Kingdom come; Thy will be done on earth as it is in heaven."* The second benefit I target is as I pointed out earlier, *'for reserving my eternal reward'*. And thirdly as Paul says, *"we seek those things which are beneficial to our brothers, without counting the cost, to help them on the way to salvation."*

As a final note in this chapter to reemphasize all that said above on loving and serving the poor in this modern but cold world, I want to illustrate a magnificent incident happened at Vatican: Pope Francis, in his first address (March 2013) to the journalists, shared how he got the idea to name himself as Francis. *"Some people didn't know"*, he said, *"Why the Bishop of Rome wanted to call himself 'Francis'. Some thought of Francis Xavier, Francis de Sales, even Francis of Assisi. I will tell you the story. At the election I had the archbishop emeritus of Sao Paulo next to me. He is also prefect emeritus of the Congregation for the Clergy, Cardinal Claudio Hummes [O.F.M.]: a dear, dear friend. When things were getting a little 'dangerous', he comforted me. And then, when the votes reached the two-thirds, there was the usual applause because the Pope had been elected. He hugged me and said: 'Do not forget the poor.' And that word stuck here [tapping his forehead]; the poor, the poor. Then, immediately in relation to the poor I thought of Francis of Assisi. Then I thought of war, while the voting continued, until all the votes [were counted]. And so the name came to my heart: Francis of Assisi. For me he is the man of poverty, the man of peace, the man who love and safeguards Creation. In this moment when our relationship with Creation is not so good—right?—He is the man who gives us this spirit of peace, the poor man . . . Oh, how I wish for a Church that is poor and for the poor!"*

Chapter-12:
'Giving Tithes'
according to my Realreligion

"You shall help to provide for the needs of the Church."
(Precept of Catholic Church)

T his Church's Precept implies that the faithful are obliged to assist with the material needs of the Church, each according to his/her own ability. Needs of the Church include those of the local church (parish and diocese) and of the universal Church as well. The kinds of needs in the churches are commonly: 1. Expenses for their Maintenance and renovation of the church properties; for payment of salaries and remunerations to their staff including parish priests and other ministers; and for running office and pastoral programs. 2. Expenses for local almsgiving and for donating to various evangelical, missionary and social programs of the diocesan and universal churches. Every parish, according to its situation, has its own annual budget for all its expenses. Parishes can be also experience occasionally big expenses that are called extraordinary ones such as major repairs, remodeling or even new constructions and so on. It is general practice of the churches in Christianity to invite their congregational members to contribute regularly-weekly, or monthly toward meeting out the above-listed regular expenses. For extraordinary expenses special fundraisers will be planned out and executed.

My Realreligion, based on the Scriptures and Church Tradition, urges me to offer regular contributions and if need be, some occasional donations and gifts to my church where I am registered in. Christian writers and preachers name this sharing my possessions with the Church as Tithes, Gift Offerings, Donations, and Stewardship and so on. Among them I love the term 'Tithes' for the reasons that it has its origin from Judaism, my Realreligion's birthplace. Also, it includes all elements of ethics and codes for my true sharing with my Church; and it spells out splendidly the authenticity of my Church's continued Tradition in this regard.

What is 'Tithe'?

The word "tithe" is simply an old English word meaning "tenth." It refers to the giving to God a "tenth" of our income or any of our life's increase. The tithe is the tenth of all the increase that God gives to us. "Increase" here indicates everything that increases the value of earthly possessions that God places into our trust, whether it is earned income or unearned gifts. Historically among the Jews tithes were required and paid in kind, such as agricultural products. Today, tithes are normally voluntary and paid in cash, checks, or stocks. It is paid usually as a contribution to a religious organization. In the light of the Scriptures it is believed that Almighty God directs that this 'tenth' be given to Him as if directly, through His true ministers in His religion and not just to be handed out anywhere.

Tithing to God through the religion was a compulsory duty for every Jew before and after the time of the Lord. In early Christianity, however, it was not practiced, but within that period, as we read in the Book of Acts, the custom was that *all who believed were together and had all things in common; they would sell their property and possessions and divide them among all according to each one's need.* (Acts 2: 44-45) Each member of Jesus' Community-the Church sold out all their possessions and brought the proceeds (money) to the apostles who then distributed to each according to need. (Acts 4: 34-37)

Later on when the Church spread and extended itself from Jerusalem to the non-Jewish countries, as the New Testament scriptures verify, in all churches the act of "freewill offerings" was practiced as a means of supporting the poor churches: *"Now in regard to the collection for the holy ones, you also should do as I ordered the churches of Galatia. On the first day of the week each of you should set aside and save whatever one can afford, so that collections will not be going on when I come. And when I arrive, I shall send those whom you have approved with letters of recommendation to take your gracious gift to Jerusalem."* (1Cor. 16: 1-3) In later life of the Church we find tithes were mentioned in councils at Tours in 567 and at Macon in 585. They were formally recognized under Pope Adrian I in 787.

Why should I tithe?

First of all, I confess that I have no any qualms about obeying God's financial law of tithing, because I recognize that all the strength and ability with which I produce in my line of work, all the materials I use, all the food I eat and air I breathe in order to gain strength come from my God, mu Provider, my Proprietor, my Father, my Creator and Life-giver. In return for all that He is to me He only asks me to pay Him one-tenth of what produce and posses.

I am told that God doesn't need all my offerings in the form of money or in kinds for His Divine Purpose. He says it very plainly: *"What do I care for the multitude of your sacrifices? says the LORD. I have had enough of whole-burnt rams and fat of fatlings; in the blood of calves, lambs, and goats I find no pleasure. When you come to appear before me, who asks these things of you?"* (Is. 1: 11-12) Nor should I ever think that my tithes would solve all problems of my life, specifically cleansing of my sins. This is because I have been enlightened by the Scriptures in which my God has expressed his displeasure and hatred against humans' tipping Him with their material goods. The Author of the Letter to the Hebrews declares this eternal truth: *"It is impossible that the blood of bulls and goats take away sins.* (Heb. 10: 4)

He expects me rather to show my worthy submissiveness to Him-my surrender to His Will with wholehearted love. We find in the Scriptures that the Lord expects from us obedience to His Will rather than their offerings. When Saul defended himself on his obedience to the fulfilling the mission on which the Lord has sent him, Samuel pointed out Saul's disobedience to God as he offered to Him the spoils disapproved by God: *"Does the LORD delight in burnt offerings and sacrifices as much as in obedience to the LORD's command? Obedience is better than sacrifice, to listen, better than the fat of rams"*. (1Sam. 5) And this is why my Master Jesus was careful in his obedience to God even from his very conception: *"For this reason, when he (Jesus) came into the world, he said: "Sacrifice and offering you did not desire, but a body you prepared for me; holocausts and sin offerings you took no delight in. Then I said, 'As is written of me in the scroll, Behold, I come to do your will, O God' . . . By this "will," we have been consecrated through the offering of the body of Jesus Christ once for all."* (Heb. 10: 5-10)

Nonetheless God never disqualifies my eagerness to give my tithes and other offerings in His Name and for His Services for humanity. That is why as I pointed out earlier, He made it as a Law. Therefore my Realreligion tells me that tithes are overt symbols of my commitment to my covenantal Relationship with God. Human relationship and interaction with God is solely founded and built up on the mutual covenant between God and His people. While God performs all His marvelous deeds towards humans according to His covenantal promises, humans are obliged to live their entire life, especially to carry out certain spiritual, social and physical actions, pleasing to their Creator in accordance with their promises given to Him. In my Realreligion I am pleased to call these human covenantal acts as a package of religious practices.

The act of giving tithes in the Church is one of those religious practices. It is based on the command of God in the Bible: *"Do not appear before the Lord empty-handed, for all that you offer is in fulfillment of the precepts. The offering of the just enriches the altar: a sweet odor before the Most High. The sacrifice of the just is accepted, never to be forgotten. With a generous spirit pay homage to the Lord, and do not spare your freewill gifts. With each contribution show a cheerful countenance, and pay your tithes in a spirit of joy. Give to the Most High as he has given to you, generously, according to your means. For, he is a God who always repays and will give back to you sevenfold. But offer no bribes; these he does not accept! Do not trust in sacrifice of the fruits of extortion, for he is a God of justice, who shows no partiality."* (Sir. 35: 6-15) We notice God being very meticulous and serious about tithing to Him. As He does to explain about all His Commandments He offers detailed explanation to the people of how and what this act of tithing (gift offerings, etc.) should be practiced. *"You shall take bran flour and bake it into twelve cakes, using two tenths of an ephah of flour for each cake. These you shall place in two piles, six in each pile, on the pure gold table before the LORD. With each pile put some pure frankincense, which shall serve as an oblation to the LORD, a token of the bread offering. Regularly on each Sabbath day the bread shall be set out before the LORD on behalf of the Israelites by an everlasting covenant. It shall belong to Aaron and his sons, who must eat it in a sacred place, since it is most sacred, his as a perpetual due from the oblations to the LORD."* (Lev. 24: 5-9) *"You shall make its plates and cups, as well as its pitchers and bowls for pouring libations; make them of pure gold. On the table you shall always keep showbread set before me."* (Ex. 25: 29-30)

We, as God's creatures and His Kingdom's citizens, through tithing are paying our Creator a very nominal amount that He requires as our Maker, our Sustainer, our Landlord, our Protector and our God! God orders us saying: *"Honor the LORD with your possessions, and with the firstfruits of all your increase."* (Pro. 3: 9) Through tithing I show outwardly my loyalty and honor to the Great God who made me; who gave me my life, my talents, my minds; and He is my Proprietor who continues to bestow the strength with which I work and the very land and materials which I employ in my work. The tithe of my increase, one of my mentors suggested, is not mine to give to God; it is God's for me to give to God, and it is a privilege for me to have it to give to Him.

God's main reason for compelling me to give regular tithes is, besides making me fulfill my covenantal love-commitment toward Him, to continue His Son's Love-deeds among His humans. In Scriptures He clarifies the secondary purposes of our tithing. First of all, a good portion of it should be spent on the needs of the poor and the weak and the rest of the tithes must be spent for the establishing, managing and maintaining of His Kingdom in the form of local and universal church. I know my God desires even the second portion of collected tithes sincerely and deliberately spent not on constructing luxurious, pompous or decorative buildings or monuments, not on hoarding wealth in the name of His Church, and not on any extravagant deeds but totally only on those expenditures rising from the uninterrupted evangelical and charitable services of the Church.

Appropriate manner of tithing

I make sure anything I offer to God as tithe coming out of love and gratitude to Him and ethically being sincere and it is much true in the context of tithing. I listen carefully to Jesus' condemnation of the Pharisees in the Gospel: *"Woe to you, scribes and Pharisees, you hypocrites. You pay tithes of mint and dill and cummin, and have neglected the weightier things of the law: judgment and mercy and fidelity. But these you should have done, without neglecting the others."* (Matt. 23: 23) Those words of Jesus can be misconstrued to mean that Israel's religious leaders were doing evil by being very careful to bring God tithes of all that entered as increase in to their homes. But adding the words, *"these you should have done, without neglecting the others,"* Jesus points out that those men were evil, not because they brought God tithes of everything that was increase to them, but because they neglected the love and truth of God.

I feel exactly as Prophet Malachi perceives that I am robbing God if I am not sincere in tithing. Prophet writes: *"Can anyone rob God? But you are robbing me! And you say, 'How have we robbed you?' Of tithes and contributions!"* (Mal. 3: 8) From my childhood I have been noticing, hearing and reading about how people of my church who practice Reelreligion of their own with no guilt-consciousness rob God our very Creator and His work. There is very little Realreligion left on earth today! It is very sad to observe that there is so much confusion and deceit going about in the name of Christianity! In my pursuit of practicing true religion I am convinced everything I possess or earn by my own IQ, tactics, qualifications and talents is God-given gifts. Naturally He is the owner and Master of me and my possessions. Hence I have the duty first and foremost to surrender all my earnings and increases to Him and after getting His blessing and approval I can use as my life demands. This first most important duty to God is vividly expressed by giving the firstfruits and the tithes to Him through His Church. If I don't fulfill my first duty then Malachi is right when he declares such thing is a sort of robbing God.

Realreligion teaches me not to make my tithing an act of 'tipping' the Lord as if I am doing Him a favor. God certainly is not my servant. Tithing should never be focused on getting some blessings from Him. Nor should it be a kind of favor I do to Him as if He were a waiter, forced to take whatever I deem Him worthy to receive. There are a number of people who practice Reelreligion whose money, I am absolutely certain, the Lord would not receive when they bring it. Their lives are unworthy of the Lord and He pierces through their hearts and sees how silly they are in their thinking that by their offerings and tithes they can blind God to their iniquities. They don't perceive that money is no substitute for repentance. I will never follow my brothers and sisters who practice this kind of Reelreligion. They hoard wealth and properties by unjust and unethical way; but in order to pacify their pricking conscience annually they donate very large portion of their possessions to a god or goddess whom they think they are worshipping. In my Church I can see this abhorrent custom of giving to their local churches either to tip God or to silence His frightening voice as conscience or to add one more idol to their worship, namely their own fake self or ego.

On my part I don't want to be like those 'big and crooked tippers'; I cannot use tithes to force God to bless me. Tithing is acceptable to God only as part of my godly lifestyle. The blessings that come from tithing come because of the kind of life I live, not because of the money I give. I cannot live a sinful life and then expect to be blessed by God just because I bring tithes to the Lord. I try to give Him as tithe regularly as much as I can afford but always with my whole heart and mind and soul in contrition and in gratitude as the 'Widow' in Jesus' parable. I dare not to throw few coins in the collection basket as I do to the beggars on the streets. I am convinced that God doesn't need my charity or my pity for His poor priests and ministers and that He has not commanded that his faithful servants must live on my tips.

I hate to act before God as one of 'bribe-bringers' who are trying to mask a sinful heart with deeds that appear to be upright but are not. Their giving is a crime, and it would be better for them not to give at all than to give with a sin-stained heart. Before I begin to plan or cash out or write a check as tithes to God, I should look at my heart from my Master's perspective so that I make sure that what I bring to God, I am bringing out of a sincere and contrite heart. Otherwise, I know well it is worse than a waste of my money; I don't want to make my tithes venomous curses to my very life. Tithing is after all a God's commandment, not a suggestion. When I have brought to God His tithes and His offerings, I should understand that I have not given God anything. All I have offered are His own gifts out of his immense goodness. I am just doing my duty of bringing to God what is already His. It is good to do my duty, by which I express myself being a faithful handler of God's possessions and avoiding becoming a thief. Jesus' words ring all the time in my ears as I offer my tithes in the Church: *"When you have done all you have been commanded, say, 'We are unprofitable servants; we have done what we were obliged to do.'"* (Lk. 17: 10)

As my Realreligion clarifies to me, I also try to give my tithing willingly and freely. Stephen L Richards, in his pamphlet, *The Law of Tithing*, rightly highlights on this issue: *"When one pays his tithing without enjoyment he is robbed of a part of the blessing. He must learn to give cheerfully, willingly and joyfully, and his gift will be blessed."* Stephen only reiterates the instruction of Paul: *"Each must do as already determined, without sadness or compulsion, for God loves a cheerful giver."* (2 Cor. 9: 7)

The benefits of Tithing

While I am careful not to be damned by the Lord's anger who says: *"You are indeed accursed, for you, the whole nation, rob me. Bring the whole tithe into the storehouse, that there may be food in my house"* (Mal. 3: 9-10), I too don't want to miss His promised blessings for tithing.

The Almighty promises, saying to us that if we pay our tithes to Him, *"Your barns will be filled with plenty, and your vats will overflow with new wine"* (Pro. 3: 10). Accordingly if we are faithful in obeying God and paying Him the first tenth of our income, He will bless our life in many physical and material ways. He has promised it and God never breaks His Word! The Creator God speaks to all those who come to know about His law of tithing with a challenge of testing Him whether our obedience to His Law of Tithing brings blessings to us: *"Put me to the test, says the LORD of hosts, and see if I do not open the floodgates of heaven for you, and pour down upon you blessing without measure!"* (Mal. 3: 10) This is quite a challenge that Almighty God gives to me who knows about Him and His law of tithing. He wants me to test Him or try Him out. If we faithfully tithe, God promises to safeguard us from all evils and to make all that we establish and produce prosper: *"I will rebuke the locust for you so that it will not destroy your crops, and the vine in the field will not be barren, says the LORD of hosts. All the nations will call you blessed, for you will be a delightful land, says the LORD of hosts."* (Mal. 3: 11-12)

These verses, as my Realreligion's members believe, are nothing less than a solemn promise from the Creator to bless those who faithfully tithe and behave as those who make God their financial Partner! For example, we read in OT that God did greatly bless Abraham, who was regularly tithing, with material wealth (Gen. 13: 2); He also blessed Jacob shortly after he vowed to tithe to Him (Gen. 30: 43). He has never failed in His promises of prosperity in the lives of His children. Jesus reiterated God's promises of prosperity and countless and abundant blessings for tithers. *"Give and gifts will be given to you; a good measure, packed together, shaken down, and overflowing, will be poured into your lap. For the measure with which you measure will in return be measured out to you."* (Lk. 6: 38)

My Realreligion is never tired of warning me that I should never misinterpret these promises of God in Jesus on tithing. He does not promise to make all His tithe-payers materially rich! God's blessings will be predominately spiritual; they are more of God's spiritual strength, wisdom and love and eternal life in God's Kingdom. Jesus therefore exhorts us to be more concerned with heavenly treasures than earthly. *"Do not store up for yourselves treasures on earth, where moth and decay destroy, and thieves break in and steal. But store up treasures in heaven, where neither moth nor decay destroys, nor thieves break in and steal. For where your treasure is, there also will your heart be."* (Matt. 6: 19-21)

To God Almighty nothing is impossible; He has all power. He can and will bless any person or nation that obeys Him, faithfully paying Him the tithe that is rightfully His. It is not illogical that parting with a portion of my money will make me far better off financially than if I held onto it. My treasure will be decreased by my giving some of it. This is naturally a human law. But according to the divine law is that the more I give the greater will be its increase. *"One person is lavish yet grows still richer; another is too sparing, yet is the poorer.*

Whoever confers benefits will be amply enriched, and whoever refreshes others will be refreshed. Whoever hoards grain, the people curse, but blessings are on the head of one who distributes it!" (Pro. 11: 24-26) In my charitable ministries my primary focus is to help people for two purposes: To help themselves and to help others. I name these endeavors as 'Help-to-Help' projects. The same is true in my act of tithing. I pay the tithes and offerings that God commands, I not only bring blessings to myself; I also allow God to use me to bless others. Never do I forget that God uses my tithes to provide for other people and give them His much-needed Truth. By hard and just work I should earn and a portion of what I have earned must be offered to the Lord in the Church as my tithe. Paul in this behavior is my rolemodel who says: *"In every way I have shown you that by hard work of that sort we must help the weak, and keep in mind the words of the Lord Jesus who himself said, 'It is more blessed to give than to receive'"* (Acts 20: 35). When we are motivated by a desire to serve others, we develop a giving, sharing, caring and generous spirit.

Jesus teaches me saying, *"Seek first the kingdom of God and his righteousness, and all these things will be given you besides."* (Matt. 6: 33) God's plan of tithing is simple: "Give to gain". In other words, give to the kingdom and God will take care of your needs. Famous preacher Spurgeon quoted what one generous believer once said: *"I shovel out, and God shovels in, and he has a bigger shovel than I do."* And while the return may or may not be monetary, you can be sure that your heart will overflow with the joy of giving generously and seeing His kingdom prosper. *"By placing our riches at the feet of God as our tithes for His Projects, we are amassing imperishable riches. We have properly placed those riches where our heart is; it is a most blessed thing to work to increase such riches rather than to fear that they may pass away."* (Pope Leo the Great)

Chapter-13:
Leadership and Authority
in my Realreligion

"Christ, you decided to show your merciful love through your holy shepherds; through your vicars you continue to perform the ministry of shepherd of souls; through your leaders of your people, you served as physician of our bodies and our spirits."
(Prayer intercessions in Divine Office morning prayer for saints)

Genuine leaders' identity

Realreligion confesses that there is only one who is holy and good leader. Namely, the God, the Father of our Lord Jesus. The Scriptures name him as Good Shepherd. *"The Lord is my Shepherd. There is nothing I shall want. In verdant pastures he gives me repose; beside restful waters he leads me; he refreshes my soul."* (Ps. 23) When Jesus came from God he surprisingly claimed Himself as the Good Shepherd. He declared himself: *"I am the shepherd; I came that my sheep may have life and have it more abundantly."* He too proved his identity as shepherd by living for his sheep. In a special way he has shown it by his loving service to the sheep as their servant and sacrificed even himself for their sake. He revealed to me the real definition of a good leader. According to him, a good leader (shepherd) is a person who loves, who serves and sacrifices himself for his sheep.

Jesus' mission on earth was to bring as many disciples as possible into his sheepfold and make them faithful flock of his Father, the good Shepherd. That is his priority interest. But he too found out from his Father that he had to share with his disciples his responsibility of shepherding. When the time came for Jesus to be lifted up to his Father's right hand and thus become an invisible source of life, he wanted his followers, his own sheep to carry on his leadership or shepherdship to tend his flock. To be faithful sheep I also have to obey the call of Jesus to shepherd my needy sheep, namely to love, to serve and to sacrifice ourselves for them. Every sheep of Jesus is called to take his/her responsibility of shepherding in different ways for different reasons and occasions of serving. For example: All of Jesus' followers are called to shepherd by mercy and compassion. Most of them are called to shepherd because of duty. Many of them are called to shepherd by natural blood connection. Some of them are called to shepherd as their life-long commitment. My Realreligion points out the last category of shepherds are the genuine leaders.

We always like to lead but not to be led. It's because we wrongly think it infringes our freedom. But by our human nature whether we like it or not, whether we are conscious or unconscious we both are led by others and lead others too. There is a basic human need to lead and to be led as the need to love and to be loved. This tendency, to lead and to be led, starts even very early in our childhood. We might not have been fully aware of what it meant. For example when I studied in the school I had certain boys and girls leading me and I was subdued by them in different dimensions of life. While I was in my 3rd grade there was a big gang behind me always and those who belong to this gang call ourselves the village heroes because under my direction the whole team frequently staged many dramas around my village. At the same time I belonged to another gang and followed one of the boys as my leader and guide in all educational issues. This is how every one of us are brought up and grown to this level. No one in the world is to be solely a leader and only a follower. Both qualities are intertwined to make a human baby into a full-grown adult.

Jesus, the Guru of my Realreligion, though he was originally the Shepherd, he behaved like a Lamb staying inside my humanfold as one like me, even like a voiceless one to be taken to the slaughterhouse. In order to offer me abundant life, a qualitylife, he has to be in that condition, as he declared: *"I came that they may have life, and have it abundantly and for that I will lay down my life for the sheep."*

I love to imitate him in his sacrificial, self-effacing service. Peter writes: *For to this you have been called, because Christ also suffered for you, leaving you an example that you should follow in his steps.* I know to be a humble and serviceable shepherd and leader is not to live in a cozy safety-net of life. The abundance and qualitylife that Jesus refers to is not something showered like 'miraculous manna' from the sky. It is something made possible by every Christ present inside the fold. Every sheep that is inside the fold acts like their Shepherd, as gate, as shepherd as protector, as guide, as provider, as sharer, above all, as a voiceless lamb that is even taken to slaughterhouse for the sake of caring and saving and uplifting the other weak sheep and lambs inside the fold.

We are born to be leaders

Realreligion's positive belief is that humans are by birth leaders. We are told that we the humans were made in the image of God. We would, then, expect to have His power also. Of course we have power. We truly possess great powers of the mind—we can invent, create, and manipulate the things of the universe. We have powers of personality, and also physical powers. Scriptures proclaim God has granted humans great authority, power and glory. God bestowed human race a power of domineering the whole universe: *"God blessed them and God said to them: Be fertile and multiply; fill the earth and subdue it. Have dominion over the fish of the sea, the birds of the air, and all the living things that crawl on the earth."* (Gen. 1:28) Admiring at the love of God for his humans Psalmist sings to the Creator: *"You have made him little less than a god, crowned him with glory and honor. You have given him rule over the works of your hands, put all things at his feet."* (Ps. 8: 6-7)

The Book of Sirach expounds about it little more: *"God granted them authority over everything on earth. He endowed them with strength like his own, and made them in his image. He put fear of them in all flesh, and gave them dominion over beasts and birds. Discernment, tongues, and eyes, ears, and a mind for thinking he gave them. With knowledge and understanding he filled them; good and evil he showed them."* (Sir. 17: 2-7) Ecclesiastes goes as far as to say *"Thou hast put eternity into man's heart."* Proverbs 4:23 says that the very issues of life flow from the depth of humanness. We call them the moral issues, such as love, goodness, righteousness, holiness and truth. They are the issues which greatly affect the life of the world.

We too are born-again leaders

Besides getting leadership from our Creator, through the redemptive work of God the Son, we have received a lion's share of divine power and authority. Paul explains very logically our present power-filled status after we have been baptized in Christ and empowered by Holy Spirit: *"For those who are led by the Spirit of God are children of God. For, you did not receive a spirit of slavery to fall back into fear, but you received a spirit of adoption, through which we cry, "Abba, Father!" The Spirit itself bears witness with our spirit that we are children of God, and if children, then heirs, heirs of God and joint heirs with Christ, if only we suffer with him so that we may also be glorified with him."* (Rom. 8: 14-17) He too enlists the elements of power and authority we have received by this divine adoption: *"We know that all things work for good for those who love God, who are called according to his purpose. For those he foreknew he also predestined to be conformed to the image of his Son, so that he might be the firstborn among many brothers. And those he predestined he also called; and those he called he also justified; and those he justified he also glorified."* (Rom. 8: 28-30) Paul is very firm in his belief that our ultimate victory is certain in Christ: *"What will separate us from the love of Christ? Will anguish, or distress, or persecution, or famine, or nakedness, or peril, or the sword? . . . No, in all these things we conquer overwhelmingly through him who loved us."* (Rom. 8: 35-37)

As a confirmation of what Paul believes, Peter writes about our new identity as baptized Christians: *"You are a chosen race, a royal priesthood, a holy nation, a people of his own, so that you may announce the praises of him who called you out of darkness into his wonderful light."* (1Pet. 2: 9) John in his visions he sees and hears about our remarkable regal power shared by Christ: *"Blessed and holy is the one who shares in the first resurrection. The second death has no power over these; they will be priests of God and of Christ, and they will reign with him for [the] thousand years."* (Rev. 20: 6) *"Jesus Christ, who is the ruler of the kings of the earth, loves us and freed us from our sins by his own blood, and made us a royal nation of priests in the service of his God."* (Rev. 1: 5-6)

Gospel Writers highlight relentlessly about the truth that Jesus directly handed over to his disciples the power and authority of: casting out evils, healing the sick and preaching his values; *"Then he called his twelve disciples together, and gave them power and authority over all devils, and to cure diseases"* (Lk. 9:1; Matt. 10:1; Matt. 10:7-8); of governing and guiding others; *"I will give you the keys to the kingdom of heaven. Whatever you bind on earth shall be bound in heaven; and whatever you loose on earth shall be loosed in heaven"* (Matt. 16: 19); and of preaching and teaching God's words. *"All power in heaven and on earth has been given to me. Go, therefore, and make disciples of all nations, baptizing them in the name of the Father, and of the Son, and of the Holy Spirit, teaching them to observe all that I have commanded you."* (Matt. 28: 18-20) Until you are clothed with power from on high." Jesus shared both his power and authority: Power is from on High will be given to every disciple to be filled within. They have only authority exteriorly to preach and witness. (Lk. 24)

My Realreligion acknowledges this mystery of God's power and authority-sharing with humans as we found pervasively in most of II Vat Council's Documents. Describing the Church as a sheepfold of God, the Council teaches that it is *continuously led and nourished by Christ Himself, the Good Shepherd and the Prince of the shepherds.* (LG 6) Inside that Christ's sheepfold, we are again and again confirmed in many documents of the Council that, *"there is a diversity of ministry but a oneness of mission. Christ conferred on the Apostles and their successors the duty of teaching, sanctifying, and ruling in His name and power. But the laity likewise share in the priestly, prophetic, and royal office of Christ and therefore have their own share in the mission of the whole people of God in the Church and in the world."* (AA 3) Therefore the Council encourages all members of the Church to be actively exercising their power-filled roles for Church growth. *". . . they are called upon, as living members, to expend all their energy for the growth of the Church and its continuous sanctification, since this very energy is a gift of the Creator and a blessing of the Redeemer.*" (LG 33)

As a member of Realreligion I fully believe that I am not merely a subject in God's Kingdom; I am also one of his partners in the making, in the bringing about of his Kingdom. As I read in NT Books, while Jesus Christ is the head, the entire Realreligion-Church is his body. That means that, as one of the members of his body I share in his kingly power and priesthood and all the responsibilities that brings! This is the power of Jesus my Lord, his power to generate life in others. I firmly hold that all members of Realreligion are kings and queens because they are his people, kith and kin, and because they are chosen and anointed by him.

The wonder of wonders in my Realreligion is the belief that my Super Leader has been benign to me and to all the members of my Realreligion, promising that he would share some of his power and authority with us. Jesus promised to His disciples before He ascended into heaven: "*You will receive power when the Holy Spirit comes upon you and you will be my witnesses . . .*" (Acts1:8) It is historical truth that once I start abiding in the risen Jesus his power enters and dwells in me. I become powerful within. It is from there you get that conviction, determination, and authority. This is what happened in the lives of Jesus' disciples after their encounter with Jesus Alive. The book of Acts describes an event when they were exposed to the reality of life: a life that is haunted by struggles between human authority and divine one; between truth and lie; between pride and innocence; between flesh and Spirit. These disciples had a strong determination and conviction. When they were interrogated, the high priest was stunned to see their determination and stubbornness. The disciples answered to their human authorities this way: "*Better for us to obey God than men!*" (Acts 5: 29) There are so many incidents like the above depicted in the Bible especially in the Acts of the Apostles that describe the strange and peculiar authority with which Jesus' disciples conducted themselves in critical situations.

As my Realreligion instructs me, I can testify this: The risen Jesus, once he befriends me, grants his Spirit who starts integrating Himself with my human spirit and simultaneously my whole life-perspective, world-view, and attitude change. I begin to live in a total different realm of life. People around me watch and find out certain strangeness about my behavior. They may have different names or labels to call me: Crazy, fool, naive, stubborn, hardheaded and so on. This is because they find certain peculiarity in my conduct. One of those strange but very explicit and disturbing manners, found in me is my way of walking through life's events with certain tenacious authority. Realreligion's members know very well what is left to their fragile human ability is to prove their worth to be victorious kings and queens in his kingdom. They too are well aware of the fact that it is possible not by their wealth, IQ, glamour, power and other human abilities but only by following Jesus' command of love.

The misuses of Leadership in Reelreligion

At our baptismal anointing, we were initiated into the saving mysteries of Jesus who conquered his life and others' too by his humbleness, obedience and service. He wanted us to manage his godly power shared with us very carefully and thus we are to live and serve and die accordingly. We all must firmly believe except the power that is shared by Jesus with us other powers, such as natural intelligence, bodily valor, and creative talents, are many times turn out to be shallow, risky and dangerous. Unfortunately even this godly power is not properly handled by most of us.

It is a common fact that the immature humans misuse and abuse their powers, including religious and spiritual power. As Lord Acton states that *"Power corrupts, and absolute power corrupts absolutely."* In 1771, Edmund Burke shared a similar sentiment: "The greater the power, the more dangerous the abuse." A year earlier, in 1770, William Pitt had pointed out that "unlimited power is apt to corrupt the minds of those who possess it." Specifically, on the above-mentioned two creative and redemptive grounds everyone, who claims to be Jesus' disciple, possesses certain power of leadership, a power to rule, to control, to form, to train, to guide and if needed, to share one's life. However I know that throughout the history of the church there have been persons, who practice Reelreligion and whom I call the 'control freaks', misusing this heavenly power and right of truth in many disgraceful ways.

This is why, late Pope John Paul II, in one of his encyclical letters, asked all church-members to examine our conscience and repent our mistakes in this regard. In the name of misinterpreted-truth and due to over-enthusiasm towards discipline and justice, many people holding authority have used coercion, intolerance and even violence against other church and other religious members. They have been, like some Pharisees of Jesus' time, feeling more self-righteous, thinking they were closer to God than others whom they discriminated and hated as Devil's children. These control freaks of Reelreligion always think that they are the only persons who have the whole truth and others are progeny of the lie.

Realreligion's view of leadership

Soon after my ordination when I was doing my pastoral ministry as an associate with a senior pastor in a city parish I had lots of debates with him about many church issues in the light of Vatican II. One among them was about leadership. At one time while I was highlighting the importance of democratic manner of administering in the parish my pastor was very adamant insisting about a traditional view about it. He nailed his approach on my head this way: "Father, you should never forget that our Church is neither democracy nor aristocracy but theocracy". Though I was at that time little upset about the term he used, later he helped me to understand the true meaning of theocracy adopted by Jesus.

Members of Realreligion espouse the exact view of the risen Jesus about Leadership. Amazingly Jesus' view of leadership is very different from that of humans. The risen Jesus, who was elevated by the heavenly Father to the most supreme authority of ruling the entire universe, indicated very splendidly what kind of leadership he would hold. Being asked by Pilate whether he was a king, Jesus, never minding about any name others might attribute to him, categorically attested what kind of leadership he would be holding. John quotes him: *"My kingdom does not belong to this world. If my kingdom did belong to this world, my attendants [would] be fighting to keep me from being handed over to the Jews. But as it is, my kingdom is not here . . . You say I am a king. For this I was born and for this I came into the world, to testify to the truth. Everyone who belongs to the truth listens to my voice."* (Jn. 18: 36-37) Jesus' claim of his leadership therefore is spiritually-powered one and focused on spiritual realm of human life and his main role as Leader is nothing but to testify to the Truth.

Jesus' perspective on his leadership is another source of shock to humans. He emphasized that his style of authority and leadership is totally being always humble and serviceable. He was a humble and simple person. *". . . I am meek and humble of heart . . ."* (Matt. 11: 29) He too preferred only such persons to share his leadership. *"Whoever humbles himself like this child is the greatest in the kingdom of heaven."* (Matt. 18: 4) He considered himself as God's servant: *"The Son of Man did not come to be served but to serve and to give his life as a ransom for many."* (Matt. 20: 28) And his delegates too were directed to be so in their lives: *". . . whoever wishes to be great among you shall be your servant; whoever wishes to be first among you shall be your slave."* (Matt. 20: 26-27)

Psychologically speaking, every human being craves for both to control and to submit. It may sound glitch; but it is the fact of our life. We have an innate desire both to subdue others and to surrender ourselves to others, to be master and slave as well. Almost all parents, for example, think that their children are their own products and properties and therefore they like their kids being obedient to them and to contact them for any advice and guidance as their masters. Nonetheless what is happening is, many a time, parents become slavish in a way and subservient to their love, cry, and their pains. Every new-born baby reigns supreme over our time, privacy, leisure and self—esteem by her or his continued cry and he/she behaves adamant to turn our attention on him or her and make us fulfill her or his desires. Parents, if they are genuine parents, feel so happy to subdue themselves to their child and find certain pleasure in it, otherwise they feel a prick of conscience if they have not done so. Like this, there are thousand and one examples to show the human nature's tendency to be slave to others.

The humans therefore always need masters, leaders and superiors to subdue them and under whom they can be secure and happy, and keep up their mental and psychological equilibrium in their life. This is why, as we read in the Bible, the kingship came into existence. The 1st Book of Samuel, chapter 8 gives us an account of how the people demanded for a king, how God considerately explained to them the dangerous consequences that would follow the erection of a king in their midst, and how people were obstinate in their demand and how finally God yielded to their request.

Even now, such a demand still exists, despite the death of traditional value of kingship and so on. The followers of Reelreligion do not obey the Values and Ideas about God. Unfortunately these people choose wrong leaders and become wrong leaders too in their turn. The leaders whom they follow many times are not just persons. Many of them are led by traditions; by customs, by codes, and by habits. Almost all pastors and ministers encounter such traditions-led group of friends in their ministries. Whenever they go to a new parish and plan to introduce something that can bring renewal in that parish invariably they would hear immediate outcry from them: 'Father! For many years we have been doing this way. This is the best way. No need of new things.' Thus customs and traditions stand as their leaders. Many sophisticated modern people are slaves to other godly symbols called Technology and Science; they may not belief the Infallibility of the Pope, but they trust the infallibility of the Journalism through Mass Media such as Printed news and Broadcastings and pay their obeisance to them not having any doubt whatsoever on.

Our balanced subjection to human leaders

God of Realreligion appreciates our innate of subduing to the others as leaders and at the same time he indicates to us what kind of leadership we should bow down to. All the things that are substituting God and Christ are either temporary, or intermediary or sometimes injurious to our call to eternal destiny; Christ has been installed by God as the leader of the whole world; undoubtedly he has been rewarded with a powerful dominion, glory and kingship from his Father the Almighty. His leadership is eternal, his dominion is an everlasting dominion that will not be taken away; his kingship shall not be destroyed.

However we should be aware of the fact that while he was walking in Palestine as human as we are, namely as Jesus of Nazareth he never called himself as king. He never liked to be made king. This was shown in many events in his life: After his miraculous act of multiplying 5 loaves and feeding more than 5000 people the beneficiaries *wanted to make him king but he denied and disappeared from their sight.* When Pilate asked him whether he was the king Jesus answered, *"My kingdom does not belong to this world. If my kingdom did belong to this world, my attendants would be fighting to keep me from being handed over to the Jews. But as it is, my kingdom is not here."* Pilate, out of fear and with his own political and career interests in mind, had Jesus flogged. Soldiers mockingly put a crown of thorns on his head and jeeringly bowed to the "King of the Jews". Then Jesus was brought out by Pilate. "Ecce homo", he said to the crowds'. In this piteous state, Jesus was rejected in favor of a murderous gangster.

Practitioners of Reelreligion misuse their religion as their coverup, to conquer others by their anger, by their hate, by their terrorism, by their harsh words, by their gossips, by their coldness, by their prejudices, by their superiority complex and so on. But in Realreligion the followers of Jesus, just like him, never let those grumpy personalities win them over. They have read many events in Jesus' life that inspire them. For example, when Peter took him beside and told him not to go to Jerusalem with all his friendly human love or affection Jesus never yielded to be conquered; at the end of his life the rulers, the bystanders, even one of the thieves shouting at Jesus, mocked him, jeered at him and asked him, 'if you are king of the Jews, save yourself'; but Jesus never offered himself as a victim to them.

At the same time Realreligion's members always conquer others as Jesus did. Their mode of winning others is not by any coercion or outward exploitation with trickeries or arms. They conquer others by their love, by their self-sacrifice and even by their death. *"I have come that they may have life and have it in greater abundance."* To give them that life, he sacrificed his own. His power is precisely in his ability to let go of his own life for the sake of others. But he did it by shedding his blood; by forgiving others; by patient endurance; by humble and simple life; by poverty; by impudent prayer; and by sacrificial love. In the shallowness of his ordinary life engagements he was extraordinary, self-controlled, disciplined, patiently enduring, forgiving, and loving.

There was vast difference between how Jesus viewed leadership and what humans think of it: Jesus' leadership over his followers was not an imposed dominion but a warm welcome extended to one who was loved and admired as king of all hearts; Jesus was a king like no other, in that he did not have a scepter but he did have a towel with which he washed his disciples' feet. Jesus had no standing army, but he did have followers. He did not sit on a throne but on the back of a donkey. He wore no crown of gold, but one of thorns. He did not use his authority to take life but to give it. He did not set boundaries or entertain only the nobility; he welcomed prostitutes, tax collectors, foreigners and thieves. He did not exploit people but spoke sympathetically of widows, prodigals, Samaritans and the poor. He did not wield the sword of punishment but extended mercy and forgiveness. He did not coerce, he invited. Rather than tax his subjects to pay the debts of his monarchy, he laid down his own life so that the "debt" of human sin would be forgiven. He did not come to conquer but to save.

That was the strategy of Jesus to conquer the entire universe. He made so many kings and queens in the past prostrate before and declare, *'you the Galilean, you conquered me.'* He had conquered millions of people in history, who for his cause left everything and followed him. These are none other than the members of Realreligion.

My Realreligion continues to believe that this unthinkable secret of power and authority holds well even this day in the lives Jesus' true disciples. The real power and real authority are not in positions or titles but in the inner strength of the person. Jesus' power and authority is not dominating but enabling and empowering. Only the weak feel the need to dominate. In this vein, I am proud to testify the greatest impact I inherited from a charitable agency *'Green Cross Ministries Inc.'*, working in the State of Oklahoma. I am so much inspired and energized by the same agency's vision and mission statement that spells out why and how a disciple of Jesus should use his/her power and authority if he/she has taken a leadership in Realreligion: *I was empowered . . . so I want to empower others; I was helped . . . so I want to help others; I have received . . . so I want to give others; I was served . . . so I want to serve others; I was cared for . . . so I want to care others.*

Jesus had his own way of making himself a leader. He became winner, victor and ever-conquering king not as our human political and religious leaders did and do. He never used diplomacy or people-pleasing spotlights appearances and performances. Rather, he does not control by domination but by love, not to be stuck with the devotees and righteous people but to search out the lost ones like the lost sheep and the lost coin. Christ is not King of diamonds desirous of wealth, glory and glamour but a King of love and service. He is a different Leader because of what he did for us.

The right way to covet and uphold the leadership

Giving some tips for how to earn authority one secular writer lists out: Serving others; allowing one self to be influenced by others; building healthy relationships; persuading others rationally; inspiring others on the way you want them to travel with you; and being a role model to others.

Jesus, a Jewish from Nazareth, son of a carpenter, became king not by any political maneuvering, lobbying, shrewd diplomacy or purchasing people with unethical and undoable promises which simply lies born out of lies. Rather here is the road to his incredible Leadership mapped out by Paul in his Letter to Philippians (Phi. 2: 6-10). Paul recognizes Jesus' astounding Leadership held now: *"God greatly exalted him and bestowed on him the name that is above every name, that at the name of Jesus every knee should bend, of those in heaven and on earth and under the earth."* He also portrays the steps by which he was elevated to this unthinkable supremacy:

Step-1: "Though he was in the form of God, did not regard equality with God something to be grasped.

Step-2: Rather, he emptied himself,

Step-3: Taking the form of a slave, coming in human likeness; and found human in appearance.

Step-4: He humbled himself, becoming obedient to death, even death on a cross.

Step-5: He behaved truthful and with integrity to God and to people, accepting who really he was and what kind of job description he was entrusted with and fulfilling those jobs perfectly: Jesus' first job was to testify to the truth. *"For this I was born and for this I came into the world, to testify to the truth."* His second job was to establish and run only a spiritual kingdom and not worldly or earthly one. And the third job was to die for witnessing to this Truth. *Jesus Christ is the faithful witness, the firstborn of the dead.* The fourth job was to free us from our sins and make all of us naturalized as his citizens: *"He has freed us from our sins by his blood, and he has made us into a kingdom, priests for his God and Father."*

Nothing he endured was wasted; all were resourceful and very productive. All the wages he got at every step of his life though it was very short period were not lost. He gave his very life-we got his life back; he gave out his breath-we were filled with his spirit; he was buried-we with him rise up. He was a slave before God for our sake-then we with him became kings and queens in his kingdom.

I clearly understood in my middle age how I should be truthful to my godly power. One of my spiritual mentors, a religious sister, taught me this: My power must come out of my obedient relatedness to three outside authorities: Authority of God's Words; Authority of the Church; and Authority of the Spirit of Charity. However much I may be intelligent, educated, well-read and talented, I know my weakness: I will waste or misuse or abuse all my power as individual unless I obey to these three authorities. The words authority and obedience may sound for some irritating. But this is the way Jesus kept himself normal and genuine despite the unthinkable power and authority he possessed within.

My Authority from within or without?

Realreligion's members are not freedom-freaks to tell that they don't need any control and not listening to others especially to the church, the community of believers. At the same time they are cautious in what spirit the orders and promulgations from their leaders are proclaimed. They totally believe the same Spirit of the Lord does work within them-groaning and mourning in prayer; reasoning out in debatable issues; and enlightening the mind for right judgment; and surely bending the will to surrender to the Truth, nothing but the Christ's Truth.

Humans live and work with two kinds of authority: *functional and personal.* Functional authority is authority that is built into particular jobs or functions. For example, Parents, teachers, CEOs, supervisors, pastors, and so on. All of us have functional authority that works from the outside. This authority comes out of election, selection, promotion, appointment, and ordination conferred by community or society. This authority can be bought and sold at our own as well as others' expenses. It can be denied, it can be coveted, or it can be misused or abused. Most of us think that is the only authority we can have; and most of the time we are satisfied with it or many times we regret over it. There is another kind of authority. It is called 'personal authority'. Personal authority is the power to choose and be responsible for our own feelings, behavior, needs, and dreams. Personal authority works from the inside. It is this personal authority which, as my Realreligion upholds, the risen Jesus imparts within every one's inner sanctuary. At every time I deploy my authority in the service of others, I am reminded of Peter's advice: *"As each one has received a gift, use it to serve one another as good stewards of God's varied grace. Whoever preaches, let it be with the words of God; whoever serves, let it be with the strength that God supplies."* (1 Peter 4: 10-11)

Personal Authority with love and service

My friends in Reelreligion, on the contrary, misuse such personal authority due to their adherence to various ideologies and isms pervading today's human race. I saw with my own eyes in a central prison India a man on death roll smiling and so happy about his killing his own mother and awaiting eagerly his death. When I told him what he did was a sin against God. But he retorted saying, "Father, I did a very good thing. I was told by God to kill my mom." What a strange god he worshipped! It is not just one case. There are now thousands of groups today in this modern world who are craving to murder people, and annihilate certain portion of the human race by bombs and machine guns. They are totally abusing their personal authority received from God. They say it is the will of their God and even justify their bloody actions by certain verses from their own Scriptures.

This sort of hideous perversion can be traced out over the centuries: Those holy bloody wars in the middle ages; those compulsory conversions from one religion to the other; those wars of crazy Hitlers and Stalins; those Gurus and Masters of different cults like Dr. Jones; those modern suicide cults and Satanic religions; and the current unholy massacres done by religious terrorists. These are all in the name of God; and in the name of personal authority! Much worse is happening even in the families of reelreligion-followers. Husband one day comes to his wife and tells, *Honey, I will kill you if you go to that church.* Another night wife tells her husband, *Jesus tells me I have to do His works; I leave you; if you want to follow me with our children, OK. Otherwise let us divorce. That is what the Lord wants me now.* Is it the true personal authority coming from God?

The only way to find out whether our personal authority emerges from the risen Jesus is to check sincerely 'yes' to Jesus' perennial question: *'Do you love me more than these?'* (Jn. 21: 15) Jesus has been very candid in this matter. He has told us that our authority must start with love and end with service. Love and service are the only criterion with which we can measure the source of personal authority. In my daily life one of my religious act is to examine my actions, engagements, plans, projects and so on all in the name of God, Jesus, and religion will fall short of their credibility. I, as a faithful member of Realreligion, frequently ensure whether my own authority-based actions are emerging out of love for Jesus alive and whether they are producing services to the others and the universe.

Requirement for leadership in Realreligion

My Realreligion proclaims that all authorities in the world are from God. Therefore whether I like them or not I should obey them as if I obey God. It may sound horrible as in olden days it was called as 'blind obedience.' However Jesus pointed out to me this very hard truth when Pilate compelled Jesus to speak pointing out his governing power. *So Pilate said to him, "Do you not speak to me? Do you not know that I have power to release you and I have power to crucify you?" Jesus answered him, "You would have no power over me if it had not been given to you from above."* (Jn. 19: 10-11) Peter the first Pope writes: *"Be subject to every human institution for the Lord's sake, whether it be to the king as supreme or to governors as sent by him for the punishment of evildoers and the approval of those who do good."* (1Pet. 2: 13-14) Paul recommends that I should *'be under the control of magistrates and authorities, to be obedient and to be open to every good enterprise.'* (Titus 3: 1) He too gives the reason for it: *"Let every person be subordinate to the higher authorities, for there is no authority except from God, and those that exist have been established by God."* (Rom. 13: 1) While such powerful position is granted by the God Supreme to all authorities, God also demands from them higher responsible, holy, and morally-bound character, attitude and personality in them.

This is more applicable to my authorities in the Church. My Guru in this regard is seen very careful and picky about initiating the authoritative system in his Church. There are two beautiful narrations in the NT that depict the drama of investiture of authority on Peter, the first of his choice. From the Gospels of Matthew and John we come to a deep realization of two requirements for being chosen or ordained for sharing Jesus' leadership: Faith and Love. In the Gospel of Matthew (16: 13-19), we read Jesus, by giving Peter the keys to the kingdom of heaven, entrusting him with the first dimension of his power and authority of ruling and governing his sheep. For such sharing we see Jesus demanding from Peter an indomitable personal faith toward Him. *"Peter, who do you say that I am?* Peter responds immediately *"You are the Messiah, the Son of the living God."* John, in his Gospel (21: 15-18) indicates that Jesus hands over to Peter the second dimension of Jesus' Leadership, namely of caretaking. For this Jesus requires from Peter a personal and total love for him. Jesus asks Peter three times, *'do you love me more than these?'* And Peter responds *'Lord, you know that I love you.'*

The members of Realreligion believe that this twofold demand of Jesus is directed not only to Peter or the Apostles but to all his disciples who esteem every action of theirs in this world as the vocation or profession or job entrusted to them from Jesus. This is totally true in their leadership and engagement of feeding, nourishing and tending the needy people in and around their lives. This may be in various manners: As parents and guardians, they may tend and feed their children and grandchildren; as lovers and spouses and friends, they may tend and feed their life-partners or friends with their love and concern; anything they perform toward their customers as their duty in the office, business or at home or even as volunteers in the community and parish is simply because of the power and authority Jesus has entrusted to them to feed and tend others. They too know well such attitude and value of their lives is impossible to be upheld consistently unless and until they respond sincerely to Jesus' two demanding questions as he asked from Peter: *"Who do you personally say that I am?"* and *"Do you love me personally and totally more than others?"* They try their best in answering to Jesus' questions positively in prayer and live up to it in daily chores. Because of such approach when they are given or delegated certain power and authority to take care of the weaklings, needy and vulnerable in the society through election, selection, or promotion, they don't become the cause and source of political infights; nor is there any abuse and misuse of their power among them. There does not exist any dangerous powerplay.

Everyone in the Church has been vested with some kind of control and power over certain people. Each one like me becomes authorized in certain things of life. Parents have got authority and control over their children; teachers over their students; political leaders and lawmakers over their citizens; and religious leaders, bishops, priests, and superiors, over their communities. If I, who have such privilege of power and authority, lose sight of the demands and conditions of Jesus namely, the personal faith in Jesus and pure and sincere love for Jesus who expects me to follow his leadership policy of humility, self-discipline, of service and sacrifice I will fail myself and fail others too.

On the contrary, the Reelreligion-followers handle such power and authority and leadership toward others in a very natural way or as taking it for granted attitude. Church's and Religions' history proves that there have been always these sorts of people using their leadership and authority mere naturally. For example, in Acts we come across one group of Roman and Jewish leaders misusing their authority. The captain and court officers of Roman curia and the high priest and his Sanhedrin abused their authority and power because they literally behaved in their natural way; their pride, jealousy and even political fear marooned their spiritual conscience and tried their best to annihilate Jesus' Way of Religion. These kinds of perverted leaders can be found in many families, neighborhoods, towns and cities, in associations, in the parishes and very sad to say, even in the campus of church leaders. I know how many people climbing up to the Church's high position by maneuvering with honey-quoting lips-service or exploiting the weakness of other people. Once they grab the pedestal and sitting on the throne of leadership they misuse or abuse their authority and power and live a self-indulging life and never care for other people's needs; they totally forget the orientation of their power and authority is solely to feed the lamb and tend the sheep. The most abominable scenario is this sort of misuse and abuse of God-given power and authority is found in church circle. It exists at the top level as well as among the ordinary parish communities.

This critical situation of the modern Church urged Pope Francis preaching aloud in many of his extempore talks with leaders of the Church. One of Pope's informal addresses to the pontifical representatives was titled by Vatican Information Service (June 21, 2013) as *"We need Pastors and not princes in episcopacy."* Pope was describing the life of pastors of the Church as a "nomadic" one and he warned them against the 'spiritual worldliness' the expression coined by Henri de Lubac, which means, "Giving in to the spirit of the world, which leads one to act for personal realization and not for the glory of God in that kind of 'bourgeoisie of spirit and life' that urges one to get comfortable, to seek a calm and easy life." Pope continued to advise the Nuncios that in their episcopal appointments they should *"be attentive that the candidates are Pastors who are close to the people, fathers and brothers; that they are gentle, patient, and merciful; that they love poverty, interior poverty as freedom for the Lord and exterior poverty as simplicity and austerity of life; that they aren't ambitious.'*

Pope Francis has rightly hit the black spot inside the Church. Those who follow their Reelreligion in the Church are unworthy of holding the authority and leadership in God's kingdom. I mean they are stupid, fools, criminals and literally satanic ambassadors in Jesus' terminology who try to covet and still possess such power and control of the Church. It is very sad thing to note that those who hold tremendous power and authority over others, either they got it by lobbying, maneuvering, and politicking or they misuse their power to exploit others for their comfort and subliminal pleasures.

Realreligion's members are very much hurt by the hypocritical behavior of leaders. But they are content with the hope and faith in the marvelous deeds of God. Over the centuries these abusers of leadership in the Church have been terribly punished by the Lord. Mary our Mother has portrayed the end of these wicked leaders in her Magnificat Song: *'The Lord has shown the strength of his arm, and has scattered the proud in their conceit. He has cast down the mighty from their thrones and has lifted up the lowly.'* My Scriptures continuously warns such people: *"Because authority was given you by the Lord and sovereignty by the Most High, who shall probe your works and scrutinize your counsels!"* (Wis. 6: 3) In Scriptures I find God dethroning so many of his authority-representatives from their august positions and so I witness in human history to this day. He gives power to them as master of his household and once he is not pleased with their performance he tells them directly: *"I will thrust you from your office and pull you down from your station"* and throwing them out of their regal position offers it to another person. God acts always as the sole Master and Proprietor of human life-management. He is the prime CEO but plays a low key and invisible in all his undertakings.

Throughout my life I have been watching and witnessing many of my neighbors and friends of Reelreligion shining in public as very good politicians and diplomats, many as bishops, priests, preachers, teachers and elders; they would shine at the pulpits, podiums, and in front of the audience. But one day some of them will be cursed and humiliated by God. Surely all these spotlight people were once started well their carrier and they were counted as blessings from the Lord. But at one time they have turned out to be curses and contemptible in the eyes of God. How is it possible? In course of their lives God has been sidelined and their puffed self took their priority. They have created their petty kingdom where they are the kings and queens and form their own convenient laws for which they become strongly opinionated. Their unaccounted supremacy replaces God's own and they use even God's authority, his podium, his words, his signs and symbols for their glory and power. They forget there is only one Father, one Source, one Parent, one Master and one Superior and that is none other than God. All the titles and recognitions they covet out of their performances and accomplishments delete God's power and glory.

This is the reason why common folks are not very happy with authority today. They aren't keen on trusting someone's judgment just because of the role they have, whether it is the police, the medical professional, law maker, teacher or clergy—all have to justify themselves. People don't accept anything today just because they are told it. They want to know why. I suppose this is because those in authority have abused their power. They have taken short-cuts and caused hurt and harm. It is understandable that they resent those who have exercised their authority badly. They feel let down, they feel that their trust has been abused; and they feel they can't rely on anything anymore.

In my Realreligion I look to Jesus as my rolemodel for handling my authoritative roles in a fruitful way. I observe Jesus played the roles of preaching, teaching and leading. People, among whom he exercised those roles, never felt that they were let down. This is what I read in the Scriptures: *"The people were astonished at his teaching, for he taught them as one having authority and not as the scribes . . . All were amazed and asked one another, "What is this? A new teaching with authority. He commands even the unclean spirits and they obey him."* The authority Jesus carried with him put all the evil spirits down and even driven out. Besides, his authoritative words calmed the storm, healed the sick and consoled the afflicted. His authoritative words even today rule the world and all hearts of human beings. They give food for life, mind, heart and soul. They cast out demons. Every word he uttered will not leave the world without effecting what it intended for.

I used to wonder what made Jesus possess such incredible authority. A word that is uttered by any human being usually carries authority because of two important factors: a) who is speaking and b) what is being said. In the preaching of Jesus I witness what he said was always truthful; but more than that, who he was who spoke gave greater weight, credibility, and authority to his teaching. He used to preach 'forgive your enemies and love one another.' As he preached, on the cross he forgave those who tortured and killed him. He was always benign loving and understanding person to everyone including his enemies. I strive to exercise my leadership in the footsteps of my Guru Jesus. In this post-modern world I am blessed with three rolemodels for my ideal leadership: Blessed Pope John Paul II who has been a model for People-oriented Leadership; Pope Benedict XVI, a pattern for Status-ripped Leadership; and Pope Francis, an example for Humble and Simple Leadership

Chapter-14:
Money management in Realreligion

"Make friends with dishonest wealth, so that when it fails, you will be welcomed into eternal dwellings." (Lk. 16: 9)

The naked truth is no one can survive in this world without money in any form. Money is a means of bargaining for our livelihood among one another. It is only a symbol of what we give and what we get. It is a basic instrument for any human interaction. Most of the relationships, however intimate they may be, are built on this 'money'. It has played an important role in human life as a necessary medium of transaction and trade, especially for those living in a complex civilization. Primitive peoples were able to bargain through goods, for example, "I will give you two fish and you give me a basket of corn." Later days, when the transactions were going beyond the frontiers and boundaries of one's community and nationality, people began using small coins in gold, silver or bronze. Then came currency bills, and now those checks and magic plastic credit cards!

Therefore, money is as good as my body. It stands as a symbol of my own identity and worth. I labor and through the wages, my labor is acknowledged. Money by itself is not the root of all evil. However as any earthly man-made systems, money, the most important financial instrument in the hands of humans can become source of good or evil by how it is handled. Money can become an evil force first in its acquiring unjustly and unethically. It can be corrupted also by hoarding it like the stagnant water filled in a tank. But mostly it can be the greatest instrument of evil if it is used with bad intentions, disobeying God's commandments and making oneself as the one only proprietor of money.

In this money-deal my Realreligion does not ask me to hate the money; rather it warns me to be cautious in its appropriating, possessing and spending. When my Guru Jesus said, *'you cannot serve two masters: God and Mammon'*, he never intended to put a conflict between God and the money, rather he pointed out only to the war being waged between the Supreme God and the possessor of money. I am well convinced of this conclusion from the manner Jesus treated money and money-owners, or moneylenders in his life. Rather, as the correct translation of the Biblical verse *'Cupiditas est radix malorum'* indicates: "The love of money is the root of all evil."

Therefore Scriptures teach me how I should handle money with care both in acquiring and using it as well. Prophet Amos warned those rich people who acquire wealth by exploiting the innocent, the poor, and the ignorant of the society. (Amos 8: 4-7) Scriptures indicates: *"Those who trust in their riches will fall."* (Pro. 11: 28)

Jesus many times cautioned rich people who misused and abused their treasures and properties like the rich man in Jesus' parable (Lk.12: 16-21); he cursed them for their misusing riches. *"How hard it is for those who have wealth to enter the kingdom of God!"* (Lk.18: 24) *"Owe to you who are rich, for you have received your consolation."* (Lk.6: 24) Jesus too used many parables (Lk.16: 1-8); (Lk.16: 19-30) to teach me how to put my money in proper use.

Jesus in his life acquired money that was provided by his own friends out of their resources (Lk.8: 3); he also carefully used it for different purposes (Mt.17: 24-27). He was praising those who use their money, even be it a dime, for good causes and with a cheerful heart: *"She (widow) from her poverty, has contributed all she had, her whole livelihood."* (Mk.12: 41-44). His words to the young rich man clarified the excellent way of using money: *"If you wish to be perfect, go, sell what you have and give to the poor and you will have treasure in heaven."* (Mt.19: 16-30)

Jesus therefore wants me to acquire money in a right and just way, by my sweat and blood, by my toil and talents and by my sincere efforts and smartness. At the same time, he demands from me to start using this money in his ways, as his faithful stewards, because he is the giver and owner of all my resources. He advises me to use this money in order to make numerous friends so that they can assist me in reaching my Home sweet Home . . . Heaven. Money should help me not to buy people for my own gratification and self-glory but for the greater glory of God and for earning my reward in the Life to come after my death. What a wonderful gift of God is the money, which can be earned and used for my 'Eternal Salvation'!

Many friends in Reelreligion feel God expects them to hold an aversion for earthly and material things and possessions. But the God of my Realreligion does not. Undoubtedly the Scripture proclaims that *'vanity of vanities, all things are vanity'*, meaning all that I hold as my material possessions will be one day gone from me or I from them. Moreover, I know that money can buy me a good bed, but not a peaceful sleep. It will provide me with the best of cosmetics, but not the inner beauty of a loving heart. It can fill my life with amusements and pleasures, but never lead me to that inner peace and joy. I can go on enumerating like this, but the message is the same." Money or any other material possessions can never bring me lasting peace and security."

As Jesus said, my life does not consist of possessions. This does not mean my God desires me to be lazy, to be broke, to be pauper, and living on others' pockets. He commands me to work and labor and to earn my livelihood. He wills I should be blessed with his riches, with his talents, with his energy and power. He wants me to enjoy the rich harvest and fruits of the earth. He desires that I should be fertile and enlarge my territory.

Human history proves that my God blessed all his sons and daughters who were close to him with abundance of possessions. However his blessings were only to those who were entirely depending on his sovereignty and power. He ignored those who forgot him while they were in pursuit of material possessions. Nor was he near to them when they were filled with abundance as the rich fool in Jesus' parable. He blesses me with his riches and material goods to be always useful to me and others and not to be harmful if I keep myself accountable to three people: First to him because he is the source of everything I possess. As Job said, *'He gave them, and He can take them back.'* As the Psalmist asserts, *'He created us from dust, and one day He will say, 'return o, children of men.'* He is a God of love and benevolence. He can give anything that is good for my life.

Secondly, I have to be accountable to others. I am always inclined to think that whatever I earn through my work and labor is solely mine. That is not true in the eyes of my God. I should remember that I am being paid from the pockets of other people as my salary or remuneration. It comes from their sweat and blood, from their taxes, from their social security or social welfare checks, from their pensions and from their savings. Besides, every human being has the right to eat, to drink, to clothe, to rest and to be merry. If many poor and needy around me have not got that luxury, one of the reasons is many like me fail to disperse that money to them, rather we hide the possessions and store it in our barns with no conscience. Do you know the fact that 80% of earthly goods are possessed by only 20% of the population and 80% of humanity live by 20% of earthly resources? The only reason why God blesses those 20% of the humanity with riches is that they in turn bless the 80% with riches on his behalf. Thirdly, I am also accountable to myself. I am accountable to my welfare. With the money, with the talents, with the opportunities given to me, I should develop my physical and emotional life, plus my spiritual life. As I have to take care of my physical growth, I too must care my spiritual life. I am born for greater things. My home is not here. I am only on my journey to my Father's house.

It is said that an English nobleman of tremendous wealth gave his Jester a scepter, saying "Keep this scepter until you find a greater fool than yourself" The Jester laughingly accepted the scepter and used it on a festive occasions. One day, the nobleman lay dying. Calling the Jester to his beside, he said, "I am going on a long journey." "Where to?" asked the Jester. "I don't know", came the reply. "What provisions have you made for the trip?" the Jester asked. The noble man shrugged his shoulders. "None at all." "Then" said the Jester, "Take this" and placing the scepter in the nobleman's hands. He added," It belongs to you." You are a greater fool than I". My Realreligion tells me that my life in this world is a journey, not a home. The end of my journey is not death; death is only a golden key that opens the palace of eternity where God reigns. Material things are very useful in my life and so I am called not to become greedy and cling to my riches. By giving and by giving of myself I hoard treasures in heaven and become rich in the sight of God. This is what Jesus my Guru pointed out when he said, *"Sell your belongings and give alms. Provide moneybags for yourselves that do not wear out, an inexhaustible treasure in heaven that no thief can reach nor moth destroy. For where your treasure is, there also will your heart be."* Paul writes to Colossians, *"Seek what is above, where Christ is seated at the right hand of God. Think of what is above, not of what is on earth. When Christ your life appears, then you too will appear with him in glory."* I am accountable therefore to use all my possessions to inherit what I am born for.

Jesus, in his Sermon on the Mount, advised all his followers not to call anyone a fool. Because, he said, 'we will be in danger of the hell of fire.' However the inspired Book in many places calls certain people 'fools.' The fool in the Bible means someone in whom there may be intelligence but who is lacking in wisdom. Foolishness or folly is wisdom's opposite. It is usually some unwise action, but often it is actual wickedness. Proverbs says: *"Fools think their own ways are right." (12: 15) "The fool throws off restraint and is careless." (14: 16) "A fool takes no pleasure in understanding, but only in expressing personal opinion." (18: 2) The mouths of fools are their ruin, and their lips a snare to themselves." (18: 7) "Those who trust in their own wits are fools.* Very surprisingly in a Gospel story Jesus makes God call a rich man 'fool.' To think of somebody a fool and say it verbally expresses the hateful and destructive attitude of a person. So my Realreligion asks me to think seriously why God speaks that way to a particular person. Jesus uses this word to tell me how God rejects a person of that stature spoken in the parable who is always 'consumption mad,' pleasure-minded, self-indulgent, materialistic and selfish in his whole life. God himself gives reason why he calls the rich man a fool: *'You fool, this night your life will be demanded of you; and the things you have prepared, to whom will they belong?' Thus will it be for the one who stores up treasure for himself but is not rich in what matters to God."* (Lk. 12: 20-21)

The hero in this Gospel story behaves exactly the way the Bible describes about a fool. Though he procured and hoarded wealth and possessions by using his intelligence and industriousness he was not wise enough to hold them and use them in a right manner. To answer to the legitimate question of life, 'what should I do with all the material goods and wealth I possess?' the rich man makes a practical and conservative choice. In this he surely uses his intelligence. But God tells him that he should use his wisdom. Namely, he wants him to use the earthly things in God's standards and not in human standards. He should use them as a steward of God and the universe. He should use them with a sense of responsibility and accountability before God the Creator and Provider. He should be blessed by the blessings of God rather than being cursed by them.

I am practicing Realreligion that proposes the eternal truth that *I am only a pilgrim on my journey to the Ultimate. Earthly things to me are transient.* Therefore it instructs me that during this journey whatever blessings come to me in the form of material goods, properties, riches and possessions are to be handled with respect for future life and God. They should be used for higher purposes since, as Paul wrote, I am born for what is above and so I should seek what is above, think of what is above, not of what is on earth.

Jesus leaves to me to judge how I deal with material goods, especially money. My Realreligion reminds me daily about this responsibility and accountability and makes me ask myself: Am I a typical consumerist as the world calls me consumed madly by buying and selling? Do I keep God in my mind and heart in my dealings with these transient earthly goods? While I live healthy and sharp-minded and intelligent do I use my talent, time and treasure as steward of God for making others in the family and community happy and living? And I surrender willingly to my Realreligion's Voice.

I have been observing in my life in fellowship with my friends of Reelreligion that almost all of them have so many dreams such as: some day of being rich, to be able to buy all the things they would love to have, to be able to travel and to have no worries. They also hold in the depth of their hearts a belief, which they see contradicted every single day, that once they have financial security, all their problems will be solved: housing, children's education, cars and other desirable luxuries, retirement and old age. Wealth, it is believed, is a sign of "success" though it is not quite clear where the "success" really lies. It also brings "respect" and "status". For all my friends in Reelreligion these priorities often take precedence over their following of Christ.

In Realreligion however Jesus my Guru invites me to leave everything, even to deny myself and follow him and his values. It is important to emphasize that Jesus is not saying, *"You must give up all these things and lead a life of bleak misery for my sake."* On the contrary, he is offering a much more secure way to happiness and a life of real enjoyment than the way that most people insist on believing in even though it is seen to fail again and again. Against the greed that obsesses many people Jesus offers me an opposite alternative to security and happiness—sharing. Jesus suggests that what I am is of far greater importance than what I have. His suggestion sounds as counter-cultural because it clarifies so clearly that the true quality of life in the world is not to be found in money and material possessions. Jesus instructs me to avoid greed and to grow rich by the standards of God rather than by the standards of the world. Many of my contemporary friends in Realreligion explain this fact in some pithy words: 'You can't take it with you.' 'There is no sense being the richest man in the cemetery'. 'Do you own your stuff; or does your stuff own you?' 'Do I possess things, or do things possess me?' 'Life is not a destination in itself but a journey to God.'

It is human life's fact that I who have labored wisely, skillfully and successfully must leave what is my own to someone who has not toiled for it at all. David very well sings in 90th Psalm: *God makes an end of them in their sleep; the next morning they are like the changing grass, which at dawn springs up anew, but by evening wilts and fades.* Hence God instructs me to rely on his eternal love more than this fading and passing and transient material goods and riches. They too will become dangerous elements in life to live restless, arrogant, hard-headed and hard-hearted and sometimes instigate me to go for immoral and perverted fun and game. Many times those riches and goods which supposed to serve me as blessings turn out to be curses and misfortunes. This is what the Bible proclaims in a poetic way: *"For what profit comes to man from all the toil and anxiety of heart with which he has labored under the sun? All his days sorrow and grief are his occupation; even at night his mind is not at rest."*

This is why I am advised by Jesus that I must fully rely on God as my Master and Proprietor. He is the Owner and Source of all I acquire and possess. All the riches and material goods I get hold of through my intellectual caliber or physical strength or as family heritage must be esteemed as his blessings. I should be very clear about my identity: I am dust, at the same time born for heavenly things. There is life continued even after death. I am capable of living eternally with God if I uninterruptedly walk with God while I still alive in this world. Absolutely God wants me to procure material goods as much as I can but in His way and not in any immoral way. These material goods and riches can tempt me to go for wrong choices injurious to my relationship with God and my own neighbors. So I have to work and labor for acquiring wealth and other life's necessities and conveniences and luxuries in a way that Jesus proposes to me. Once I earn all these material goods and riches I will be again tempted to misuse or abuse them for my self-gratifications. Therefore God in Jesus expects me to manage them with prudence and discipline. This means I should never yield to the greed and avarice and become slaves to them. Jesus says therefore: *"Take care to guard against all greed, for though one may be rich, one's life does not consist of possessions."*

God also demands from me to, besides using properly for mine and family's basic needs, share whatever I have acquired with the community, especially to keep God's values stay alive in the world and to uplift the poor and the needy. Jesus commands me *to go and sell everything, to give to the poor and then follow him.* This means he asks me to be responsible ambassador on his behalf to share his blessings with others who are deprived of them or searching for such blessings.

In one of the Parish Sunday Bulletins I wrote an open letter to my parishioners. It was all about money-management. It was titled: *"Earn justly>>>Save wisely>>>Spend generously >>> Store heavenly!"* My Guru Jesus expects me to be good steward in managing my material goods. To be a good steward I must be honest, sincere and faithful in my responsibilities and accountabilities. I must be faithful in the effective management of my gifts. *"Any one who is trustworthy in little things is trust worthy in great; any one who is dishonest in little things is dishonest in great"* (Lk 16:10). God has given me many gifts and talents. These gifts are given so that I may use them for my own good and the good of others. *"If you are not trustworthy with what is not yours, who will give you what is your very own?"* (Lk 16:12). The possessions I have surely don't belong to me. They belong to God. What is my own, what fits me, what corresponds to my nature, is the salvation that God gives me in Jesus. Once, a prize was offered for the best essay on 'money'. The winner summed up the essay as follows: "money is a very useful commodity, and can purchase everything but happiness; it is a passport to everywhere but to heaven." However if it is handled properly itself becomes the ladder to heaven.

People of Reelreligion with no exception have been behaving dishonest regarding the handling of worldly things, properties and especially the money. From the moment they feel the need of money, the need of good name, the need of property, the need of all conveniences they start procuring them either dishonestly or unjustly. They, in their sleeping attitude of forgetting their boundaries and limitations, act as if everything is theirs and they are bold to say even to God, 'it's my money. I can do with it whatever I want.' A day comes. May be it is today or any day when their conscience acts as God. They are being caught redhanded. It demands them to act quickly for straightening out their sham. Jesus tells me, *"Make friends with dishonest wealth, so that when it fails, you will be welcomed into eternal dwellings."* These friends, I know, are the poor. Charity covers multitude of sins. I know this from what Christ says about his being the recipient of what I do for them. The poor, St. Augustine said, are, so to speak, my couriers and porters: They allow me to begin transferring my belongings now to the house that is being built for me in the hereafter.

I do know some of my Catholic friends always hold a grudge against their pastors who, talking about money and its need for today's church, pestering them by their begging to contribute more toward the church maintenance and other charities. However the pastors who are dedicated to their vocation love their dual role of not only interacting between God and their people as spiritual ambassadors but also connecting God and mammons as holy beggars. Mammons are the personification of richness and of those persons who covet wealth and possess it for their own self-gratification, incense them daily as their idols, hiding it from other people's eyes and die leaving everything for court cases.

Realreligion's God does not expect me to be broke, to be pauper, and living on others' pockets. He commands me to work and labor and to earn my livelihood. He wills I should be blessed with his riches, with his talents, with his energy and power. He wants me to enjoy the rich harvest and fruits of the earth. Historically and Scripturally He blessed all His sons and daughters who were close to Him with abundance of possessions. But one thing is sure. He blessed only those who were entirely depending on His Sovereignty and Power. He ignored those who forgot him while they were in pursuit of material possessions. He distanced himself from those, who disregarded his justice and love, when they were filled with abundance as the rich fool behaves in Jesus' parable. Therefore as Jesus has proclaimed, I try to be poor in spirit in order to be blessed with inheriting the kingdom of God.

Chapter-15:
Sex, Marriage and Family
in my Realreligion

"Father you have made the union of man and wife so holy a mystery that it symbolizes the marriage of Christ and his Church. Father, by your plan man and woman are united, and married life has been established as the one blessing that was not forfeited by original sin or washed away in the flood." (Wedding Blessing Prayer)

Sex & Marriage are God's supreme blessings

It is statistically true that one in every two marriages ends in divorce around the globe. People who follow their Reelreligion forget the true God and his instructions about sex, marriage and family; they conveniently either ignore or despise the Scriptures; they find no meaning in family system, which to their esteem is only a tribal instinct; and they become delinquent and lost their immune power to bear the hardships and hurdles of this married life.

According to Jesus, marriage is a consecrated life. In this married life a man is consecrated to God through his wife and a woman consecrated to him through her husband. There is no difference between the consecration of a celibate religious and that of a married couple. The widows and the other singles are consecrated to God through their current lifesituation. And so is every couple. I

239

read in Scriptures that matrimony is holy and therefore the sex also is holy, birth of a child is holy, the ritual of changing the diaper of a baby is holy, and so on and on. Holiness comes out of how the couples handle everything as consecrated to God who is all Truth, all freedom and all Love. My realreligion points at Jesus as a rolemodel for any consecrated life. He did not hesitate to humble himself and suffer even death for fulfilling the demands of such life. This is why Paul, one of my religion teachers writes to the couples *"to be subordinate to one another out of reverence for Christ. Wives should be subordinate to their husbands as to the Lord. For the husband is head of his wife just as Christ is head of the church, he himself the savior of the body. As the church is subordinate to Christ, so wives should be subordinate to their husbands in everything. Husbands, love your wives, even as Christ loved the church and handed himself over for her to sanctify her, cleansing her by the bath of water with the word, that he might present to himself the church in splendor, without spot or wrinkle or any such thing, that she might be holy and without blemish. So (also) husbands should love their wives as their own bodies. He who loves his wife loves himself. For no one hates his own flesh but rather nourishes and cherishes it, even as Christ does the church, because we are members of his body."*

Following thus the footsteps of our Lord, Realreligion's couples lead their married life in his humble and sacrificial consecration to God for others. People of Reelreligion prefer to get married in the church building just to use the Church as a backdrop for pictures; most of them really don't understand marriage as a sacrament any more than the people who bring their children to First Holy Communion but then don't return with them until Christmas understand what the Eucharist is all about.

My Realreligion wants its members to get married in the Church because marriage is the most important decision of any adults in their lives. It wants Jesus to be present in the way of a sacrament not just at the wedding rituals, but as it is celebrated daily. The sacrament of marriage is not just a prayer during the wedding, it is not just a blessing of a union; it is far more than this. The sacrament of matrimony is the union of God with people establishing a new unit of his Church. The sacrament of matrimony establishes the Christian home with Christ at the center. It is a fact of human life, as any other living creatures, to get connected to opposite sex, copulate together, and while enjoying the pleasure of sex they exchange and enhance their love and bring forth children. It is nothing extraordinary. God has already inserted it into his creative plan, the intelligent design. Jesus Christ came and revisited it and made it into a sacrament, which means as a consecrated act of humanity. As he wanted all his disciples should be consecrated to God, their human acts and performances in this world, he demanded married life too must be a consecrated life on earth as the religious and priests live with their vows. Remember the prayer we say during wedding ceremony: *"Father you have made the union of man and wife so holy a mystery that it symbolizes the marriage of Christ and his Church. Father, by your plan man and woman are united, and married life has been established as the one blessing that was not forfeited by original sin or washed away in the flood."*

Through the sacrament of marriage a man and a woman begin to live a consecrated life of sex, love, family and work. Couples make a triple permanent vow before God, not just a promise or a contractual agreement, but a lifelong commitment to each other to be together, to love, to serve and to sacrifice their very life till their death: Vow of Love, Vow of Togetherness and Love of Fidelity. By these vows to each other and God couples make their acts of marriage holy and sacred. Consecration means making something or somebody holy and sacred. That is what is done during the blessing of marriage in the Church.

As Bible says, 'it is not good for any human person to be alone. Every one of us is a social animal. So by nature we are born to be one in two, in other words to be together. Two to be one in a way is easy if one satisfies certain human thirst, hunger, like sexual gratification; if one becomes a guardian of the other for safety and security with one's savings, insurance policies, properties and other items that can make earthly life fulfilling. When all these are done well, the command of God that 'what God has joined together, no human being must separate' has no value there. The rib story enumerated in the Bible is not necessary for that period of glamorous days when two human beings, likeminded, saying always yes to the other, and gratifying each other's bodily, emotional and social needs. But that is not what we see in real life.

241

First of all human nature is never satisfied completely with what is available in this world. It is so limited, so temporary and so transient; nothing will offer a complete satisfaction. So in married life, where two persons want to live together and share the same bed and table together and rear up children and try to make a family of their own to become part of the human society, cannot satisfy each other in everything, at all times and forever. Therefore Church in the light of Christ invites a man and woman to consecrate their life of togetherness with willful vows to God the Almighty, who is the only satisfier of every human being. As Jesus himself consecrated his very life to his Father, every disciple of Jesus is called to consecrate his/her life to God as Jesus himself did.

While every disciple of Jesus is to be consecrated like Jesus to God for their life fulfillment, the act of marriage is in no way become an obstacle or barrier to it; rather it enhances each disciple's consecrated life as both assist each other in reaching the summit of consecration. When a couple begins to lead such consecrated life in marriage every thing they perform turns out to be holy and sacred: So the sex they enjoy is holy, birth of a child is holy, the ritual of changing the diaper of a baby is holy, and so on and on. Holiness comes out of how they handle everything as consecrated to God who is all Truth, all freedom and all Love. Submissiveness for example as Paul instructs will not be in any way a source of violence of individual freedom.

Many would agree that a love-oriented life in marriage may be easy to sing and to devise stories and fairytales but not possible in reality. Yes, as we read in Scriptures, by humans it is impossible but with God this is possible. Those who realize that marriage is the most important decision of their life come to Church so that Jesus the miracle-worker can be present in the way of a sacrament not just at their wedding, but as they celebrate their marriage throughout their lives. The sacrament of marriage is not just a prayer during the wedding, it is not just a blessing of a union; it is far more than this. The sacrament of matrimony is the union of God with people establishing a new unit of his Church. The sacrament of matrimony establishes the Christian home with Christ at the center. It is a fact of human life, as any other living creatures, to get connected to opposite sex, copulate together, and while enjoying the pleasure of sex they exchange and enhance their love and bring forth children. It is nothing extraordinary. God has already inserted it into his creative plan, the intelligent design.

However Jesus Christ came and revisited it and made it into a sacrament, which means as a consecrated act of humanity. As he wanted all his disciples should be consecrated to God, their human acts and performances in this world, he demanded married life must be a consecrated life on earth. My Realreligion upholds that as in any other consecrated lives in the Church, through the sacrament of marriage a man and a woman begin to live a consecrated life of sex, love, family and work; couples make a triple permanent vow before God, not just a promise or a contractual agreement, but a lifelong commitment to each other to be together, to love, to serve and to sacrifice their very life till their death: Vow of Love, Vow of Togetherness and Vow of Fidelity. By these vows to each other and to God the couple makes their acts of marriage holy and sacred. Consecration means making something or somebody holy and sacred. That is what is done during the blessing of marriage in the Church.

I heard one preacher describing the psychological difference existing in man and woman: Usually, he said, man expects from his wife three things: Food, Sex and Admiration. At the same time a woman longs for from her husband not only these three but also the fourth one: Emotional relationship. In order to attain their wishes, both man and woman play win-and-win game with each other. Even one of those needs are not fulfilled, there start confusion, doubts, misunderstanding, disobedience and separation. But once both satisfy each other's needs they continue to lead a successful marriage that includes: Surrender, commitment, cooperation, tolerance, and so on.

Most of the marriages do find such success for a limited time. But according to the revelation we heard from our Scriptures, an ideal marriage is not for few months or limited time. It is forever. It must be qualified with two important characteristics: Stability and fidelity. Made for each other for eternity, in life and death, in uphill and downhill, in joys and sorrows and in sickness and health never depart from each other. These characteristics are eternal, ideal, and divine. These will never be attained only by eating and drinking together, making sex, admiring each other and even by emotional relationship. This is possible only by divine help.

Realreligion is convinced that while the bride and bridegroom are at the altar of God, Jesus consecrates them and their marriage in truth, intercedes for them telling his Father *'Father bless them. They are your gift to me. I want them to enjoy the same glory as you shared with me.'* Jesus also wants them to be convinced of his inseparable connection with them and his deep involvement in their lifesituation. *"Who will condemn? It is Christ Jesus who died, rather, was raised, who also is at the right hand of God, who indeed intercedes for us. What will separate us from the love of Christ? Will anguish, or distress, or persecution, or famine, or nakedness, or peril, or the sword?"* (Rom. 8: 34-35) Jesus' main demand from the wedded couple is that each one takes the other lifepartner, not just for lust but for God's purpose and design to be accomplished through them in His kingdom. This is what every couple, especially the bridegroom, of Realreligion pray to God ceaselessly: *"You made Adam and you made his wife Eve to be his helper and support; and from these two the human race has come. You said, 'It is not good for the man to be alone; let us make him a helper like himself.' Now, not with lust, but with fidelity I take this kinswoman as my wife."* (Tobit 8: 6-7)

I hear many senior couples in Realreligion, who fortunately celebrate the silver or golden jubilee of their marriage, testifying to me of the main reason for how they have survived so long in married life. They approve that it is all because of God's grace. It has made one partner silent and deaf while the other behaved like non-stop CD player; it melted some one's heart to forgive and forget what another has done hurting; it helped them to give and take a balanced diet of food, sex, admiration and emotional relationship.

Once I asked an ideal elderly couple in a parish, who had lived together for 65 years in their married life: "What is the secret of your successful married life?" The lady was the first to answer: "We do not believe the old saying about marriage being a 50-50 proposition. Marriage is for us a 100 percent proposition; each one gives 100 percent to the other, without counting the cost and without demanding any return." Then I turned toward the husband. He said: "100 percent she is right. My married life was successful and happy because in our daily communication I always tell my wife: "You are 100 percent right. And I will never stop saying this. She is 100 percent right." This couple may be an exception while the majority may not agree that one single partner takes the predominant role of dictating the other all the time. There is a time for one to order and the other to salute and another time the reverse. This is the way of getting all the blessings in married life. Lack of that balanced yes-quality in a marriage brings failure and pains and ends in separation.

Family in its true identity

Family is the only place where human beings learn the reality of life. Research studies indicate majority of social criminals and imbalanced personalities come out of broken or abnormal family background. In Realreligion's families members get closer to the life's reality in a beautiful and fitting environment where not only certain things are taught but also many more things are caught. The environment of a God-blessed family is the fitting source of life-experiences. When a boy and a girl, with a limited and more theoretical and hearsay background of their own truths and facts about love, sex, marriage and family, begin to build up their own family, they start realizing that what they experience is not the same as they had once learned, heard, and discussed. They begin to see even the truths are not realties. So they get closer and closer to reality of life: what is sex, what is love, what is relationship, and what is family management. Added to it, if they are truly Christian and religious they face the lion in its den. They experience hardships, trials, disappointment, and unexpected problems as they lead a family crowded with children, relatives and friends. They suddenly feel the need of God, His power, His nearness, and prayer. They catch up gradually the meaning of faith, the importance and victory of prayer, and the vital role of God's commandments, sacraments, and moral code of conduct. As the modern saying goes, "If you are very religious before marriage, you are little bit crazy and mad, but if you are not religious after your marriage you are a typical and pitiable fool ever lived."

Once the same young couple experiences some hard realities of life and faith, in their normal family situation they start sharing it with one another. It happens consciously and unconsciously. When each member is exposed to every step of life, in its handling of sex, love, relationship, finance, childbirth, rearing of children, sickness, and other problems, every member of the family is affected and gets a load of joy, pain, suffering and hurts. Again here family offers an environment for sharing each one's experiences. Look at a child. By the age of four, according to the behavioral scientists, a child has developed one-half of his/her total mental capacity, and eighty percent by age eight. During these critical years, more is caught by the child than it taught to the child. This means children learn more from what we share with them in the family than what we say or teach in outside classes. We do not teach a child to love, rather we give love to the child and he/she reciprocates it.

In a healthy family environment both experiencing and sharing of life, love, and faith are intrinsically connected to sacrifice. To make even with husbands, most of the wives respectfully and willingly sacrifice their own tastes and even dreams. The same is true with the husbands. Parents naturally are prone to give, to bear all the pains of their children; they work hard with sweat and blood to buy food, to find home, and to clothe their children. Many times parents sacrifice even their legitimate pleasures and individual ambitions for the sake of their Children. Parents suffer, they are hurt, and their freedom is infringed. But they let not show their feelings to their children because it would hurt and harm them. Such a sacrificial environment is found in a true and genuine family.

Family is a Domestic church

As II Vatican council proposed, Realreligion's members hold firmly that their family is a domestic church. This is not something new. In early days of the Church, since there were not church buildings, families let their homes to be used by the Apostles and disciples to conduct the Eucharistic celebrations. When the Church became extended, grown and developed, separate church buildings were constructed and people began to be divided for convenience and easy management. A big separation occurred between family and church. The church became something a family went to, belonged to, and participated to. Family and church turned out to be two separate experiences. Therefore in the spirit of Vatican II Realreligion's practitioners started rethink about the identity and relationship of both family and church. They proudly call their families 'domestic churches'. A family is not a group of people who gather because they like each other. That is a circle of friends. A family is not a group of like-minded people. That is a service club. It is not a group gathered for some specific action. That is a social action group. All these groups choose to form a community. It is always nice to see all the above-mentioned are found in a family. Even if they are not there it is still a family. People do not form a family. Rather people are constituted as people by the family. Their individual lives are rooted in the family.

Realreligion inspires us to believe that every Christic family is the church because it is founded on the sacrament of marriage. As the church community is a gathering founded on the baptismal commitment so the family members are gathered in a home founded on the marriage commitment. Family is ordained by God to create, to preserve and to grow life for God's Kingdom. Family is a church because each individual who lives in that environment is sanctified by different sacraments and sacramentals, rules and regulations, codes and customs formed by that particular family. Family becomes a church by its love meals shared together daily. Bethlehem means 'house of bread.' Each home is Bethlehem where food is prepared and served to its members with TLC: Tender, Loving, and care. Family is church because the real and original altar of sacrifice is found there. In many homes of Realreligion members have special shrine of saints and prayer room. Family is the church where the Word of God is preached and taught more by living than speaking, more by deeds than words.

Most families of Reelreligion-practitioners seem to be domesticated systems rather than being domestic churches. In order to keep fake peace and preserve fake family-prestige in the community every member in their families has been domesticated by one or two selfish and arrogant member of the family. Children are domesticated like animals and changed into pets and so women in many countries. Wives are domesticated to act like sexual toys, child-bearing machines, and professional butlers and cooks. Even men in some families are domesticated and therefore we call them 'hen-becked husbands.' Many families are being torn to pieces by globalization, industrial injustice, and economical and political upheavals. They become either renegades or being separated from each other daily, for months, and for years. Families of Reelreligion are formed by people for various reasons: curiosity and playfulness;

lust and self-gratification; romanticism and human fulfillment; fear and shame; dumbness and blindness; and purely law and tradition. Nonetheless, families of Realreligion are 'domestic churches', built on God's love and His Will, where honoring, respecting, revering, obeying, trusting, forgiving and helping one another are found; and where working harder, taking the challenges and risks of life, making choices for life's security and prosperity with one and one heart, paying the price of family peace and joy is experienced.

Family is a 'Service-Station'

Etymologically the word 'family' is derived from Latin root *'Famulus'* which means 'servant.' What an appropriate word it is to signify the exact role and identity of our families where we are all born and which we are proud to build up. Family first of all is a place of servicing. It stands as a service station where we build up our personality, repair and maintain tame and groom ourselves. We too fill ourselves with all that we need as fuel for traveling safely and securely in our future lives. Secondly family is that place where each serves the other, placing the needs, interests, desires and delights of the other before their own. Thirdly family is a place where boys and girls are recruited for different services in the society. To make our choices for life, in education, business, job, marriage and so on, family offers all possible free services to help us choose the best for us.

Members of Realreligion in their family environment discover who they are and what they are capable of becoming. All exaggerated self-importance, all extreme inhibitions and all fears are ripped off by the services performed in the families. They know that it is the 'family spirit' that makes a house into a home sweet home; it turns any isolated island into a prosperous land of the living; it makes the deserted life into an oasis, a resting place of green pasture. They watch their friends of Reelreligion, even be they grouped together by blood, by color, by race or by the name of Jesus or God, not holding the family spirit and consequently failing to attain their goals. Therefore my friends of Realreligion abide by certain godly principles and achieve the fruits of a family. Principle one: Their families worship the Lord as their primary duty. God is the biggest Dream of their lives. To worship Him means to walk with Him, to talk with Him, and to act with Him daily. This may be called a faith walk. They choose any day as His Day, as the Day of the Lord. The whole world considers even in this 21ˢᵗ century the Sunday as the day of the Lord, a day specifically dedicated to Him. So Realreligion's families choose an appropriate day, a proper and convenient time, and a place conducive to worship Him. But always it must hold Him as its biggest dream. Principle two: They preserve morality as their family code of conduct. Every member of the family moves and breathes fidelity, honesty, purity and justice in its dealings with one another. Principle three: They shape their families by charity. It means that each member of the family goes beyond oneself. The whole family goes beyond itself, its club, its association, its race, its group, its nation, and its world to the entire universe. It does not stay or be stuck in micro family but go to the macro family as Jesus their Guru lived and taught.

Family System is God's Choice

Family means a group of people affiliated by consanguinity, affinity or co-residence. Family is defined as a fundamental social group in society typically consisting of one or two parents and their children. Or two or more people who share goals and values, have long-term commitments to one another, and reside usually in the same dwelling place. These members of a household live under one roof. It is a group of persons, who share common ancestry. This means it is a group of individuals derived from a common stock: *the family of human beings.* This is a right description of what we used to call the 'traditional family'. In this modern world such a form of family system is becoming a smaller and smaller majority. We encounter different forms and shapes of family such as single-parent families, foster families, and blended families which make up a large percentage of the families in today's society. In addition to these families, for many people family can mean more than those to whom one is biologically related. Some understand family as that group of closely linked, mutually supportive persons with whom they most frequently interact. All of these don't water down the beauty and reality of our Human Family system.

Family system is not man-made; rather it is God who established it for the good of humanity. When God created humans, He found out "man cannot be alone." He too decided humans should live as His replica-to be life-sourcing as He is; to be governing and controlling the entire creation as He is; to be holy as He is; to be going out of themselves in celebrating Life as He is. For all these to be achieved, He thought it is good for humans to build up their own family system in which 'two or three gathered in His name He will be present.' To facilitate such family system which He found humans are limited to handle, He created them in His image and likeness. One of God's nature is to be a family within Himself.

God is basically a family. Realreligion honors this revelatory truth about the Trinity of God which is commonly ignored or neglected by the majority of humans. Many of us continue to damage this wonderful identity of God. Namely He, as Triune God, is a Family, is a Community. We are told that God created the humans, male and female, "in the image and likeness of God." The particular Hebrew word employed for "image" is the same word our sacred authors use when talking about idols of pagan gods and goddesses. When someone in sixth-century B.C.E. Palestine asked why Israelites had no idols of Yahweh, the response was, *"We do. Each of us is an image of our God. Our God is as diverse as we are."* However the same diversified God is after all One. He is a Community, a Family, yet he is One. What makes our faith so exceptional, so unique is the belief that our God is a family! Our God is a community of persons, a fellowship of Love that has burst forth in ecstasy to the point that St. Paul can say in the reading we heard today: "The love of God has been poured into our hearts by the Holy Spirit which has been given to us" (Romans 5:5). What this tells us about the God we believe in is that he is One who is constantly communicating infinite Love between the Father, the Son and the Holy Spirit. Our God is a sharing God, a God who wants to invite us into becoming a similar community of love among ourselves. Our God, then, is a model for how we are to be in relationship with one another.

What is a Happy and Holy Family?

Every time a preacher talks about marriage and its dignity, he has to face in his audience three kinds of people: First group is those who think marriage is a fun and game. They feel anything they can do or undo until everything goes well with their self-gratification.

The second set of people are those who had started their married life with that approach but got up in broken family situation, divorce, separation and single parenthood. They lead a life of misery and mental agony but for the sake of survival in the society with kids they put on smile on their faces. The third group of audience is some elderly couples and widows and widowers who took marriage seriously, started the marriage with an objective of building up a family according to God's will and go on still enduring the burdens of family life. When they experience the hard situations in life they go beyond themselves and turn to God.

There are many families in the Bible shown to us as the rolemodels for running happy and successful families. One among them is the Holy Family of Nazareth. Jesus, Mary and Joseph lived a beautiful family life full of joy, peace and love. The only reason for this was all three went beyond their selfish ambitions and pleasures, beyond their natural situation and relationship. In the Gospel we have a tiny glimpse of that family factor depicted. When Mary and Joseph lost their only son in festive crowd, like any other parents were in tension and worry. But Jesus as the messenger of God told them that it was true he was their child but above all he was the son of God. He reminded them how they consecrated him in the Temple while he was a baby as Hannah did in OT. Hannah prayed for a child and when God granted her request, she rejoiced and returned the child to God when he became old enough to be weaned. Children are not only blessings of God but also belonging to Him and they are entrusted to their parents to give back to God. As John writes, we are first the children of God, conceived and birthed in love, in the Spirit of Jesus, the Word made flesh. This is who we truly are! We were created to love, each in our own singular way. This is the principle with which Realreligion families are created and managed. They are told by Realreligion that, as Mary and Joseph had learned, their children are not theirs, but belonged to God alone. Kahlil Gibran, a mystic poet, very succinctly puts this excellent truth in one of his poems: *Your children are not your children. They are the sons and daughters of Life's longing for itself. They come through you but not from you. And though they are with you, yet they belong not to you. You may give them your love but not your thoughts. For they have their own thoughts. You may house*

251

their bodies but not their souls. For their souls dwell in the house of tomorrow, which you cannot visit, not even in your dreams.

The Word was made flesh and dwelt among us. Yes. It is true the Word of God dwelt among us. Emmanuel, God with us. But do we know, what was his first dwelling place? First he dwelt in the womb of Mary very closely for only ten months. Then? Where did he dwell for longer time? Surely it was in a family circle. Nearly 30 years he dwelt there. Only three years he was dwelling physically among the human crowd, a macro family.

God selected Family of Nazareth as his first dwelling place on earth because first and foremost Mary and Joseph who build this family were individually made themselves as His dwelling place. They offered a dwelling place for God in their hearts. They were like Abraham and Sarah, who practicing Realreligion, allowed God to stay in their hearts by faith. They remained grounded permanently in the Lord and His Will.

As Mary and Joseph my Realreligion friends are determined to provide the best for their children. The best of all the best they offer to their children is witnessing to children that they remain relentlessly grounded in the Lord. They make prayer a part of their home life. They pray with their children at bedtime and pray for them after they fall asleep. They take them together to the Lord's Day and Holy Day's celebration at their parish church. They teach their children fear of God and respect one another. They let the children witness their respect for them, for each other, and for others and demand that they respect others, including themselves.

We have two lives, a private or family life and a public or professional one. These two lives should be in harmony but in the lives of Reelreligion-practitioners we observe very often they are in tension. Whereas Jesus resolved the tension by giving priority to his private life, they, unfortunately, try to resolve it by giving priority to their professional life, leaving their family life to suffer. Rose Sands writes about the unhappy man who thought the only way he could prove his love for his family was to work hard. *"To prove his love for her, he swam the deepest river, crossed the widest desert and climbed the highest mountain. She divorced him. He was never home."*

According to the Spirit of God and the Scriptures every traditional family is not necessarily to be called family or even holy because they fall under the definition-package we saw earlier. Look at Jesus' family. Joseph is believed he was a widower who married Mary and all his children from previous marriage were esteemed as step-sons and daughters to both and step-brothers and sisters to Jesus. And Jesus was a foster Son to Joseph and not real son. Hence you observe the Family of Nazareth cannot be included as one among traditional families. In OT, Hannah, the mother of Samuel, left her son entirely in the hands of high priest Eli at the temple. No more then he belonged to his family. Jesus' behavior both in his teenage and adulthood as well seems to be again telling us living under one roof is not going to make the family holy. Very sadly Jesus abruptly leaves his Mom one day telling her he wants to do the Will of his Father. There are so many examples such as these found in the Scriptures where we see all those families even 4000 years back did not comply with the right definition of a family.

Therefore we have to search for the true definition and meaning of 'holy family.' First of all any group of humans that lives in commune with one another in the bond of loving, selfless sharing and sacrificing is to be named the 'family.' Every one longs for relationship, a binding of togetherness with all humans or atleast with some. And that is what all about our family system. A family we create or belong to, is not just a living under one same roof nor its togetherness bound by laws and principles, nor a place where goods and possessions are distributed evenly and justly. But it is 'living together in spirit and in truth. It is 'communing of feelings, temperaments, knowledge, and the very self with each other mutually.'

Secondly if a family is to be called 'holy' it should be bonded, grouped, united on the basis of one ultimate principle, namely the Will of God. This was a continuous obsession of Jesus from the moment he entered into this world. Occasionally he showed it in his life with the questions: To his parents—*"Why were you looking for me? Did you not know that I must be in my Father's house?"* To the crowd: *"Who are my mother and (my) brothers?"* And looking around at those seated in the circle he said, *"Here are my mother and my brothers. (For) whoever does the will of God is my brother and sister and mother."* Jesus too number of times told his disciples and to those who wanted to follow him: *"If any one comes to me without hating his father and mother, wife and children, brothers and sisters, and even his own life, he cannot be my disciple.''* This is how Jesus defined the true family concept. Any togetherness other than this is simply a fake, deceptive and sometimes very dangerous.

The family-members of Realreligion listen to Jesus keenly who wants them to treasure and cherish any kind of family-surrounding they have been led in. They accept their only duty as his disciples is to base this togetherness on the Will of God whose desire for all of us is to live happily and make those who are around us happier. Like Jesus and Prophets and Sages, practitioners of Realreligion see to it that every member of their families must be first dedicated to the Lord and consequently become God's beloved children. Once they become fully conscious of God's presence and relation with them they listen to him what his will for them. And His Will is that *we must love one another as we have been commanded.*

As soon as I left my traditional family environment, I thought I am sent to hell and continued to regret so many years of my life priest for such misfortune. But when I began my journey within my Realreligion, and from the light of Jesus' own life and family background and from the inspiration I got from Scriptures I realized that being part of a traditional family setup is one among many opportunities offered to mankind for reaching their destiny. There are so many manners and modes of such family living. Being a priest and become a sole member of the macro-family of Christ is something big. Jesus belonged to not only his flesh and blood family (micro) but also his faith family (Macro) of those 'who do the will of my Father.' Like Jesus, who recognized themselves as sisters and brothers of one another because of their union in him. Therefore I cherish this position of today more willingly and more meaningfully. Nevertheless one fact is true: If I had not been there in an environment of 'traditional family' that had been built, preserved and kept intact always in faith and goal of fulfilling God's will, I would never have dreamt of coming out of myself and become such intrinsically and intimately united with the Church, the macro-family of Jesus.

The Family of Nazareth became 'holy' not because it was up to the characteristics of a traditional family but rather, because it was built and maintained as the meeting place of heaven and earth, where God reached out to us humans in an act of bonding. It has now become the model of an ideal family life where the fully grown mindsetup of loving sincerely, serving selflessly and sacrificing totally takes origin and grows. It is around such family hearth that true relationships are nurtured, laying the foundation of human personality. It is there that parents mirror God's love to their children and children bloom as God's precious gifts to their parents.

In this postmodern Age Realreligion's view of God-made family system is being distorted and disturbed by the factors of cultural disintegration, a cultural breakdown of healthy principles and standards, in areas like education, family life, crime and drug abuse, as well as in secular attitudes toward sex, individual responsibility, civic duty and public services. In the midst of these obstacles for families, Benedict XVI had words of encouragement for couples, in one of his Angelus messages: *"Being conscious of the grace they have received, may Christian husbands and wives build a family open to life and capable of facing united the many complex challenges of our time. Let them not to be do swept away by modern cultural currents inspired by hedonism and relativism; let them be ready instead to carry out their mission in the Church and in society with generous dedication."*

Chapter-16:
Suffering according to Realreligion

"Endure your trials as 'discipline'; God treats you as sons. For what 'son' is there whom his father does not discipline?" (Heb. 12: 7)

W hen I cry out that I am suffering I mean that I am experiencing some unpleasantness and aversion associated with the perception of harm or threat of harm in me. In suffering I feel certain kind of pain both physically, emotionally and mentally. I call this feeling of pain in various names: Distress, sorrow, unhappiness, misery, affliction, woe, ill, discomfort, displeasure, and disagreeableness, chagrin, and so on. By nature I have been terrified personally even in thinking or witnessing sufferings.

However in the light of Scriptures my Realreligion tells me that every person born in this world, if he/she is truly the servant of Yahweh, he/she has to be a 'Suffering Servant' who passes through the vale of tears and the dark valley. However that journey of suffering will finally lead this suffering servant to a life of resurrection and elevation. Scriptures too project Jesus as the typical Servant of Yahweh. He has learned or grown himself through his sufferings as a compassionate and understanding person. Jesus asserted that his commitment to Yahweh has led him to drink the bitterest chalice of life and going through the Baptism of blood. He demanded his followers to drink the same bitterest cup and be bathed by the same bleeding Baptism. Jesus does not talk about anything that is new to the humanity. Suffering, pain, sickness, and death are some inevitable consequences of human life. They are part of my life's game. The Lord's only contribution to me in this regard is offering me some tips by his teachings and living how to accept my own sufferings and elevate them into some instruments of my own happiness and eternity.

I had a friend in Oklahoma, USA. Two years back she was knocked down by a stroke, and hit her head and her brain damaged very badly. She became unconscious on that day. There were many operations done. Nothing was successful. For nearly 3 years she was bedridden, unconscious, living by feeding tube and died oneday and gone to the Lord. Whenever I visited her at the nursing home I was moved to tears as my mind went back to my past days with her being very active and supportive to all kinds of ministries in the parish. I, as her spiritual director, had many conversations with her. In one of the last conversations she was explaining to me about a dream she had at night in which the crucified Lord appeared to her with his bleeding. She wanted my interpretation of it. I responded to her by the impulse of my knowledge of Scriptures that perhaps the Lord might have wanted her to answer to him whether she was ready to drink the bitter chalice and be bathed in his bleeding baptism. I also told her, 'please do not pray for more sufferings as St. Francis of Assisi did, nor should you pray for healing from your suffering.' She could not accept the second part of my suggestion. Therefore I corrected myself and told her 'any physical healing you pray for is only very temporary. But you should pray for the wholistic healing, which is eternal and spiritual.' I too added, 'please pray hard for the glory of God who is in you through your suffering.'

That is what my Realreligion teaches me. Like every one in the world I should undergo certain sufferings at different levels and at different degrees. But I must be sure that it is not what I suffer that makes me great but the way I suffer that makes me stand on the high pedestal in God's kingdom. This is the Gospel of my sufferings; the Gospel of my glory; and the Gospel of Jesus Christ the Suffering Messiah. I am told in the Bible that God is pleased to crush us in infirmity; human suffering becomes the source of salvation for the entire humanity; human suffering turns out to be the source of justification and vindication; through human suffering the will of God is accomplished; and through human suffering a person would see the light in fullness of days. In particular Jesus in his life made much of the glorification of sufferings. People who follow their own Reelreligion, which preaches a cheap and cozy way of earthly life, never accept that God and his Son Jesus endorsed human sufferings. But my Realreligion provides me a proper interpretation about human suffering and elevates it as the way of glory and fullness of joy.

The Glory of 'Suffering'

Suffering is simply a physical, emotional, mental and spiritual pain I feel and sense. It is an imbalance I encounter within my spirit. It is a state of peacelessness, restlessness and a loss of tranquility. How does it come? Where and what is it generated? There are various reasons for human sufferings. The Bible says the main cause is my sinfulness that generates ignorance, pride, stubbornness in making wrong choices in life. It induces to go for overdoses of bodily pleasures and uncontrolled emotions and feelings leading to perversions and violations. Due to these reasons many people suffer with ill health, and social evils. However God in Jesus surely does not glorify these sufferings. He is not delighted to crush me with these infirmities. He is rather the eternal healer of the human body and soul.

So there should be another way of explaining God's glorification of human suffering. What is the kind of human suffering God in Jesus talking about? Suffering is possible only in those beings that move. A stone or a dead body is incapable of feeling the pain and suffering. So suffering enters into my system when I get up and move to do something, even to move my members of the body, to move from the womb of my mothers to the outside world. It is a move from higher level to lower level. It is a move to serve the other and become even a slave of love and compassion to the other. This is what Jesus means when he highlights human suffering as the greatest resource from heaven. He says to his disciples: *"You know that those who are recognized as rulers over the Gentiles lord it over them, and their great ones make their authority over them felt. But it shall not be so among you. Rather, whoever wishes to be great among you will be your servant; whoever wishes to be first among you will be the slave of all. For the Son of Man did not come to be served but to serve and to give his life as a ransom for many."*

Jesus' handling of his sufferings became a model for my own suffering-management. He experienced acute suffering when he emptied himself, lowered himself down from his eternal glory and lived as a slave to serve his fellowmen. God stripped himself of his omnipotence; from being "omnipotent," he made himself "impotent." (Phil. 2: 7). In his acceptance all the above-sufferings, Jesus transformed power into service. As the Prophets foretold, Jesus in his life was an impotent redeemer. *"He grew up like a sapling before him, like a shoot from the parched earth . . . . He was spurned and avoided by men, a man of suffering, accustomed to infirmity."* This is the suffering Jesus glorifies in; exemplifies; designs it for me as the program of life. There is nothing wrong in it. It is purely a practical suggestion for me to act courageously and wisely and joyfully in life's moves and changes, especially when I face certain situations where I have to bow down to the nature, to my destiny and other people's too.

Why to suffer?

Every religion has tried to answer this question in its own inspiration. Buddhism, for example, considers our human desires are the cause of sufferings; Hinduism holds that suffering follows naturally from personal negative behaviors of individuals either in their present life or in their past life. Islam contends humans suffer according to Allah's will as a test of faith. Judaism started holding that sins are the causes of human sufferings, but later on after encountering the greatness, holiness and mercy of God as well as their own stiff-necked attitudes and behaviors during their desert-journey, insisted that every suffering is a test from God either to chastise us or to prove our obedience to Him. *". . . But the Lord chastises those who are close to him in order to admonish them."* Judith 8:24-27; Ex. 20: 18-2; Deut. 8:5; Tobit 12:14; Ps 94:12; Pro. 3:11-12; Wis. 3:4-6; Sir. 2:1-6; Heb. 12:5-6. While God does use the sufferings for testing us and chastising us, He too makes use of them as steps to a more prosperous life. *"He guided you through the vast and terrible wilderness with its seraph serpents and scorpions, its parched and waterless ground; he brought forth water for you from the flinty rock and fed you in the wilderness with manna, a food unknown to your ancestors, that he might afflict you and test you, but also make you prosperous in the end."* (Deut. 8: 15-16)

Certainly, when Jesus came into this world and preached his Gospel, he emphasized all that had been said of human sufferings in the past. In his Gospel light the author of the Letter to the Hebrews writes: *"Endure your trials as 'discipline'; God treats you as sons. For what 'son' is there whom his father does not discipline? If you are without discipline, in which all have shared, you are not sons but bastards. Besides this, we have had our earthly fathers to discipline us, and we respected them. Should we not then submit all the more to the Father of spirits and live? They disciplined us for a short time as seemed right to them, but he does so for our benefit, in order that we may share his holiness. At the time, all discipline seems a cause not for joy but for pain, yet later it brings the peaceful fruit of righteousness to those who are trained by it."* (Heb. 12: 7-11) However Jesus added some more nuance to it.

When the mother of James and John came to Jesus and told him that he should make her two sons sit, one at his right and the other at his left, in his kingdom, Jesus asked his candidates, "Can you drink the cup that I am going to drink?" They said to him, "We can." Jesus always desired that his disciples should follow his bloody path of suffering. He told everyone who wanted to follow him: *"Whoever wishes to come after me must deny himself, take up his cross, and follow me. For whoever wishes to save his life will lose it, but whoever loses his life for my sake will find it.* (Mt. 16: 24-25) When Jesus told his disciples to follow him in his sufferings he did not present to them anything new to them. Suffering is a common factor in human life. Any new life comes out only out of pain, suffering, death and disappearance of the old; they are the part of its life's development. For example, a seed has to undergo a cruel annihilation in order to bring forth new plant life. *"Amen, amen, I say to you, unless a grain of wheat falls to the ground and dies, it remains just a grain of wheat; but if it dies, it produces much fruit."* (Jn. 12: 24)

Paul emphasizes the Lord's holding on the glory of sufferings (2Cor. 4: 7-18). First he says that by my suffering my whole life changes as a new life in Christ. *"We are afflicted in every way, but not constrained; perplexed, but not driven to despair; persecuted, but not abandoned; struck down, but not destroyed; always carrying about in the body the dying of Jesus, so that the life of Jesus may also be manifested in our body . . . For, this momentary light affliction is producing for us an eternal weight of glory beyond all comparison . . ."* Another reason he gives for accepting my sufferings is that through my sufferings I earn an eternal life after my death. *"We know that the one who raised the Lord Jesus will raise us also with Jesus and place us with you in his presence."* He says there is one more benefit of my sufferings, namely all that I suffer with Christ will be benefitting to my brothers and sisters in their salvation. *"Everything indeed is for you, so that the grace bestowed in abundance on more and more people may cause the thanksgiving to overflow for the glory of God."*

My Realreligion encourages me to endure my sufferings pointing out that suffering is a special call to me to develop a beautiful virtue, the virtue of perseverance, in bearing whatever disturbs and causes harm *"More than that, we rejoice in our sufferings, knowing that suffering produces endurance, and endurance produces character, and character produces hope, and hope does not disappoint us, because God's love has been poured into our hearts through the Holy Spirit which has been given to us".* (Rom. 5: 3-4)

Human Suffering made into redemptive cross

Quoting God's words from John's Gospel, *"For God so loved the world that he gave his only Son, that whoever believes in him should not perish but have eternal life"*, Pope John Paul II wrote: In this Godly mutual act of giving and giving up and handing over, *"love is manifested, the infinite love both of that only-begotten Son and of the Father who for this reason "gives" his Son. This is love for man, love for the "world": it is salvific love."* This means, Pope said that Jesus Christ conquered the cruel and venomous evil of suffering by his love.

All humans have their own crosses to carry in life. For some their wives are crosses, for wives, their husbands, to parents their children, to children their parents. Unfortunately for too many people their entire life is a cross because of their birth defect, the family diseases they have inherited, poverty and oppression from social injustice. According to the Scriptures those crosses can be of two categories: The crosses of going against the current; and the crosses of floating over the current.

Life is a river that never becomes dry. It brings lot of challenges. Individuals have to take them willingly and float over them or to swim against the unfairness of life. Often people of reelreligions salute to their self-love, which demands from too many pleasures, too many possessions, and too many slaves that can worship them, obey them and do what their selfishness demands. My Realreligion challenges me to go against my own self, which is number one enemy to my positive growth. To be a committed disciple of Jesus means to follow his Kingdom-principles, the Ten Commandments that are many times against my self-love. They become crosses to me.

To many other persons not only swimming against the current of life is a cross but also is the floating over the current. God wants me to go with the flow. This means to accept my inability to know the mind of God and to obey His Will in my life. This is the most painful cross a Realreligion member should face. Even after breathing the air of enlightenment, technical, scientific discoveries, the Lord wants me to humbly acknowledge my creatureliness. In the Book of Wisdom the Spirit of the Lord instructs me on how to relate to God realistically. I read that God is the Supreme Being beyond all human grasping. His ways are not my ways and no human being can fathom out what he is all about, how he is existing and why he does such and such a thing. I am only dust and unto dust I will return. I am very breakable, vulnerable and fragile. I also learn from the Lord that even though I am incapable of understanding God and of establishing proper relationship with him and with other human beings it does not mean those things are impossible to me. It is very possible by the grace of God. Only he must offer me first his wisdom and power because, as the Book of Wisdom says, *'who has ever known God's will unless he first gave him Wisdom and sent down his holy spirit to him? In this way he directs the human race on the right path; they learn what pleases him and are saved by Wisdom.'*

Jesus labeled all human sufferings as 'crosses'. No Jew in the time of the Lord dared to use this term because it was sign and symbol of degradation, death, crucifixion, criminal punishment, curse, and suffering. His disciples made use of this term cross referring, not only to Jesus' life-long sufferings beginning from his conception till his final passion and ignominious death, but also to their own persecution, their cost of discipleship, and mainly to Jesus' redemptive work. Jesus in a very positive way accepted the crosses, embraced them with his freedom fully, acted with them, on them as much as he could, but always used them for the greater good of the world. He made his own crosses as the wooden platform to gather people together, as the wooden ladder to take them up to greater vision and mission and as the wooden weapon to fight against the enemies who live and enjoy in injustice, in war, in hatred, in lies. As Paul clarifies about his pursuit of carrying his own crosses, with all these witnesses I too must bear my crosses in order to fill in what is undone in Jesus' redemptive project: *"Now I rejoice in my sufferings for your sake, and in my flesh I am filling up what is lacking in the afflictions of Christ on behalf of his body, which is the church."* (Col. 1: 24)

When he said take up the crosses, he meant the exterior, public suffering that results from Christian involvement in the social, political and economic issues of society. He meant the hostility, criticism, ridicule, opposition and condemnation that will come to those who publicly try—by word or action—to right any social wrong in the light of gospel principles. He meant that Christianity is not a quiet haven of private solace and security, but a challenging call to the public suffering of self-sacrificing action. He meant the public cross, out there, in the public forum, out there, in public social action. He meant the cross of thousands of great persons throughout the human history, 'so great a cloud of witnesses', who have been jailed, suffered, and died because they sought to establish the justice and peace of God's kingdom concretely in the actual structure of secular society. That is the cross that Jesus was talking about. That is the cross that we must be ready to carry as the cost of being his disciples. It also may mean: That sometimes doing the will of God is hard, and involves suffering. Being a helper in the building of the kingdom requires work. That sometimes following the example and teaching of Jesus is a real challenge. That doing the right thing and loving our neighbor can be downright dangerous. That sometimes loving demands sacrifice. *"For the sake of the joy that lay before Jesus he endured the cross, despising its shame, and has taken his seat at the right of the throne of God. Consider how he endured such opposition from sinners, in order that you may not grow weary and lose heart."* (Heb. 12: 2-3)

While I feel the cost of discipleship is too much, my Realreligion brings to my attention constantly Jesus' consoling and promising words: *'Come to me all you who labor and are burdened, I will give you rest. Take my yoke upon you and learn from me, for I am meek and humble of heart. And you will find rest for yourselves. For my yoke is easy, and my burden light.'* (Matt.11/28-30)

How to endure my sufferings?

Invariably all world religions consider the 'giving advices' to their devotees for how to endure their sufferings fruitfully. Hinduism for instance suggests that a Hindu must accept suffering consciously as a just consequence and as an opportunity for spiritual progress. In Islam the faithful must endure suffering with hope and faith, not resist or ask why, accept it as Allah's will and submit to it as a test of faith. Jews are asked by their religion to observe resignation to the will of God who is Creator, Provider as well as Lawgiver and just Judge. Toward God the human attitude should be in time of suffering: *"Naked I came forth from my mother's womb, and naked shall I go back there. The LORD gave and the LORD has taken away; blessed be the name of the LORD!"* (Job 1: 20-22) In addition, *"We accept good things from God; should we not accept evil?"* (Job 2: 10) Judaic Literatures offer some suggestions for enduring human sufferings as God's sons and daughters: *"My child, when you come to serve the Lord, prepare yourself for trials. Be sincere of heart and steadfast, and do not be impetuous in time of adversity. Cling to him, do not leave him, that you may prosper in your last days. Accept whatever happens to you; in periods of humiliation be patient. For, in fire gold is tested and the chosen, in the crucible of humiliation. Trust in God, and he will help you; make your ways straight and hope in him."* (Sir. 2: 1-6)

My Master Jesus lived and demonstrated the right and meaningful way of suffering. As he has taken his sufferings as one of the conditions to please his Father, in the Gospel Jesus puts an absolute condition for being his disciples. He says: *"If anyone wishes to come after me, he must deny himself and take up his cross daily and follow me."* His condition sounds weird and shocking mainly because of the word he uses-the cross. But if we get into Jesus' heart we discover some practical and valuable suggestion for peaceful and joyful life.

As he himself states we get better life when we accept his invitation: *"For whoever wishes to save his life will lose it, but whoever loses his life for my sake will save it."*

What was a Cross in Jesus' time? It was an uncivilized, disgraceful and dreadful instrument of punishment given to criminals. Jesus, as a criminal, carried that cross and died on it in shame and cruelty. Thus cross has become the symbol of all sufferings we endure physically and mentally. It includes death, the climax of my sufferings. It is this cross Jesus wants me to carry daily. As a matter of fact, I should know that the past abominable identity of the cross is totally erased. After Jesus used it, after he died on it, the cross has become the symbol and source of salvation of humanity. The loss has become gain; the pain has produced joy; the death changed into life; and bleeding has turned out to be living waters. Paul repeats in his Letters as a Litany that *'through faith in the cross of Christ we are all made children of God.'* Describing the historical change occurred in the identity of the cross, Pope St Leo the Great said: *"The cross of Christ is the source of every blessing, the fountain of all merit; to the faithful it gives strength from His weakness, glory from His shame, and life from His death."*

All the glory and honor the cross receives today is simply because of the person Jesus who handled and managed it with loving tender care. *"And just as Moses lifted up the serpent in the desert, so must the Son of Man be lifted up, so that everyone who believes in him may have eternal life."* (Jn. 3: 14-15) John here substitutes a verb implying glorification. Jesus, being exalted to glory at his cross and resurrection, represents healing for all. *"And when I am lifted up from the earth, I will draw everyone to myself."* He said this indicating the kind of death he would die."* (Jn. 12: 32-33) Jesus, as the Celebrity from heaven, used the cross chivalrously and properly. The cross he used contains his behavior of being defenseless in the face of opposition and violence; it symbolizes his commitment to God and longing to fulfill God's will in word and deed in spite of persecution and pain. When the disciples proclaimed that Jesus was the Christ of God, he never denied it; however he added to it one more qualification to himself that he was after all one like us, carpenter son, born of a woman, mere son of man who as any other human being, had to face the consequences of human birth. He had to suffer and die.

He freely chose to come down to the earth, lovingly took the form of slave, and willingly to do down to Jerusalem to die an ignominious death. It was by such smarty cross-management Jesus made the cross the source of life, grace, and surprisingly of true joy.

Undoubtedly Jesus' cross of suffering turns out to be first and foremost the source of my salvific healing. Therefore as Prophet foretold, Jesus wants me first to look at him crucified. This looking up to the crucified Savior makes me shedding tears and mourning for him, mainly because I am moved to remorse of conscience; I feel guilty of myself. Also, when I look at him on the cross my heart beats with longing to be like him valiant, magnanimous, forgiving, well-balanced. Secondly, I start longing for his immense love and for living like him chivalrously. This is the same reason why Paul would write: *I love and preach him crucified.* I can see this longing for the crucified Jesus on the cross portrayed in many saints' statues and pictures. Saints like Alphonsus Liguori could write volumes on their love for the cross. St Teresa of Avila very well said: *"Desire earnestly always to suffer for God in everything and on every occasion."*

As soon as I am healed and energized by the marvelous action of the crucified Jesus, I begin to hear from him to carry my daily crosses like him. Jesus underwent all his sufferings with an ultimate aim of bestowing salvation to his fellowhumans, plus demonstrating his total love for God and his human brothers and sisters. There have been in human history so many people who were edified by Jesus' cross-management and tried hard to follow his footsteps. They were convinced that only by this they can be true disciples of Jesus who invites all to follow him, not just stand by or behind the cross but take it up and accompany him. That is what Jesus preached; and that is what he lived. I get enthused to endure my sufferings in a Christic way. Whether we are Christian or pagan, religious or irreligious, every one of us suffers; everyone is naturally born sufferers. Everyone without exception meets in life pain, sickness, suffering, and at the end, death. While many handle them and manage them in natural way; but I, the Realreligion-practitioner, bear my crosses in Christic way. I unite my sufferings to the cross of Jesus and recognize that I do not bear my burdens alone; Christ and His people are there like Mary, Simeon, veronica, assisting me in carrying my burdens. As

Paul emphasizes, the true members of Realreligion suffer together as members of the One Body of Christ.

I too keep in mind not every suffering is salvific; but every suffering, even if it is a little ache and pain, can be source of salvation to others if it is borne in communion with Jesus and with his intentions. Thomas a Kempis writes in his book 'Imitation of Christ': *"He who knows how to suffer will enjoy much peace. Such a one is a conqueror of himself and lord of the world, a friend of Christ, and an heir of heaven."* The cross of shame in which Jesus hung was not a sign of failure. We need to learn that the cross was the very throne of our King. What seemed to those, standing by, to be the moment of utter failure was in fact, the moment of Jesus' greatest victory; it was a victory for life, for truth and for love; and a victory over external shame and degradation and over death itself. He used the cross, his suffering, as weapon to defeat his enemy, the devil. Whenever I see the Latin script written over the sanctuary of one parish church in Oklahoma: '*In Hoc Signo Vinces*', which means "by this sign He conquers", I am reminded of the beautiful and bewildering truth that Jesus my King, dying on the cross, was the victory of truth, of justice, of compassion and, above all, of love. The greatest love any one can show is to give his life for his friends. This is the power of my Jesus, a power that overcomes every possible evil and which nothing else can overcome.

In conclusion as a practitioner of Realreligion let me list out how I put up with my own sufferings fruitfully: I endure the sufferings voluntarily and innocently as Christ suffered. I go through the sufferings *'so that life of Jesus may be manifested in my mortal flesh.'* Being filled with hope I bear my crosses, fully conscious of the fact that *'He who raised the Lord Jesus will raise us also with Jesus'.* I too present all my bodily sufferings to God daily as a living sacrifice, holy and acceptable to Him. I undergo my sufferings smilingly as Jesus' Apostles did. *"So they left the presence of the Sanhedrin, rejoicing that they had been found worthy to suffer dishonor for the sake of the name."* (Acts 5: 41) They continued their rejoicing attitude throughout their lives as they witnessed and advised Jesus' followers to do the same: *"Rejoice to the extent that you share in the sufferings of Christ, so that when his glory is revealed you may also rejoice exultantly."* (1Pet. 4: 13) Paul, as he was suffering in prison writes: *"Rejoice, I say it again rejoice.'*

Chapter-17:
Death according to my Realreligion

"I look forward to the resurrection of the dead and the life of the world to come." (Nicene Creed)

W hy I was born? Why I am in this wretched situation while all others are in a high spirited mood? Why my pocket is not full while others' are filled and overflowing? Why is he behaving this way? Why is she not changing her way of dealing with me? Why am I left without my husband? When others enjoy long lives why my spouse was taken away from me? While most of my companions are thriving in health and wealth despite their abuses and injustice why am suffering this deprivation and disappointments? While many others are swiftly climbing up the ladder of power, success and fulfillment why me going on stuck still at the first step of my ladder? Besides all these unanswered questions there are two more dark questions, which have never been answered fully and make human beings live in depression, fear, hurt and coldness. They are: 'What will happen to me after my death?' And 'what is going to happen to this enormous universe?' As all religions proclaim, my Realreligion too offers the answers to both the questions and very succinctly added into my Creed-Package: *I believe in the resurrection of the body, and life everlasting.* This is the Apostles Creed version while in Nicene Creed my Realreligion makes me say: "I look forward (not 'I believe') those two mysterious truths about what would happen after my death. It means the Church wants me not only to hold these truths as mere intellectual possession but also to assimilate them and act on them in present life as hopefully looking forward as ultimate end of human life.

Earthly life is a 'passing cloud'

I have least doubt that my human life is temporary and transient. And so it will be with the universe because like me all that make into universe are physically made and so they will face the same destiny as myself. Recent scientific discoveries have proved that the entire universe with all its planets and beings will meet an end as they had their beginning with a 'Big Bang.' Materialists or those who do not believe in God and the spiritual world have the conviction that, by this big bang everything and everybody in this universe will be annihilated, in other words, they turned out to be nothing. But my Realreligion upholds that myself and all other beings and creations will meet our final end with a big bang but that would become the beginning of eternity, a renewed state of being with God. "New heaven and New earth" is my Realreligion's dream to be realized after a big bang. There are so many references in Scriptures about this dream of 'final end': "It shall be a time unsurpassed in distress since nations began until that time; in those days the sun will be darkened and the moon will not give its light, and the stars will be falling from the sky, and the powers in the heavens will be shaken . . . But nobody can predict the time of all these happenings. Jesus says, *"But of that day or hour, no one knows, neither the angels in heavens nor the Son, but only the Father in heaven."* So I am told about what will happen but not when it will occur.

On the contrary, Reelreligion-members have been for centuries exploited by their doomsday-prophets in this final-end mystery. An astronomer named John of Toledo calculated that a major calamity would destroy the earth in September 1186 after Christ. A group of London astrologers speculated that the world would end by a flood in February of 1524. A German monk and mathematician Michael Stiffel announced that the end would come on Oct. 18, 1533. Solomon Eccles, a Quaker prophet made a similar prediction in London in 1665. Mrs. Mary Bateman of Leeds, England claimed that her hen was laying eggs inscribed with the words, 'Christ is coming!" In York, Pennsylvania, grocery store owner Mr. Lee T. Spangler predicted that the world would end by fire during Oct. 1908. 11 years later, in San Francisco Mr. Albert Porta predicted that with the conjunction of six planets on Dec. 17, 1919, a magnetic current would pierce the sun and the earth would be completely cremated. In Los Angeles, a girl named Margaret Rowan announced that the angel Gabriel had told her the world would end on Feb. 13, 1925. The world did not end in 1931 as predicted by the Prophetical Society of Dallas, Texas. Neither was Charles Long of Pasadena correct when he wrote the end of the world would happen at 5:33 PM on Sept. 21, 1945. Many Italians in those days long believed that Rome and the world are safe as long as the Coliseum stands. When in May 18, 1954, engineers discovered huge cracks in the 1800-year-old amphitheater, the entire Italian population were in panic thinking the world was coming to an end. The same predictions were announced about the year 2000. We all know about the Y2K predictions. I know personally some men deserted their families flew to Jerusalem and lived there for months waiting for the Lord's coming. These kinds of doomsday prophets and predictors of Reelreligion still thrive in such exploitation.

The Final End

If you were truly a normal human person you would be haunted and disturbed by countless questions about thousand and one things about life. While a few questions get their answers supposedly, for most of the questions we are left in darkness. One of such questions is 'What happens when I die?' I know at least what happens to my body because many a time I write it in my will. But what about the life, which I am breathing? Many philosophers and religions tried to answer the question: The Egyptians had a highly developed doctrine of the future life and prepared diligently and meticulously for their time beyond time. The Hindus, Buddhists, Jains, and Sikhs believed that they should experience immortality by being reborn or reincarnated as another being. The Jews had believed that the Sheol was the final stop on their journey of life. In later stages of Judaism and especially just before my Guru Jesus was born, the Jews held a strong conclusion about the kind and quality of life after death. In the story of Maccabees in OT one of the Maccabee brothers says, 'the king of the world will raise us up to live again forever.' He expressed his belief that the God he worshipped is the same one who would be the king and provider even after his death. That he would live forever like his God.

Jesus has been very much concerned with our clear understanding of what would happen at the end. Therefore he is quoted in the Gospels discussing about it so much. The word 'end' is used in Scriptures for two purposes: One, to mean the climax or the full stop of all that start; two, to mean the goal, the purpose, the aim of what is going on and what I am engaged in now. As regard the first meaning, my end is not disputed. It is there. Anything in this world, that starts breathing, will one day have its last breath. Everything that is in this universe and everything I have created would have its end. Nothing remains today that had been filling, beautifying, and energizing a couple of centuries back. The same is true with any kingdom, power, culture, civilization, and so on. I have no idea when or how my world will end. The end may be a very long way ahead or, using the awesome scientific technology the humans could bring it to an end in a relatively short time.

Of much more practical interest for me is when my own personal end will come. Again it may be quite a long way off humanly speaking or, given the fragility of my human existence; it could happen in the very near future. I see examples of this every day. Therefore my Realreligion says to me that when my Guru Jesus speaks in the Gospels about these ends and the closing chapters of every human being he is not keen on passing that fact as truth to believe. End is part of human life's game. End is a common phenomenon in my life. Therefore Jesus directs my attention to the other meaning of 'end', namely the goal and purpose of my life. He asks me to answer what is the purpose of my life? Is it just to breathe, eat, drink and ease and finally end it for the sake of some insects under the earth to have good and sufficient food for some weeks? Or something new, born out of my death? Some more lessons people learn out of me? Or is it that something that will be more satisfying going to happen as continuity?

When I hear from Jesus about the end of my life and the entire universe I live in, all that he does is not with a purpose of frightening me and thus keeping me as chicken under his wings. My Realreligion explains that it is like the conversation of a couple talking about their future. Husband would say to his wife that he is planning this and that, it needs lots of money and we have to sell our property or shift our residence and hunt for another job. But his wife would tell him the pros and cons of his dreams and plans. May be, at one point, she would be recounting some future catastrophe as a prophecy that would come due to such plans. It is not that she wants to frighten her husband; rather she discusses with him on certain evil results challenging them in his future plan. Then the husband elaborates his vision of their future family status and confirms to her that they have to be together in facing the challenges in order to achieve their goal. This is what Jesus does when he describes about the horrible things happening at the end of the world. His message is loud and clear: "Hang in there because the ultimate victory will be yours."

My life after death

When Jesus was asked about humans' status after their death he answered that the life after death would be similar and dissimilar to earthly life. There will be both continuity and discontinuity of this worldly life. Bodily and materially I will be different. There is going to be no more physical structure, fall, stumbling, pain, ageing, marriage, procreation, and so on. No more mortality. Jesus explained that resurrected life would be radically different from the present one because the sons and daughters of the resurrection are sons and daughters of God. 'Also we will be like angels.' In other words, those who have gone through the passage of death to resurrected life are transformed.

In one of my sleepless nights with some heavy negative thoughts about human life, I was fed up with browsing TV Channels because most of those channels replaying some films of separation divorce, violence and killings. So I turned the Radio on. It was exactly midnight. Guess what I heard. A beautiful country-song with a repeated chorus, *"Still we are going to die."* The lead singer sings like a litany: 'we may be on strict diet.' And the chorus repeats, "Still we are going to die." 'We may walk two miles a day.' 'Still we are going to die'. 'We may quit smoking'. 'Still we are going to die'. 'We may not commit sin'. 'Still we are going to die'. 'We may be complete vegetarian'. 'Still we are going to die'. It was really melodious to listen but at that night it aggravated my depression.

Death may be a subject that is almost all of us, especially in this youth-worshipping and progress-oriented society, plan to avoid and to ignore or forget about it in our daily lives. But the fact is that death is inevitable. We will all die; it is only a matter of time. Death is as much a part of human existence, of human growth and development, as being born. It is one of the few things in life we can count on that we can be assured will occur.

Even if we don't want to hear often about the facts of death, we are indeed influenced by this truthful saying, "Still we are going to die." Most of our attitudes and views about our life's engagements are generated out of this idea about death. Since 'still we are going to die,' many of us make it a point to eat and drink as much as we can while still we are alive. There are others who are hurt so badly by this truth of 'still we are going to die,' live a life of discouragement and depression and never feel happy about themselves. A large portion of human population is affected by this truth about death subconsciously and leads a careless life in their management of lives. So they face an early death, a sudden unexpected death. And most of them carry within them, what I call, a hidden death' namely they develop within their physical system certain disease which turns to be the source of death, killing them slowly and gradually. Also there are some others who build up psychologically a fixation for certain ideas, or for certain job or position and go on fighting for it till death. I call it the 'stubborn death.' It can be either for good or bad purposes. Their hard-headedness is simply a by-product of their adherence to the truthful saying, "Still we are going to die."

The above-said attitudes are all natural to everybody. But for a Realreligion-practitioner, who has been blessed by God's revelation and light through Jesus, there is more to it. Death is not a curse or punishment but a blessing. Paul says that Jesus is not only the Lord of the living but also of the dead. He urges us in his letters to bear the death of Jesus in our bodies so that we can bear the life of Jesus. St. Jerome says, "Death is a blessing, more powerful than life itself. The Lord allowed death to enter into this world so that sin might come to an end." Death is not an end in itself but a Passover from temporality to eternity, from corruption to resurrection, from mortality

273

to immortality and from rough seas to a calm harbor. Death is not a source of disappointment but an already scheduled appointment with our creator; it is not a source of despair but an event of challenge posed to every human individual. I always feel that for many of us who walk in the footsteps of Jesus as his disciples faithfully death is an event of not just God challenging us, but rather, of our challenging him. Standing before his throne we can boldly demand from him, 'Lord, give us our reward for what we were to you.'

Connection between my final end and earthly life

Death is not to be included as an expenditure category in our life account book. But rather, it is to be respected as a source of time-consciousness, a source of inspiration to appreciate every second of our lifetime, everything in creation and every person whom we come in contact with. In the Gospels Jesus is placing before us the truth of the great importance of our lives. The death in itself is not a challenge. It is a part of life. Therefore the life itself is a challenge. Live it then fully, consciously and deliberately. This is Jesus' Gospel message. Jesus wants us to be prudent and smart to make the best use of the time of life given to us.

In my Realreligion all that I practice and perform are focused on the deep connections existing between my today's earthly life and the coming day of heaven and hell. After creating every bit of His creation, God burst out in wonder and total satisfaction seeing their goodness: *"God looked at everything he had made, and found it very good."* (Gen. 1: 31) My Realreligion tells me that there is a meaningful end to my present fading life that is filled with challenges and struggles and mixed with ups and downs; my individual struggle is part of the universal struggle that is going on between God and the devil, good and bad, truth and lie, love and hatred; to this struggle there will be an end after all. Scriptures explain in a metaphorical or figurative way the reality of heaven and hell. On the basis of revelation my Realreligion believes, as Pope John Paul II stated in 1999, that *"Heaven, or the happiness in which we will find ourselves, is neither an abstraction nor a physical place in the clouds, but a personal relation [with God]. . . . This final condition can be anticipated in a certain sense now on earth . . . . Moreover, the pictures of Hell given to us in Sacred Scripture must be correctly interpreted. They express the total frustration and emptiness of a life without God. More than a place, Hell is the state of the one who freely and finally removes himself from God, the source of life and joy."*

In order to give better explanation on the intrinsic relation between today's life and life after death the Scriptures point out there is going to be an end to the creation that would shock, jolt, and shake every human being. I already know the precarious nature of the life I am leading. I have experienced so many separations, ends and disappearances of hundreds of my friends and relatives. How hard it is for a life leaving the body, much worse its relations. Every person's death or end of his earthly life stands as unforgettable, shocking, hurting and in a way to many a calamity or a catastrophe. So it is going to be the same experience the entire humanity would encounter at the end of the entire universe.

In the light of his revelation my Realreligion wants me to hold that human earthly life is very temporal and transient but it comes very meaningful and very purposeful if I connect it to the eternal Word of God. I have to place these present hours of living in the time of the Lord. The whole humanity lives in chronological time, being calculated second by second according to the clock ticking. But God lives in *kairos*, timeless time. All the past, present and future are one in the Lord. If I compare the time of my living as the water flowing through the pipeline, God's time is seen as the large ocean of water. So the water flowing through the pipeline must travel toward the ocean and mingle with its water. So I should take the present moment as the time of the Lord. I must focus my attention only on the Lord who is coming to judge the living and the dead. The Son of Man is coming in the clouds at every moment, at every step of my moving in this world. He has a beautiful plan and huge project to be accomplished. *"Taking his seat forever at the right hand of God now Jesus waits until his enemies are made his footstool."* Therefore my Realreligion advises me that I should connect my present life which is futile, vain and very transient to the eternal plan of God in order to make it more meaningful and successful. Everything will pass away, including the good things I have accomplished except the love I bear for Jesus.

The continuity between life before and after death is nothing but my loving relationship with God. He is the God of the living.

He is the God of Abraham, Isaac, Jacob, Moses, my great grand pa, my grand ma, my parents and me. So He is the link, the base the bridge. When I begin to relate myself to him and in his name to others, that relationship remains forever. Relationship is always spiritual. I try to use the body for expressing it and experiencing it because of my limitation. Earthly style of life is not the only style. All sexual, emotional, commercial, political and social relationships are the lowest possible dimension of relationship. What to do? There is no other option in this world. After death it will be fully civilized, enhanced, resurrected relationship. The importance of this life is to establish strong relationship with that God of the living and relate one another on the basis of my relationship with Him. Added to it, as Paul indicates, I may hold on to this life with hope on the love and everlasting encouragement given by God in Jesus, continue to be good in word and deed.

I always long for a life of justice, peace, joy and freedom. Whenever I do not possess such fulfilling life today I wish for a 'better tomorrow, a better future, a better life.' This desire and dream is innate in my nature because I know God who created me is life itself. People may call him in various names, as love, truth, justice, peace and joy. However the suitable name that includes all that said-above as the intrinsic ingredients is life. When Moses asked God what was his name, God replied 'I am Who Am.' My God is a living God enjoining a fuller life that can be ever dreamed of. Being his creature naturally I am inclined to possess such life too. I am born to possess such life. If I don't get it or lose it, I am disappointed, confused and tensed. To add to the struggle the human death comes in between to worsen my problem.

My Realreligion tells me not to be afraid of facing death because I would be resurrected surely from death. Death has a very short duration. It is only a means and not an end in itself. Final resurrection as the goal of all living is a central concept of my religious faith. It is very much a matter of faith and trust in God's word as I have no proof or prior experience of such a life nor can I say very much about it. Paul puts it well when he says that "Eye has not seen nor ear heard all that God has prepared for those who love him." People of different faiths have tried using all kinds of material delights and colorful images to describe life after death. These images are not in the long run helpful and I do better going with the author of the mystical book *The Cloud of Unknowing* which suggests that I only begin to know God when I realize that I do not know him nor can I know him in any full way in his life. And the same goes for the kind of life I will live face to face with him. Though there are too many explanations and religious dogmas around this world I adhere firmly to what Jesus says in the Gospel as a revealed truth. Jesus says: *'Those who are resurrected from the dead cannot die anymore, because they are equal to angels and are the sons of God, being sons of the resurrection."* This means I will enjoy fuller life, better life than anything I dreamt of but quite different from what has been touched and explained with my limited human brain.

In this vein my Realreligion points out that there is no problem in longing and dreaming of better future and better life. The real issue is what kind of means I use to attain that 'better tomorrow.' In my childhood Catechism classes I learned a simple answer to this question. I will attain better life after death if I know God well, love him well and serve him to my fullest strength. Though this sounds as simple as an answer it contains so many demands and requirements to be fulfilled. To know, to love and to serve God faithfully demands too many restrictions, lots of discipline, and sometimes takes my very earthly life. I have an array of saints as my rolemodels in this effort. In order to possess a better life they strived to fulfill all God's laws. As the Psalmist sings *they kept their feet firmly in God's paths; there was no faltering in their steps.* They too were *watching and ready to meet the Lord's coming for he comes usually at an hour we do not expect.*

Wild dreams about life after death

People of Reelreligion are in their daily lives hesitant and negligent to be in the presence of the Lord. The main reason for it is that in spiritual presence with the Lord humans become conscious of their end. My Realreligion compels me to be consciously and continuously in the presence of the Lord for enjoying my fuller life in this world. It offers to me very convincing reason for it.

This is not simply a utopian promise. It means that in the long run Truth, Love and Justice will prevail. A review of the history of the past centuries, in spite of all that has gone wrong, has shown continuing progress in all areas of human values. My Scriptures is full of all such discussion about the closing chapters of me, the end of my nation, my culture, my civilization and the entire humanity. All that it does is to remind me how important it is to live the full life today each moment. As T.S. Elliot in *'Murder in the Cathedral* wrote, "we do not know very much of the future, except that from generation to generation the same things happen again and again. Men learn little from others' experience. But in the life of one man, never the same time returns." God of my Realreligion talking about the challenge of death and the end of everything takes me to the serious consciousness of the present. He also shares with me how to cope with the evil ends today, at this present moment and transcend them and continue to live over and beyond this short tenure of earthly life. For achieving my proper ultimate end, he offered me the following tips:

I should go on dreaming wild dreams about my end: Wild dreams of today are the practical deeds and enterprises of tomorrow. I have dreamed so many wild dreams about my life in my childhood. And that is what I experience and express and live in today. Only our dreams made us make beautiful choices for life. We have grown, developed and achieved because of our dreams. Invariably all religions are based on certain stories and dreams. My Realreligion is not exempted. My God always invites me to dream dreams and live through them. I live on wild reams about God, about life after death and so on. All of my dreams are enlisted in my creeds and dogmas. For example, I recite in my creed: "He will come again in glory to judge the living and the dead, and his kingdom will have no end. I look for the resurrection of the dead, and the life of the world to come." These things are simply my wild dreams.

As a matter of fact, I dream these dreams on the basis of the wild dreams of Jesus and the prophets. In the Gospels I often hear Jesus' prophecies and predictions, which are his wild dreams about human life and the entire creation. Prophet Malachi for instance dreams about that great day, the final day, a day of judgment, and a day of wrath. These wild dreams are perfectly necessary for me to go through this valley of tears. They make my life meaningful and my today's burden light and sweet. They are not at all nightmares. They are the source of strength and guidance for my making proper decisions in daily life. Truly if these dreams and their actualities are not connected with Jesus' dreams, many times they turn to be dangerous to myself and to the world. Other times these dreams may take me off the ground frighten me and keep me in complexes being faithless in future, ending in depression and keeping eating and drinking as the only goal in life. This is why my Realreligion cautions me to deal with my wild dreams very prudently.

I must also hold an undistracted or undistorted vision of that end: Any project planning first conceptualizes its end, goal or vision and puts it in writing. Then come the details of the objectives, activities, methods and budget so on. If my life on earth is a project I need first be convinced of its end. Then only I can describe the ways and means of achieving it.

I should have a childlike trust in God: Change is good and quitting also sometimes is good in secular life. But I cannot be a renegade in my connections with God. My Realreligion encourages me with the promise that those who persevere faithfully and in awe of God need not fear the end.

I need patient endurance: Jesus, in the Gospel, warns that pursuit of my life's goals as his disciple will be fraught with conflict, but I shall not be left to my own devices. God and God's grace will be ever near, as will Jesus' own Spirit, giving me words and wisdom and the will to persevere.

I should work while I work and pray while I pray: This is because today is the day very important for reaching the end of tomorrow. No room there for sloth, laziness, waste of minutes, self-gratification. St Paul issues very practical advice on a very earthy topic. 'Don't burden others with your piety,' he seems to be saying. Waiting for the Lord is, of course a priority, but my waiting should be purposeful. I should go to work; earn my own money; buy my own food; mind my own business and keep on going until Jesus returns.

Nothing sown, nothing reaped. It is a fact that I reap in the garden only what I sow in it. And so is in my life too. Those who have sown nothing, they will reap nothing. Many chose to go their own way without God and God will allow them to continue doing so. They will lie in the bed they have made. But for those who have based their lives on being loyal to Truth and have spent their lives in the service of their God and seeking the well-being of their brothers and sisters, "the sun of righteousness will shine out with healing in its rays". No one has permanent residence here on earth. I should live each day in the full knowledge that my life period on this earth is a prelude to eternity and that the manner in which I live here and now will determine whether I enjoy my eternity or endure it with great struggle. Mark Twain has said, *"Twenty years from now, you will be more disappointed by the things you didn't do than by the ones you did."* The last words of the French Carmelite and spiritual writer Elizabeth of the Trinity, who died a painful death from Addison's disease in 1906, at age 26, were: *"Everything passes. In the evening of life, love alone remains."* All I can do when death approaches is clinging in faith and love to the One who shall remain when my life list is completed and all else passes away.

Till the final end let me kick on, push on, struggle, combat and run the race; let me wait for the victorious end; here I am not alone in waiting; there is a whole humanity including the universe which is groaning for perfection. Let me go on fighting; let me go on waiting; let me in my own way go on contributing to the progress, betterment and growth of this universe, with its humans, all other animate and inanimate beings and the whole environment; let Him come back in His own time; I know He will come one day; and therefore with all other faithful in the church I will say boldly, loudly and meaningfully in the mass after the consecration : *When we eat this Bread and drink this Cup, we proclaim your death Lord Jesus, until you come in glory.*

Until the moment I breathe in this world I should ceaselessly recite with the Psalmist: "When will I come to the end of my pilgrimage and enter the presence of God?" (Ps. 42) However at the final moment of my life my heart should beat saying with Paul: *I know the one whom I have trusted and I am certain that he, the just judge, has power to keep safe what he has entrusted to me until that Day; I have fought the good fight; I have run the race to the finish; I have kept the faith; God's grace in me has not been without fruit."* Plus let my soul depart from my body as I lisp the final words of my master Jesus: *"Into your hands, Father, I commend my spirit; it is finished."*

Books and Authors referred

Zanzig, Thomas (2000). Jesus of history, Christ of faith. p. 33. ISBN 0-88489-530-0.

Espin, Orlando (2007). Introductory Dictionary of Theology and Religious Studies. p. 231. ISBN 0814658563.

Dictionary of Catholic Terms @ thesacredheart.com

Catholic Encyclopedia in Newadvent.org

St. Cyril of Jerusalem, "Catechetical Discourses"

St. Ignatius of Antioch, "Letter to the Smyrnaeans"

J. N. D. Kelly, "Early Christian Doctrines"

Geertz, Clifford. Religion as a Cultural System, 1973

Monaghan, John & *Just, Peter. Social & Cultural Anthropology*. New York: Oxford University Press. ISBN 978-0-19-285346-2

Harper, Douglas. *"religion"*. Online Etymology Dictionary.

Shorter Oxford English Dictionary

Max Müller, *Natural Religion*, 1889

Max Müller. *Introduction to the science of religion.*

Esptein, Greg M. *Good Without God: What a Billion Nonreligious People Do Believe.* New York: HarperCollins. 2010

Nicholas Lash. *The beginning and the end of 'religion'.* Cambridge University Press, 1996. ISBN 0521566355

Timothy Fitzgerald. *The Ideology of Religious Studies.* New York: Oxford University Press USA, 2000.

Boyer (2001). *"Why Belief": Religion Explained.* 2001

Joseph Campbell, *Thou Art That: Transforming Religious Metaphor.* Ed. Eugene Kennedy. New World Library ISBN 1-57731-202-3.

Dawkins, Richard (2006). *The God Delusion.* Bantam Books.

Bland, Byron (May 2003). "Evil Enemies: The Convergence of Religion and Politics".

John S. Feinberg & Paul D. Feinberg. Ethics for a Brave New World. Crossway Books. 0-18.

Dinesh D'Souza. "Answering Atheist's Arguments". Catholic Education Resource Center.

Daniel Dubuisson, The Western Construction of Religion

Tomoko Masuzawa, *The Invention of World Religions.* Chicago: University of Chicago Press, 2007.

George A. Lindbeck, *Nature of Doctrine* (Louisville: Westminster/ John Knox Press, 1984)

Barzilai, Gad; *Law and Religion;* The International Library of Essays in Law and Society; Ashgate (2007), ISBN 978-0-7546-2494-3

Durant, Will *The Age of Faith*; Simon & Schuster (1980), ISBN 0-671-01200-2.

Haisch, Bernard *The God Theory*: Universes, Zero-point Fields, and What's Behind It All—discussion of science vs. religion, Red Wheel/Weiser, 2006, ISBN 1-57863-374-5

Winston King. *Encyclopedia of Religion*. Ed. Lindsay Jones. Vol. 11. 2nd ed. Detroit: Macmillan Reference USA, 2005.

Brodd, Jefferey (2003). *World Religions*. Winona, MN: Saint Mary's Press. ISBN 978-0-88489-725-5.

Wilfred Cantwell Smith *The Meaning and End of Religion* (1962)

Wallace, Anthony F. C. *Religion: An Anthropological View*. New York: Random House, 1966.

Dow W. James, *A Scientific Definition of Religion.*

Bouquet, A.C. *Comparative Religion*. Baltimore: Penguin Books Inc. 1956

Sherrington, Charles S. *Man on His Nature*. New York: Cambridge University Press, 1951

The New Shorter Oxford English Dictionary. 1993. Edited by Lesley Brown. Oxford: Oxford University Press.

The Sacraments: Symbol, Meaning, and Discipleship, published by Herald House (Bolton and Gardner, eds., 2005),

Marcus Borg, *The Heart of Christianity: Rediscovering a Life of Faith* (HarperSanFrancisco, 2003, 57).

Benson, H., et al. *Study of the therapeutic effects of intercessory prayer,* American Heart Journal 151: 934-42. 2006.

Roberts, L., et al. 2000. *Intercessory prayer for the alleviation of ill health.* Cochrane Database Syst Rev (2): CD000368.

Pope John Paul II, *"Salvifici Doloris"*: An apostolic letter on 'Meaning of Human Suffering', Vatican, Rome, 1984.

James Davies. *The Importance of Suffering: the value and meaning of emotional discontent.* London: Routledge ISBN 0-415-66780-1

Thurston, Bonnie Bowman, *The Widows*, Fortress Press, Minneapolis: 1989

Faley, Roland, *Footprints on the Mountain*, Paulist Press, New York: 1994).

Joseph A. Amato. *Victims and Values: A History and a Theory of Suffering.* New York: Praeger, 1990. ISBN 0-275-93690-2

Jamie Mayerfeld. *Suffering and Moral Responsibility.* New York: Oxford University Press, 2005. ISBN 0-19-515495-9

David B. Morris. *The Culture of Pain.* Berkley: University of California, 2002. ISBN 0-520-08276-1

Elaine Scarry. *The Body in Pain: The Making and Unmaking of the World.* New York: Oxford University Press, 1987. ISBN 0-19-504996-9

Plus:

New Catechism of the Catholic Church

All Documents of II Vatican Council

Speeches, Conferences, Letters and Catechisms of Pope John Paul II, Pope Benedict XVI and Pope Francis. (Collected from Vatican Information Service online)